The Kerygma of the Wilderness Traditions in the Hebrew Bible

American University Studies

Series VII
Theology and Religion
Vol. 163

PETER LANG
New York • Washington, D.C./Baltimore • San Francisco
Bern • Frankfurt am Main • Berlin • Vienna • Paris

Terry L. Burden

The Kerygma of the Wilderness Traditions in the Hebrew Bible

PETER LANG
New York • Washington, D.C./Baltimore • San Francisco
Bern • Frankfurt am Main • Berlin • Vienna • Paris

Library of Congress Cataloging-in-Publication Data

Burden, Terry L. (Terry Lynn).
The kerygma of the wilderness traditions in the Hebrew Bible / Terry L. Burden.
p. cm. — (American university studies. Series VII, Theology and religion; vol. 163)
Includes bibliographical references and indexes.
1. Wilderness (Theology)—Biblical teaching. 2. Bible. O.T.—Criticism, interpretation, etc. I. Title. II. Series.
BS1199.W56B87 1994 221.6—dc20 93-43277
ISBN 0-8204-2253-3 CIP
ISSN 0740-0446

Die Deutsche Bibliothek-CIP-Einheitsaufnahme

Burden, Terry L.:
The kerygma of the wilderness traditions in the Hebrew Bible / Terry L. Burden. - New York; Baltimore; San Francisco; Bern; Frankfurt am Main; Berlin; Vienna; Paris: Lang, 1994
ISBN 0-8204-2253-3

The paper in this book meets the guidelines for permanence and durability of the Committee on Production Guidelines for Book Longevity of the Council on Library Resources.

Printed in the United States of America.

Contents

Abbreviations

BDB Francis Brown, S. R. Driver, and Charles A. Briggs, *A Hebrew and English Lexicon of the Old Testament*

BHS *Biblia Hebraica Stuttgartensia*

GKC E. Kautzsch and A. E. Cowley, *Gesenius' Hebrew Grammar*

JSOT *Journal for the Study of the Old Testament*

SBL *Society of Biblical Literature*

Tables

Preface

The present work is the product of not only numerous hours of research and study but that of a compassionate interest in the Hebrew Bible, especially the Pentateuch. My interest in the Pentateuch began to grow while participating in a Hebrew exegesis seminar on the book of Genesis. The class was taught by Page H. Kelley, Professor of Old Testament at The Southern Baptist Theological Seminary. My studies in the Hebrew Bible were greatly encouraged through his leadership during the time in which I served as his Garrett Fellow at The Southern Baptist Theological Seminary and his research assistant in the publication of *Biblical Hebrew: An Introductory Grammar*.

Appreciation must also be expressed to Professor John D. W. Watts. In my early years as a student of the Hebrew Bible, he encouraged me to pursue further research and writing in areas of the Pentateuchal traditions. During my early investigations into the subject of the wilderness traditions, he recognized the value of such a study and supervised the development of the topic.

I am equally thankful to Professor John B. Polhill at The Southern Baptist Theological Seminary. As one of my teachers of New Testament languages, he helped me appreciate the need for a proper balance in Biblical studies. In regard to the instruction in the proper methods of research and writing, I am much indebted to Professor Pamela J. Scalise. Professor Scalise has provided valuable assistance and supervision in previous projects as well as the present work. I am also deeply indebted to Professor Robert L. Cate at Oklahoma State University for reading my work during its first stage of preparation. His suggestions are certainly received with much respect and gratitude. His enthusiasm for the project has been very stimulating, and to him I am grateful.

Appreciation must be expressed also to Professor George W. Coats at Lexington Theological Seminary. I was privileged to study with Professor Coats in the fall of 1989. As the following research will reveal, Professor Coats' work, *Rebellion in the Wilderness*, published in 1968, has been a premier resource in the study of the wilderness traditions. Coats follows this work with numerous articles on the wilderness traditions and related Pentateuchal topics. His class lectures on the Pentateuch and private conversations with me have enriched my interests in the Pentateuch. In a conversation one autumn afternoon at Lexington Theological Seminary, he reminisced about his early days as a student of Holy Scripture. He gladly confessed to me, "I started out in the Pentateuch and never left it." The enormous value of his contributions to biblical scholarship is without question. I shall always look to his work for insights into Pentateuchal subjects and interpretation.

Acknowledgment and deepest gratitude must be extended to my family and friends who have been very supportive and encouraging during the long period of studies at The Southern Baptist Theological Seminary. Throughout the preparation of the manuscript for publication, my wife, Mary, has provided valuable assistance and support. I also wish to express my appreciation to Dr. Heidi Burns, Acquisitions Editor, and Miss Nona Reuter, Production Supervisor, at Peter Lang Publishing for their advice and guidance in the completion of the manuscript.

Terry L. Burden
Louisville, Kentucky
September, 1993

To Mary

Chapter One

Introduction

The study of *kerygma* in regard to the ancient Israelite traditions presents a wealth of possibilities for biblical interpretation. The use of *kerygma* in biblical studies normally implies a New Testament context, but as scholars such as Gerhard von Rad, G. Ernest Wright, and Hans Walter Wolff have discovered, the message of God's actions in the world constitutes the *kerygma* from the book of Genesis through The Revelation to John. The wilderness traditions, in particular, provide an important starting point for an investigation of biblical writers' use of ancient Israelite traditions. In the study of the *kerygma* of biblical texts, ancient credo or confessional statements become relevant, because such statements may reveal the theological views of biblical writers. Since *kerygma* implies the recitation of God's actions, or the announcement of God's salvation, then, through the study of *kerygma*, one can understand more fully the biblical teachings about God.[1] The Pentateuch is a recitation of God's acts of salvation; and the subsequent recollections in the Hebrew Bible of God's actions in Israel's sacred history will contain all of, or portions of, the contents of the Pentateuch. The wilderness traditions are not always recited explicitly when biblical writers retell God's actions. The present study is concerned with those moments when the biblical writers chose to recall the wilderness traditions. The nature of the present research will require the maintenance of a close relationship among the *kerygma* of the traditions, the recitation of Israel's sacred history, and the community of faith who received and embraced the message.

The purpose of the research is to examine the wilderness traditions in the Hebrew Bible. The wilderness traditions are those narratives found in the books of Exodus and Numbers that refer to the wanderings of the Israelites in the wilderness under the leadership of Moses following the exodus from Egypt. The primary concern is the manner in which the wilderness narratives are used by biblical writers to express beliefs in God by the community of faith.

The use of the term *kerygma*, in reference to the Old Testament, implies the expressed beliefs and faith of a particular community revealed in the content of holy scripture, whose message is directed to a community of faith.[2] Von Rad states that interest in biblical literature lies in the assertions of God's actions in history.[3] Therefore, there are two activities in the study of the Old Testament: one is historical and one is confessional. The testimony of traditions consists of those accounts which reveal the experienced presence and nature of God. The accounts of God's actions from Israel's sacred history constitute a record of God's revelation and its meaning for the people.[4] In tradition analysis, primary attention should be given to the development and function of those testimonies among the people. Stress, then, should be placed upon the *kerygmatic* objective of the texts and its ongoing significance to a particular cultural and historical challenge.[5]

Brueggemann suggests that the confessing stance of the community revealed in the text will always be both protest and affirmation.[6] Sanders uses different terms in stating a similar hermeneutical function: the constitutive and the prophetic. He explains the use of these terms:

> At those historical moments when Israel was weak and needed reconstituting . . . the constitutive mode was proper: our father Jacob was a wandering Aramean (Deut. 26:5); we are lost and wandering like him (in Exile); maybe like him we mark another beginning and not the end of Israel. But if that same mode of rereading the tradition of Jacob, or Abraham, was read at a time when Israel had power, and had somehow confused it with God's power . . . To continue to draw strength from the tradition would only harden the heart into further irresponsibility. At that historical moment the prophetic mode is indicated.[7]

Herein lies the dual function of *kerygma*. On the one hand, *kerygma* reveals the message of God's actions with the purpose of reviving and affirming faith in God among the people. Fundamentally, *kerygma* is the announcement of divine action intended to exhort the audience to faith.[8] On the other hand, *kerygma* is an appeal to obedient actions on the part of the community. The *kerygma* of biblical texts maintains an instructional function whereby the community is encouraged to live in a manner worthy of divine approval.[9] These two elements, affirmation and appeal, form the basic function of *kerygma*.[10] The salvation of God is a historical reality made present in the *kerygma*, and through the recitation or confession of the saving acts of God, the *kerygma* always proclaims the coming fulfillment of the salvation of God. Thus, *kerygma* is characterized by anamnesis and prophecy.[11]

In the present work, the use of the closely related term *confession* or *confessional* text will refer to statements made by biblical writers that express faith in the actions of God. Confession in this regard will not necessarily imply an ancient creed in a formal sense. For example, the statement in Numbers 14:6–9 may be understood as a confessional text expressing the belief by the community of faith that the gift of the land is the fulfillment of the promise, and such a confession should affirm a like faith by the people. In other words, the use of the term *confession* is another way to identify and explain statements of faith revealed in the biblical texts.

The frequent references to the community of faith in the present work are understood as the Israelite community, portrayed in the biblical text through whom the kerygma is presented, and the readers or audience of holy scripture in ancient Israel. The study will not seek to discover or to identify the community of faith, which stands behind the text through whom the traditions were transmitted. Instead, questions addressed to the nature of the community of faith will focus on the audience revealed by the texts and to whom the kerygma is intended. The kerygma of the texts implies a community of faith that embraces and affirms the beliefs and faith revealed in those texts. In other words, the community of faith and the kerygma belong together.[12] The description of the community of faith, therefore, will be analyzed inductively through the exegetical process of the selected texts.

The selection of materials in the Hebrew Bible that contain references to the wilderness traditions will be determined according to the shape of the traditions of the Pentateuch. Isaiah 48:20–21, to illustrate, is selected for analysis since the imagery of the second exodus utilizes the water miracle stories from the Tetrateuch. Many of the texts considered refer to specific events from the narratives in the Pentateuch (Ezek. 20; Psalms 78, 95, 105, 106). Furthermore, the close relationship between Israel's sacred history, which is derived from the Hexateuch (with emphasis on entering the land), and the wilderness traditions contained therein also influences the selection of material for the study.

The study of the kerygma of Holy Scripture is the prominent feature of the work of Hans Walter Wolff, whose methodology is revealed in a series of articles compiled in 1975 with Walter Brueggemann.[13] Wolff's methodology depends on the Documentary Hypothesis, and he remains loyal to that school of literary criticism. Each of the sources (J, E, P, and D), which together span the whole of the Pentateuchal literature, reveals its own theological agenda in the Pentateuchal traditions. Wolff addresses the kerygma of the Yahwist, the Elohist, and the Deuteronomistic Historian while Brueggemann examines the kerygma of the Priestly Writer, published in the same work with Wolff, and the Deuteronomistic Historian in an additional study.[14] The treatment of the sources or literary traditions in the Pentateuch is relevant insofar as such an analysis may contribute to the interpretation of the wilderness traditions.

The major focus of the current project, then, is the final form of the text through which, as Wolff's methodology suggests, the community expresses its faith in God. Therefore, questions of the historicity of texts, pre-written stages of the literary process, and the text's relation to other Ancient Near Eastern texts will not be considered. Questions addressing these issues, though relevant in many ways, do not have a place in the study of the kerygma.[15]

The analysis of the wilderness traditions in the Hebrew Bible proceeds under the assumption that the wilderness traditions in the Hebrew Bible were informed and shaped by the ancient traditions that were received by the community. The texts containing the traditions, and references to those traditions, were shaped by the writers of the Hebrew Bible according to how the traditions functioned in the community of faith.[16] The traditions of Israel's experiences in the wilderness developed within the life of the community, and the community was influenced and shaped by those traditions.

The traditions involving Israel's life in the wilderness were among the many elements which had the potential for providing stability and continuity within the community of faith.[17] Analysis of the kerygma of traditions of the wilderness wanderings, due to the nature of its methodology, focuses upon the dynamic nature of the traditions and how they spoke to the community of faith.[18] Although the wilderness period may appear rather minor in its degree of importance within biblical traditions as a whole, the wilderness traditions provide a means whereby the community of faith could relate to Holy Scripture and find expression for its faith.

The Scope and Idea of the Wilderness Traditions

The wilderness traditions obviously have a prominent place in the literature of the Pentateuch. In the Book of Deuteronomy the traditions of the wilderness period provide preaching illustrations unparalleled elsewhere in the Hebrew Bible. Further references to the traditions of the wilderness wanderings occur throughout the Hebrew

Bible, and in each retelling of the saving acts of God, the wilderness traditions are used by the biblical writer with a particular community situation in mind. The wilderness traditions did not remain static in their message and interpretation, for they spoke again and again to the needs of the community at particular critical junctures in the history of the people.[19] Some of the early references to God's saving acts did not include the wilderness traditions, such as Deuteronomy 26:5–9.[20] In Joshua 24:2–13 a similar credo is stated in a more elaborate fashion, but here the wilderness traditions are only mentioned briefly: "You lived in the wilderness a long time" (vs. 7b). Even in the books of Exodus and Numbers, the narratives referring specifically to the wilderness wanderings appear at times in a state of confusion with little unity.[21] In essence, it appears at first that the wilderness wanderings hold an insignificant place when compared to other traditions that record the saving acts of God. The exodus and the conquest are the major elements in most confessional texts in the Hebrew Bible. The apparent casual role of the wilderness traditions in confessional texts changes substantially in some of the writings in the Hebrew Bible (Pss. 78, 105, 106, Neh. 9).

The idea of the "wilderness" can have multiple meanings in different writings throughout the Hebrew Bible. The term can refer to a place of habitation in general or a condition depicting desolation like references found in prophetic literature such as Isaiah and Jeremiah.[22] The translation "wilderness" is derived from various Hebrew terms with מִדְבָּר, "wilderness," appearing to be the most frequently used, not to overlook the Hebrew designation for the book of Numbers (במדבר). Other terms include עֲרָבָה "dry place," צִיָּה "drought," (cf. Jer. 2:6), and יְשִׁימוֹן "waste" (Deut. 32:10). According to Israel's sacred history, מִדְבָּר designates the period between Israel's exodus from Egypt and the conquest of Canaan.[23] In the discussions throughout this book, the translation "wilderness" is used when the language and imagery refer to the traditions of the wilderness wanderings of the people of Israel.

Critical studies have been written that analyze the structure and composition of the narratives identified with the wilderness traditions.[24] Coats completed an important tradition–historical, form–critical analysis of the traditions with emphasis on the particular motif of Israel's rebellion in the wilderness.[25] Coats follows his premier work with numerous articles on the wilderness traditions and related Pentateuchal topics. Reimann investigates the wilderness imagery in pre–exilic prophetic writings by focusing on the "return to desert" motif.[26] Darr's work with Ezekiel and Second Isaiah focuses on the contributions of the imagery of "desert" for the interpretation of the two books.[27] In contrast to the above works, the present analysis considers the whole of the wilderness traditions in the Pentateuch, which reflects the period of Israel's life in the wilderness prior to entrance into the land of Canaan, and how these traditions are appropriated throughout the Hebrew Bible.

Kerygma Approach to the Study of Traditions

According to Gerhard von Rad, the records of the divine acts of Yahweh were interpretations of faith made by the community of faith. Statements about Yahweh's revelation made by the community of faith are therefore confessional in nature.[28] The divine acts of Yahweh, according to von Rad, are contained in the first six books of the Hebrew Bible. The "history of redemption," as revealed in the Hexateuch, includes the creation of the world, the calling of the ancestors, the promises made to Israel, Israel's experience in Egypt, the exodus, the miraculous demonstrations of God's power and favor, the wilderness wanderings, and the entrance into the promised land.[29] An example of a confessional or credal statement that proclaims these divine acts is found in Joshua 24:2–13; a text constituting what von Rad calls the Hexateuch in miniature.[30]

Walter Harrelson assigns these basic elements to the expanded core tradition, which initially consisted of the fundamental belief in Yahweh as the God of Israel.[31] The "building blocks" of the core tradition are Yahweh's guidance of the patriarchs, Yahweh's special favor for the poor and oppressed, and Yahweh's presence and guiding leadership of the community.[32]

Essentially, the Hexateuch reveals the faith of Israel, and its shape is influenced by the confessional or ancient credo. The manner in which faith perceives events in history has its own peculiarities; therefore, an understanding of the divine acts of Yahweh is not necessarily what critical historical scholarship might uncover.[33] Von Rad assumes that constant recurring features or patterns can be identified in traditions that could be characteristic of confessional statements.[34] The ancient creed, according to von Rad, is a summary of the principal facts of God's redemptive activity; and, in its outward form in the Hebrew Bible, the creed represents a merging of diverse materials under a more focused theological agenda.[35] Creeds, then, tend to follow a canonical pattern that provides a standard or pattern into which later ideas may be incorporated.[36] A creed might be called a confession of faith, or, rather, an enumeration of the saving acts which were the constitutive elements essential to the religious community.[37] The ancient creed is not necessarily an affirmation of Israel's faith alone, but often a creed could function as an exhortation to faith. Basically, the purpose of a creed is to encourage faith through the affirmation of the saving acts of Yahweh.[38]

An ancient creed contains diverse elements such as the references to the patriarchs, the experience of the Egyptian bondage, the deliverance from Egypt by the power of God, and the entrance into the promised land through the guidance of God. The identification of the ancient creed in biblical traditions, for the purpose of determining its kerygma, must include some or all of these elements. The kerygma of the ancient traditions of the Pentateuch constitutes the criterion for further kerygmatic statements in the Hebrew Bible.[39] The form and content of confessional statements occurring in traditions can change to include the presence of a new word for the community of faith.[40] New elements remain grounded in the old traditions while the confessional statements speak to a current situation for a particular community of faith.[41] An example of this development is found in a comparison between Deuteronomy 26:5–9 and Psalms 105–106; the former illustrates a very brief credal text and the latter illustrates an elaborate expansion or a detailed recital of Israel's sacred history.

Hans Walter Wolff's kerygma methodology follows closely the conclusions of von Rad's credo study.[42] Von Rad's purpose was to get behind the literary sources appropriated by the Wellhausen school of literary criticism, JEDP, in order to determine the development of the traditions that resulted in the J and E works. Wolff focuses on the present shape of the various literary sources of the Pentateuch, through which the faith of Israel is confessed. Brueggemann writes, "To look into a text for kerygma implies that we have somewhere, in some text, a normative statement of faith by a confessing community."[43] Wolff and Brueggemann attempt to systematize the kerygma by searching for the frequent expressions that will reveal the theological views of the writers. The kerygma of biblical texts, however, does not necessarily indicate what all generations believe, but, rather, the faith demanded and expressed in Biblical texts is that which is the measure of authentic faith.[44]

Wolff and von Rad propose that the Yahwist literary source is the primary source theologically and the great support for the traditions of the Pentateuch.[45] The theological agenda of the Yahwist's work reflects the period of Solomon and the heightened nationalistic interests of the times.[46] The kerygma of the Yahwist, revealed through the pivotal passage in Genesis 12:1–3, emphasizes blessing in which Abraham, as a great nation, will be a blessing to the nations of the world.[47] As an advocate of the Israelite monarchy, the Yahwist believed the promises of Abraham came to be fulfilled in the time of David. As Wolff correctly observes, the question arises, however, as to whether the people of Israel have in fact brought about the blessing of Abraham during the Solomonic period.[48] The response of the community to divine purpose can help or hinder the fulfillment of the promise, regardless of whether Israel lives in the wilderness or in the land.[49]

Among the sources, the Elohist literary source is the most difficult to identify, perhaps due to its fragmentary nature and themes similar to the Yahwist, thus making it difficult at times to distinguish the two.[50] The kerygma of the Elohist, in Wolff's view, has as its central motif the "fear of the Lord."[51] The Abraham and Isaac narrative in Genesis 22 provides an example of the motif, where obedience to God is revealed through the testing of faith (Gen. 22:8–14). In the wilderness traditions, the notion of fear of the Lord (יִרְאַת אֱלֹהִים Gen. 20:11) does not occur explicitly as it does in the patriarchal narratives, though the motif of obedience is certainly present.[52] In the discussion of the wilderness traditions, the analysis of the Yahwist material proceeds with the awareness of the presence of the Elohist.

According to the Deuteronomistic historical work, the history of the Israelite community is understood as the fulfillment of the words spoken by Moses at the beginning of Israel's historical records in Deuteronomy.[53] For the Deuteronomistic historian, the hope of history in the late period is found in the rediscovering of the Mosaic religion and the establishment of a stable monarchy in Jerusalem.[54] Judges 2:11f. and 1 Samuel 12, for example, indicate decisive roles for the continuation of salvation history. These passages contain the theme "return" (שׁוּב) which, in Wolff's view, enables us to recognize the historian's kerygmatic intention.[55] The notion of "return" means a restored covenant relationship with God, and such a return will result in the reversal of the judgment upon the community, though that judgment might already have been decreed.[56] The notion of שׁוּב is reflected in the message of the work as a whole, and for the community, a renewal of the pre-587 covenant is possible, if Israel will make the necessary changes.[57]

The key element in Wolff's return motif is the notion of the "mercy" and "forgiveness" of God. The kerygma appeals to a faith in the actions of God who forgave and delivered the people in times past by instilling hope of forgiveness in the present. The Deuteronomistic historical prologue in Deuteronomy 1–4, to illustrate, records the saving acts of God which are intended to establish faith and confidence in a forgiving God so that a "return" can be made by the community. A return, according to Deuteronomistic work, is prompted by listening to the voice of Yahweh, the God of the community, according to the instruction of Moses. Turning back to Yahweh and listening to the voice of Yahweh have become inseparably related in the theology of the Deuteronomistic History.[58]

The Deuteronomistic History intends to help the community of the exile revive its purpose in life as the people of God. In addition to Wolff's use of שׁוּב, "return," Brueggemann's kerygma study identifies the key element expressed through the notion of "good" (טוֹב). The "good" motif discerns the graciousness of God and encourages the community to look beyond its present despair and hold onto the promises of God. The message of the Deuteronomistic History, that centers upon goodness, does not stress what Israel must do, as Wolff implies with שׁוּב, but the notion of goodness relates to the gracious actions of God. In order for the exilic community to revive its faith in God, the community must understand the actions of God in a fuller sense. The actions of God in history point to a future for the Israelite community, because its future remains within the good purposes of God. The kerygma of the Deuteronomistic History, in this perspective, builds not only on the past actions of God but, most importantly, on the present and future actions of God.

The Priestly Writer is the last major influence in the development of the Pentateuchal literature.[59] Bentzen, likewise, suggests that the Priestly Writer gives the Pentateuch its plan.[60] The Priestly Writer, therefore, presupposes the presence of J and E which are earlier sources for Israel's traditions. Due to the editing of the traditions throughout their history, the previous agenda of the J or E source may have been incorporated into the priestly material or reshaped by another redactor.[61] Within the priestly material, and other material subsumed under its agenda, a program has developed for the reconstruction of the community after the exile, which also includes the revival of the despondent community in the post-exilic period (cf. Hag. 1:2–11).[62] The uncertainty of the exilic period influences the Priestly program of restoration and heightens the emphasis on the Mosaic tradition in an effort to present the options to follow in order to insure the future and the survival of Israel.[63] Brueggemann notes, for example, that the Priestly Writer emphasizes the fidelity of God to the community and the assurance of its well-being even in exile.[64]

The kerygma of the Priestly Writer, according to Brueggemann's observations, can be identified in the blessing in Genesis 1:28. Mankind is blessed, and will continue to be blessed by God; and, furthermore, external circumstances do not nullify the reality of God's purposes for mankind. According to this interpretation of the priestly kerygma, the blessing in Genesis 1:28 gives the community the hope and the power to act toward the future.

In Sue Boorer's study of the kerygma of the Priestly Writer, she reinterprets the traditions of prominent periods in history to give a comprehensive account of the direction which the history had taken, thus providing a basis for hope for the future.[65] The elements in the covenant promises to the patriarchs include descendants, land, and the promise of God's presence as Israel's God. The last element, according to Boorer, unfolds in the wilderness traditions where God manifests his power and presence through the exodus and the wilderness. The exilic community came to understand that the covenant promise to Abraham did not end with the conquest and possession of the land. Since the exile created a theological crisis, which may be understood as a threat to the validity of the promises of Abraham, the Priestly Writer intends to stress this point. The monarchical period, therefore, is to be understood as only a step toward the final fulfillment of the promise of permanent possession of the land.[66]

In conclusion, the identification of the kerygmatic objective in Holy Scripture, as Brueggemann explains, became a serious concern for the Confessing Church in Germany during the 1930s.[67] At that time, individuals like von Rad and Wolff believed the Church had begun to compromise the message of the Bible to accommodate the National Socialist movement in Germany. Accordingly, the Church sought to exegete for themselves the biblical text in order to find the kerygmatic intention of the writers of biblical texts.[68] The crisis of compromise within the community of faith, however, is not an issue characteristic of contemporary times alone. The crisis of the Babylonian exile, for example, created the same concern among the religious leaders and scholars in sixth-century B.C.E. The redactors of the Hebrew canon sought to discover, and recover, the confessional elements in the ancient Israelite traditions in the hope that Israel's traditions might speak to the needs of their community by addressing the community's particular cultural and historical challenges.[69] As a late contributor in the history of Israelite writings, the Chronicler, for example, is concerned with Israel's past, from which the community should take seriously the lessons of that past.[70] Certain kerygmatic elements, such as those present in von Rad's ancient credo, that were passed down through the generations, held a prominent place among the religious writings. Traditions spoke new messages to the community, thus redefining or shaping new interpretations of the old traditions.[71] The Chronicler's History, of course, provides an excellent example of new interpretations of traditions. The historical situation for the community, along with the whole historical process, contributes to the reception and interpretation of the traditions by the community; whereby, the community confesses its faith in relevant new ways.[72] The kerygmatic content of ancient Israelite traditions will reveal the confessing stance of the community. The changing shape and adaptability of the confessional stance of the community of faith are related to and formulated for particular situations in the life of the community. The kerygma of any biblical tradition is therefore always to be considered in relation to the experiences of the community of faith.

Although a large portion of the Pentateuch has Israel outside the land, the wilderness traditions constitute a small element in the overall shape of the Pentateuchal traditions. Because of their highly dependent nature, a study of the kerygma of the wilderness traditions must consider the kerygma of the Pentateuch, and, for that matter, the Hebrew Bible as a whole. Wolff's basic methodology provides an adequate starting place, but his apparent neglect of the wilderness narratives provides an additional challenge for identifying and understanding the kerygma of the wilderness traditions. When the kerygma of a literary tradition is discussed, the patriarchal narratives almost always provide the point of theological and historical origin, while the Israelite narratives in Exodus through 2 Kings provide the historical periods in which the kerygma unfolds. The wilderness traditions appear to be the cross-roads where the ancient traditions of Israel's beginnings meet.

Notes

[1]G. Ernest Wright, *God Who Acts: Biblical Theology as Recital* (London: SCM Press, Ltd., 1952), p. 18.

[2]Karl Rahner and Karl Lehmann, *Kerygma and Dogma* (New York: Herder and Herder, 1969), p. 17, suggest that the use of the term *kerygma* can describe both the act and the content of proclamation. James I. H. McDonald, *Kerygma and Didache* (Cambridge: Cambridge University Press, 1980), pp. 1-8, explains the use of the term *kerygma* in one respect to refer to the form of the preaching and in another respect to refer to the content of the message preached. In the present research, *kerygma* will refer to the content of the message presented in Holy Scripture.

[3]Gerhard von Rad, *Old Testament Theology*, vol. 1, trans. D. M. G. Stalker (San Francisco: Harper & Row, 1962), p. 106.

[4]Douglas A. Knight, "Revelation Through Tradition," in *Tradition and Theology in the Old Testament*, ed. Douglas A. Knight (Philadelphia: Fortress Press, 1977), p. 149.

[5]Ibid., p. 150.

[6]Walter Brueggemann, "Wolff's Kerygmatic Methodology," in *The Vitality of Old Testament Traditions*, 2nd. ed., ed. Walter Brueggemann and Hans Walter Wolff (Atlanta: John Knox Press, 1982), p. 31.

[7]James A. Sanders, "Hermeneutics," *The Interpreter's Dictionary of the Bible*, suppl. vol., ed. Keith Crim (Nashville: Abingdon Press, 1962), p. 405, and *Canon and Community* (Philadelphia: Fortress Press, 1984), p. 90.

[8]C. H. Dodd, *The Apostolic Preaching and Its Developments* (London: Hodder & Stoughton Limited, 1936), p. 8, stresses the dual nature of proclamation to be evangelism and instruction. See Klaus Koch, *The Growth of Biblical Tradition*, trans. S. M. Culpitt (New York: The MacMillan Publishing Company, 1969), p. 70.

[9]McDonald, *Kerygma and Didache*, pp. 4-7.

[10]Alan Richardson, *An Introduction to the Theology of the New Testament* (London: SCM Press, Ltd., 1958), pp. 24-25; Dodd, *The Apostolic Preaching and Its Developments*, pp. 21-24.

[11]Rahner and Lehmann, *Kerygma and Dogma*, p. 19.

[12]Ibid., p. 17.

[13]Walter Brueggemann and Hans Walter Wolff, ed., *The Vitality of Old Testament Traditions*, 2nd. ed. (Atlanta: John Knox Press, 1982).

[14]Walter Brueggemann, "The Kerygma of the Deuteronomistic Historian," *Interpretation*, 22 (1968), 387-402.

[15]Brueggemann, "Wolff's Kerygma Methodology," p. 30.

[16]James A. Sanders, *From Sacred Story to Sacred Text* (Philadelphia: Fortress Press, 1987), p. 162.

[17]For a study of continuity in Israelite traditions, see Peter R. Ackroyd, *Studies in the Religious Tradition of the Old Testament* (London: SCM Press Ltd., 1987).

[18]Bruce C. Birch, "Tradition, Canon and Biblical Theology," *Horizons in Biblical Theology*, 2 (1980), 113-125; Douglas A. Knight, "Canon and the History of Tradition: A Critique of Brevard S. Childs' Introduction to the Old Testament as Scripture," *Horizons in Biblical Theology*, 2 (1980), 127-149.

[19]James A. Sanders, "Adaptation for Life: The Nature and Function of Canon," in *Magnalia Dei: The Mighty Acts of God. Essays on the Bible and Archaeology in Memoriam G. E. Wright*, ed. F. M. Cross (Garden City: Doubleday & Co., 1976), pp. 531-560.

[20]Gerhard von Rad, *The Problem of the Hexateuch and Other Essays* (London: SCM Press Ltd., 1984), suggests that the Sinai material (Exodus 19 through Numbers 11) and the narratives describing the wanderings in the wilderness are separate traditions that have been assembled by a redactor. The present study will consider the relationship between the wilderness traditions and the Sinai material where the issue is relevant to the analysis of the wilderness traditions. The origins of the two traditions, however, are beyond the scope of the present research.

[21]Martin Noth, *Numbers: A Commentary*, The Old Testament Library, trans. James D. Martin (Philadelphia: Westminster Press, 1968), p. 2.

[22]Robert W. Funk, "The Wilderness," *Journal of Biblical Literature*, 78 (1959), 205-214.

[23]Shemaryahu Talmon, "Wilderness," *The Interpreter's Dictionary of the Bible*, suppl. vol., ed. Keith Crim (Nashville: Abingdon Press, 1962), p. 947. Also, see his "The 'Desert Motif' in the Bible and in Qumran Literature," in *Biblical Motifs: Origins and Transformations*, ed. Alexander Altmann (Cambridge: Harvard University Press, 1966), pp. 31-63.

[24]Volkmar Fritz, *Israel in der Wüste* (Marburg: N. G. Elwert Verlag, 1970); Ulrich Mauser, *Christ in the Wilderness* (Naperville: Alec R. Allenson, Inc., 1963); Martin Noth, *A History of Pentateuchal Traditions*, trans. B. W. Anderson (Atlanta: Scholars Press, 1981), and *Numbers: A Commentary*; Brevard Childs, *The Book of Exodus*, The Old Testament Library (Philadelphia: The Westminster Press, 1974); various articles and publications.

[25]George W. Coats, *Rebellion in the Wilderness* (Nashville: Abingdon Press, 1968)

[26]Paul A. Riemann, "Desert and Return to Desert in the Pre-Exilic Prophets" (Ph.D. dissertation, Harvard University, 1964).

[27]Katheryn Pfisterer Darr, "Breaking through the Wilderness: References to the Desert in Exilic Prophecy" (Ph.D. dissertation, Vanderbilt University, 1984).

[28]Douglas A. Knight, "Revelation through Tradition," in *Tradition and Theology in the Old Testament*, ed. Douglas A. Knight (Philadelphia: Fortress Press, 1977), p. 162.

[29]Von Rad, *The Problem of the Hexateuch*, p. 2. See Wright, *God Who Acts: Biblical Theology as Recital*, p. 13, who proposes that the Bible relates history in a confessional manner, because the recitation of Israel's sacred history is a religious act of the worshiping community. Martin Noth follows von Rad's work with general approval. For Martin Noth, *A History of Pentateuchal Traditions*, pp. 46-62, five themes suggest the kerygmatic scope of the Pentateuchal traditions, the exodus from Egypt, the leading into Canaan, the promise to the patriarchs, the leading of Israel in the wilderness, and the revelation at Sinai. Various traditions were linked together with these five themes to form the Pentateuchal traditions, but the five themes remain the major elements. The exodus theme is the oldest theme around which other traditions were formed.

[30]Von Rad, *The Problem of the Hexateuch*, p. 8.

[31]Walter Harrelson, "Traditions and the Tradition," *Perspectives in Religious Studies*, 6 (1979), 184-189; "Life, Faith, and the Emergence of Tradition," in *Tradition and Theology in the Old Testament*, ed. Douglas A. Knight (Philadelphia: Fortress Press, 1977), p. 19.

[32]Harrelson, "Life, Faith, and the Emergence of Tradition," p. 30.

[33]Gerhard von Rad, *Old Testament Theology*, vol. 1, trans. D. M. G. Stalker (San Francisco: Harper & Row, Publishers, 1962), p. 106.

[34]Ibid., p. 108.

[35]Von Rad, *The Problem of the Hexateuch*, p. 2.

[36]Ibid., p. 6; Peter R. Ackroyd, *Studies in the Religious Tradition of the Old Testament* (London: SCM Press Ltd., 1988), p. 14.

[37]Von Rad, *The Problem of the Hexateuch*, p. 4.

[38]Dennis J. McCarthy, "What was Israel's Historical Creed?" *Lexington Theological Quarterly*, 4 (1969), 46-53.

[39]Rahner and Lehmann, *Kerygma and Dogma*, p. 15.

[40]James Barr, *Holy Scripture: Canon, Authority, Criticism* (Philadelphia: The Westminster Press, 1983), p. 70.

[41]Von Rad, *Old Testament Theology*, vol. 2, p. 130; Joseph Blenkinsopp, "The Structure of P," *The Catholic Biblical Quarterly*, 38 (1976), 275-292.

[42]Walter Brueggemann, "Wolff's Kerygmatic Methodology," in *The Vitality of Old Testament Traditions*, 2nd. ed., ed. Walter Brueggemann and Hans Walter Wolff (Atlanta: John Knox Press, 1982), pp. 29–39.

[43]Ibid., p. 29.

[44]Ibid., p. 30.

[45]Hans Walter Wolff, "The Kerygma of the Yahwist," trans. Wilbur A. Benware, in *The Vitality of Old Testament Traditions*, 2nd. ed., ed. Hans Walter Wolff and Walter Brueggemann (Atlanta: John Knox Press, 1982), pp. 41-66; von Rad, *The Problem of the Hexateuch*, p. 74. In keeping with common scholarly views, Wolff dates the Yahwist to the Solomonic era. See Rolf Rendtorff, "Tradition-Historical Method and the Documentary Hypothesis," *Proceedings of the Fifth World Congress of Jewish Studies*, vol. 1 (Jerusalem: World Union of Jewish Studies, 1969), 5-11, where Rendtorff initiates his argument for the rejection of the notion that the Yahwist is a formal narrative source that extends from Genesis to Numbers, or the Hexateuch. Subsequent studies that focus on his fresh approach to the Pentateuch include the *Journal for the Study of the Old Testament* 3 (1977), and his primary work, recently translated into English, *The Problem of the Process of Transmission in the Pentateuch*, JSOT Supplement Series 89, trans. John J. Schullion (Sheffield: JSOT Press, 1990).

[46]Terence Fretheim "The Theology of the Major Traditions in Genesis-Numbers," *Review and Expositor*, 74 (1977), 301-320.

[47]Hans Walter Wolff, "The Hermeneutics of the Old Testament," trans. Keith Crim, in *Essays on Old Testament Hermeneutics*, ed. Claus Westermann (Richmond: John Knox Press, 1964), p. 191. Peter F. Ellis, *The Yahwist: The Bible's First Theologian* (Notre Dame: Fides Publishers, Inc., 1968), pp. 205-211. G. H. Davies, "The Presence of God in Israel," in *Studies in History and Religion*, ed. Ernest A.

Payne (London: Lutterworth Press, 1942), p. 13, suggests that more attention should be given to the universalism of the Yahwist. Gerhard von Rad, *Genesis*, 2nd. ed., trans. John H. Marks (Philadelphia: Westminster Press, 1972), p. 200, states that both the Yahwist and the Priestly Writer share this element of traditions that connects the hope in the Abrahamic covenant to its universal scope.

[48]For a survey of blessing, see Claus Westermann, *Blessing in the Bible and the Life of the Church*, trans. Keith Crim (Philadelphia: Fortress Press, 1978).

[49]Fretheim, "The Theology of the Major Traditions in Genesis-Numbers," p. 308.

[50]Martin Noth, *A History of Pentateuchal Traditions*, trans. B. W. Anderson (Atlanta: Scholars Press, 1981), p. 36, assigns very few passages to the Elohist within the wilderness narratives in Exodus and Numbers. The Elohist is to be found visibly in Exodus 18, but is not recognized by Noth in the book of Numbers until after the Meribah narrative in Numbers 20:14.

[51]Hans Walter Wolff, "The Elohist Fragments in the Pentateuch," trans. Keith Crim, in *The Vitality of Old Testament Traditions*, ed. Walter Brueggemann and Hans Walter Wolff (Atlanta: John Knox Press, 1982), p. 67.

[52]Numbers 14:9, which is attributed to the Priestly Writer, speaks of fear, but the fear is not fear of God. In Exodus 18:21, in which Exodus 18 is attributed generally to the Elohist, the motif appears at its clearest. In Numbers 12:8, Aaron and Miriam were not afraid to speak against Moses. George Buchanan Gray, *A Critical and Exegetical Commentary on Numbers*, The International Critical Commentary (Edinburgh: T. & T. Clark, 1903), p. 124, does not follow the assumptions of Noth, but allows for the presence of the Elohist in Numbers 12. The implication is that, since Aaron and Miriam did not fear the Lord, they were not afraid to challenge Moses.

[53]Hans Walter Wolff, "The Kerygma of the Deuteronomic Historical Work," trans. Frederick C. Prussner, in *The Vitality of Old Testament Traditions*, 2nd. ed. (Atlanta: John Knox Press, 1982), p. 84.

[54]John F. A. Sawyer, *From Moses to Patmos* (London: SPCK, 1977), p. 50.

[55]Wolff, "The Kerygma of the Deuteronomic Historian," p. 90.

[56]Ibid., p. 91.

[57]Brueggemann, "The Kerygma of the Deuteronomistic Historian," p. 388.

[58]Ibid., p. 98.

[59]Scholars disagree as to the full nature of the Priestly work in regard to its role as a narrative source. Peter R. Ackroyd, *Exile and Restoration* (Philadelphia: The Westminster Press, 1968), p. 91, has the Priestly work as a narrative work. Frank M. Cross, *Canaanite Myth and Hebrew Epic* (Cambridge: Harvard University Press, 1973), p. 301, claims that P is not a narrative source that existed independently of the JE strands. Von Rad, *Old Testament Theology*, vol. 1, p. 232, proposes that the Priestly Writer is a genuine historical work. Noth, *A History of Pentateuchal Traditions*, p. 7, states that the Priestly source has a theological concern for history, but a different one from the Yahwist. As a historical work, the Priestly Writer endeavors to show that the cult entered history with Israel and is the goal of creation. The present study will assume that the priestly writing, whether redactional or historical in its work, is a narrative work in its relation to other literary sources (JED), but this is not to suggest that the Priestly document existed independently as a literary source.

[60]Aage Bentzen, *Introduction to the Old Testament*, vol. 1 (Copenhagen: G. E. C. Gad Publishers, 1959), p. 33.

[61]Cross, *Canaanite Myth and Hebrew Epic*, p. 324.

[62]Ibid.

[63]Ackroyd, *Exile and Restoration*, p. 101, proposes, for example, that Numbers 13-14 parallels the uncertainty of the exilic age.

[64]Walter Brueggemann, "The Kerygma of the Priestly Writers," in *The Vitality of Old Testament Traditions*, ed. Walter Brueggemann and Hans Walter Wolff (Atlanta: John Knox Press, 1982), p. 117.

[65]Sue Boorer, "The Kerygmatic Intentions of the Priestly Document," *Austin Biblical Review*, 25 (1977), 12-20.

[66]Ibid., p. 17.

[67]Brueggemann, "Wolff's Kerygmatic Methodology," p. 31.

[68]Ibid.

[69]Knight, "Revelation through Tradition," p. 150.

[70]Jacob M. Myers, "The Kerygma of the Chronicler" *Interpretation* 20 (1966), 259–273. Also, see John Goldingay, "The Chronicler as a Theologian" *Biblical Theology Bulletin* 6 (1975), 99–126.

[71]Sanders, "Adaptation for Life," p. 538.

[72]Douglas A. Knight, *Tradition and Theology in the Old Testament*, ed. Douglas A. Knight (Philadelphia: Fortress Press, 1977), pp. 3-4.

Chapter Two

The Wilderness Traditions in Exodus and Numbers

The present study of the wilderness traditions in the Hebrew Bible has its starting point in the Tetrateuch, specifically the books of Exodus and Numbers. The wilderness traditions contain narratives which reflect the period of time that Israel spent in the wilderness following the exodus from Egypt and extending to the period prior to Israel's entrance into the land of Canaan. The material found in Exodus, Leviticus, and Numbers can be divided into three popular sections, but the traditions of the wilderness wanderings do not appear in all sections. The three sections are the exodus from Egypt (Exod. 1–18), the Sinai narratives (Exod. 19–Num. 10:10), and the journey from Sinai to the Jordan (Num. 10:11–36:12).[1] A distinction is made between the wilderness narratives occurring prior to the Sinai narratives and those that follow. The three-fold division recognizes the distinct nature of the Sinai traditions with the wilderness traditions occurring primarily within the first and the last divisions.

Identification of the Wilderness Traditions

The divisions in the Book of Exodus traditionally include the exodus from Egypt (Chapters 1:1–15:21), the wilderness journey from the Reed Sea to Sinai (Chapters 15:22–18:27), and the covenant at Sinai and its ordinances (Chapters 19–40).[2] These divisions can be broken down further into smaller individual events or traditions such as the plagues narratives (Exod. 7:1–11:10) and the exodus tradition (Exod. 13:17–15:21). Structural analysis of the book of Exodus reveals the complex nature of the relationship of the various traditions, thus making the task of defining some of these divisions rather difficult. One of the issues debated among scholars, for example, centers upon where the wilderness traditions actually begin in the Book of Exodus.[3] The debate normally considers the relationship of the Reed Sea narrative to the exodus tradition and the narratives of the wilderness setting.[4]

The wilderness narratives in the book of Exodus represent a structured journey with its immediate destination at Sinai (see Table 1 below). Although the destination at Sinai is not mentioned within the wilderness narratives, the structure of the text from the exposition of the journey in Exodus 13:17–22 to Exodus 19:1–2 takes the form of a specific short journey to a definite place. The command of Yahweh to Moses (Exod. 3:12) seems to refer to this destination; otherwise, there is no apparent explanation for the structure of the exodus and wilderness traditions that assume a knowledge of the destination.

Table 1

THE WILDERNESS NARRATIVES IN EXODUS

Exodus 3:12 Journey command

13:17–22 Exposition
  14:1–15:21 Reed Sea event
    15:22–27 Marah narrative
      16 Manna and Quails event
        17:1–7 Massah and Meribah event
          17:8–16 War with the Amalekites
            18 Jethro and Moses visit

19:1–2 Arrival at Sinai

Unlike the narratives in Numbers, which will be discussed below, the Exodus narratives do not have a high point prior to the entrance into the Wilderness of Sinai. Each narrative, instead, contributes to the journey as a whole with the journey's climax at Sinai. The overarching structure to the wilderness traditions in the book of Exodus is therefore determined by the theme of the journey to Sinai.

The divisions in the book of Numbers are (1) the conclusion of the Sinai narratives (Num. 1–10:10), (2) the journey to the transjordan (Num. 10:11–21:9), and (3) the period associated with the transjordan prior to the entrance into Canaan (Num. 21:10–36:13). The first two divisions are fairly clear as to the point of separation from one period to the next. Numbers 1–10:10 is linked by its content and context to the Sinai experience in the books of Exodus and Leviticus. The transition from one setting to another occurs in Numbers 10:11–12 which has the Israelites departing from the Wilderness of Sinai.

However, the point of separation of the wilderness narratives in the second division to that of the transjordan narratives in the third division is debatable. One view proposes that the division should lie at 22:1 where the Balaam narratives record Israel at the plains of Moab.[5] When the transjordan is reached (Num. 22:1), the journey of Israel through the wilderness is completed. The views of scholars such as Fritz suggest that upon entering the plains of Moab the scene shifts from the wilderness period to the traditions of the "Jordan valley."[6] At this point in the journey to Canaan, the stories of Israel shift in focus to Israel's encounter with the nations of the transjordan and the preparation for entrance into the land of Canaan.

Table 2

THE WILDERNESS NARRATIVES IN NUMBERS

Exodus 32–34 The Golden Calf Event

10:11–28 From Sinai to Paran
10:29–34 Hobab
10:35–36 The Ark
11:1–3 Taberah murmuring
11:4–35 Quail and Manna
12 Miriam leprosy
13, 14 Spy story
15 Various laws
16 Korah rebellion
17 Aaron's rod
18 Tribe of Levi venerated
19 Laws of defilement
20:1–13 Water of Meribah
20:14–21 Edom conflict
20:22–29 Death of Aaron
21:1–3 Hormah
21:4–9 Bronze Serpent

25:1–18 Baal Peor event

Milgrom adds that the serpent narrative in Numbers 21:1–9 is the last event in the wilderness period.[7] Still another opinion maintains that the vengeance on Midian in 31:1–20 should be included as part of the wilderness wanderings.[8] In essence, the identification of the Biblical texts which should be assigned to the wilderness traditions remains unclear due to the ambiguity regarding the point of separation between the wilderness period and the narratives attributed to that period, and the subsequent period in the transjordan.

The narratives associated with the wilderness traditions in the book of Numbers can be listed as above in Table 2, bearing in mind the problem of identification stated above. The chiastic shape of the list of narratives reflects the high point of the wilderness traditions which occurs with the spy narrative (Num. 13–14) and the Korah rebellion (Num. 16).

The wilderness traditions are bracketed by the incident of the golden calf (Exod. 32–34) and the apostasy at Baal Peor (Num. 25:1–18).[9] The major portion of the wilderness narratives appears between these important events (Num. 10:11–21:10) with the most prominent traditions recorded in Numbers 13–17. Unlike the Exodus narratives that reveal less about the situation within the life of the community during the journey to Sinai, the traditions in Numbers reveal a community organized to some degree with its social affairs and laws in constant conflict. The development of the community is demonstrated in the spy narrative (Num. 13–14) and the Korah rebellion (Num. 16). The two events reflect Israel's efforts to gain control of their own life situation now that the community is confronted with problems that threaten their survival. Of course, the stories reveal a community that repeatedly fails to follow the leadership of God and God's appointed leaders.

Numbers 10:12–14:45 are wilderness traditions that are clustered at the beginning of the period of Israel's journey from Sinai into the wilderness. Numbers 20:1–21:10 are traditions clustered at the end (Table 2).[10] The Korahite rebellion (Num. 16–17) can be placed somewhere in between the two periods, though the incident is without explicit reference to any location. The rebellions in Numbers 16–17 represent several events with different persons involved which reflect the experiences of the Israelite community over a period of time.[11] The vicinity of Kadesh (10:11–20:13) is traditionally understood to be the place where the Israelites spent the major portion of the forty years in the wilderness.

The Reed Sea Tradition

The Reed Sea narrative (Exod. 13:17– 15:21) is among those narratives that are considered in the identification and analysis of the wilderness traditions. Should the Reed Sea event be included among the wilderness narratives that comprise the wilderness traditions? Martin Noth regards the deliverance at the sea to be the center of the exodus theme. All the miraculous acts of God in Egypt point to the decisive event at the Reed Sea.[12] According to this view, the exodus event concludes with the miraculous sea event and the Israelites' departure from the Reed Sea (Exod. 15:22) thus marking the beginning of the wilderness narratives.

One suggestion has the exodus narratives concluding when the Israelites depart from Egypt (Exod. 12:50). In contrast to the previous view, the Reed Sea narrative would be included within the wilderness traditions and placed among the many miracles that occurred during the Israelites' wilderness journey from Egypt to Sinai.[13] The Reed Sea narrative, then, marks the beginning of the wilderness theme and provides the literary link between the exodus and the wilderness theme.[14] Coats argues that if the Reed Sea event is the climax to the exodus event, as Noth and others propose, then the exodus theme is independent from other Pentateuchal themes.[15] The presence of the Egyptians in both the exodus and the Reed Sea events does not necessarily suggest that the two events form one tradition. If the Reed Sea tradition is placed within the wilderness traditions, the conclusion to the plague tradition (Exod. 13:16) would mark the end of the exodus theme, and the summary statement in Exodus 13:17 would therefore begin the account of the wilderness journey. The setting for the Reed Sea in all three sources (Exod. 13:17–18 [E], 13:20ff. [J], 14:1–2 [P]) also places Israel outside of Egypt and in the wilderness.[16]

Other views challenge the conclusion that the Reed Sea event belongs in the wilderness setting.[17] The view that makes a distinction between the Reed Sea tradition and the wilderness traditions states that at an early stage, represented by the Yahwist source, the sea event was not included in the exodus tradition but was considered a part of the wilderness cycle.[18] As Childs observes, the later emphasis from the Priestly Writer united the Reed Sea event with the exodus tradition. Exodus 14:1–2 (P) is a key passage that suggests the Reed Sea narrative belongs to the exodus tradition. In Exodus 14:1–2, the Israelites are ordered to turn back and camp in Egypt, close to the sea. The itinerary in Numbers 33:5 further states that Israel reached Etham located "on the edge of the wilderness," indicating a location distinct from a wilderness setting. The wilderness wanderings, therefore, would not begin until after the Israelites leave the area of the Reed Sea, thus completing the exodus from Egypt.[19] Coats, however, argues that, even for the Priestly Writer, the distinction is yet made between the exodus (Passover) and the Reed Sea event thus placing the Reed Sea event in the wilderness setting.[20]

Considering the validity of the debate, perhaps the initial stage of the Israelites' departure from Egypt and the Reed Sea is not a wilderness situation. Exodus 12:37 and 13:20 are stations in the itinerary concerned with the departure of the Israelites from Egypt. Davies suggests that these two notes in the itinerary are placed unnaturally within a series of incidents that occurred during the departure.[21] Both stations in Exodus 12:37 and 13:20 are linked by the name Succoth: "And they moved from Succoth, and encamped at Etham" (Num. 13:20a). After stating the Israelites traveled from Succoth to Etham on the edge of the wilderness, there is no further reference to a journey through or out of that setting. No connection is therefore made between the itinerary in 13:20 and the next station in 15:22, a station undoubtedly in the wilderness. A connection is made, however, between the statement in Exodus 13:18a and Exodus 15:22. The itinerary link between these two passages appears to speak more in favor of, but with some uncertainty, the notion that the Reed Sea event is an integral part of the overall wilderness theme.

וַיַּסֵּב אֱלֹהִים אֶת־הָעָם דֶּרֶךְ הַמִּדְבָּר יַם־סוּף	"But God led the people round by the way of the wilderness toward the Reed Sea." (Exod. 13:18a)
וַיַּסַּע מֹשֶׁה אֶת־יִשְׂרָאֵל מִיַּם־סוּף וַיֵּצְאוּ אֶל־ מִדְבַּר־שׁוּר	"Then Moses led Israel from the Reed Sea, and they went into the wilderness of Shur." (Exod. 15:22a)

The debate over the placement of the Reed Sea event appears to center upon the itinerary station at Etham (Exod. 13:20). Etham is located "on the edge of the wilderness." In Exodus and Numbers the term קָצֶה is used to refer to a border or outskirt of an area.[22] The language in Exodus 13:20 suggests that the edge of the wilderness does not necessarily mean to be within a wilderness setting. A syntactical ambiguity is noted by Childs, with respect to the relation of the "way of the wilderness" to the "sea of reeds" (Exod. 13:18).[23] The translation of דֶּרֶךְ הַמִּדְבָּר יַם־סוּף is potentially difficult. The construction can be translated in the accusative of direction, "by way of the wilderness toward the sea," or as a construct relationship, "by way of the wilderness of the Reed Sea." The translation could likewise be "in the direction of the wilderness and the Reed Sea." Further ambiguity exists in Numbers 33:8 where the sea that the Israelites passed through is located, according to the priestly itinerary, within the "Wilderness of Etham," a location not included in the

Exodus account.[24] The Septuagint has τῆς ἐρήμου αὐτοι instead of the reference in the Masoretic Text to Etham, thus indicating another attempt to deal with the problem of Etham's relationship with the wilderness setting.

A summary point is evident from the above discussion regarding the itinerary. The ambiguity in the wilderness itinerary associated with the exodus tradition is central to the problem of determining the relationship between the exodus and wilderness traditions in their final shape within the canonical text. The identification of the wilderness traditions, in the fullest sense, is certainly influenced by this relationship. The present study will assume that the exodus tradition concludes with the Reed Sea event, to include the Song of Moses (Exod. 15:1–18) and the Song of Miriam (Exod. 15:19–21).

Exodus 32 and Numbers 25

The task of determining where the wilderness traditions end in the book of Numbers is similar to the problems encountered in the previous discussion. The problem concerns the relationship of the Balaam narratives (Num. 22–24) and the episode at Baal Peor (Num. 25:1–18) to the wilderness and transjordan traditions. This relationship can be further clarified by establishing a relationship between Exodus 32 and Numbers 25.

The period following the exodus from Egypt is marked by two extreme sins. One is the apostasy of the golden calf (Exod. 32–34) and the other is the faithlessness of the scouts (Num. 13–14).[25] Exodus 32–34 is of particular significance to the task of identifying the scope of the wilderness traditions in the book of Numbers. The golden calf incident in Exodus 32 and the Baal Peor incident in Numbers 25, may contribute to the shaping of the traditions of the wilderness period since the two events resemble each other in their inner detail. Both narratives present Israel as a rebellious and unfaithful people, traits of the community common to the wilderness traditions as a whole. Exodus 32:21–22 is a key passage that reveals the rebellious nature of the people:

וַיֹּאמֶר מֹשֶׁה אֶל־אַהֲרֹן	And Moses said to Aaron,
מֶה־עָשָׂה לְךָ הָעָם הַזֶּה	"What did this people do
כִּי־הֵבֵאתָ עָלָיו	to you that you have brought
חֲטָאָה גְדֹלָה׃	a great sin upon them?"
	(Exod. 32:21)

וַיֹּאמֶר אַהֲרֹן אַל־יִחַר	And Aaron said, "Let not
אַף אֲדֹנִי	the anger of my lord burn
אַתָּה יָדַעְתָּ אֶת־הָעָם	hot; you know the people,
כִּי בְרָע הוּא׃	that they are set on
	evil." (Exod. 32:22)

The passage is difficult to translate due to the ambiguity of the Hebrew in the reference to the nature of the people in the final clause of verse 22.[26] However, the characterization of the community in this passage and their behavior revealed in Numbers 25 indicate a similar nature inherent in the wilderness generation. Other similarities between the two passages include the worship of other gods (Exod. 32:8 and Num. 25:2) and the wrath of God shown in the punishment of the guilty (Exod. 32:26–28 and Num. 25:7–8).

The Golden Calf event and the Baal Peor event, furthermore, could reflect the actions and experiences of the wilderness community at the beginning and the end of the wilderness traditions proper (Table 2, p. 19). The punishment for the sin at Baal Peor can also be interpreted as the fulfillment of the judgment at the golden calf incident. In Exodus 32:34, to illustrate, the writer appears to be referring to the coming event in Numbers 25. In the fullest expression of the traditions surrounding Israel's sin and subsequent judgment, Baal Peor could be an extension of the golden calf incident.[27]

The apparent relationship between Exodus 32 and Numbers 25 helps to validate the proposition that Exodus 32–34 and Numbers 25 constitute an inclusive statement of the destiny of the first generation: "A day will come when I will punish them for their sin" (Exod. 32:34). If these two events represent an inclusive statement, then the scope of the wilderness traditions may include the Balaam narratives as well as the Baal Peor incident, but, on the other hand, the sins and rebellions of the exodus generation transcend the various traditions in the books of Exodus and Numbers and should not be understood as restricted solely to any single tradition.

NUMBERS 26–36

Dennis Olson proposes that the census lists in Numbers 1 and 26 control the primary structure of the book.[28] The occasion for the census suggests that a new generation of Israelites has arisen. The first generation of Israelites has died in the wilderness, and now a new community continues with anticipation of entrance into the promised land. Emphasis on the transition from one generation to the next by

Biblical writers has likewise placed stress upon the motif "death in the wilderness," one of the key motifs that has come to epitomize the fate of the Israelites in the wilderness period. Death in the wilderness is the punishment for and the result of the community's rebellion against Yahweh, a judgment even Moses and Aaron do not escape. In this respect, the census in Numbers 26 can be the place of departure from the wilderness period so marking the conclusion of the wilderness traditions. The balance of the book of Numbers is concerned primarily with the prospective occupation of the promised land. In effect, the view that Numbers 26 represents a transition is likewise compatible with the view that Numbers 22–25, linked to the wilderness period by the itinerary in Numbers 22:1, should be included in the wilderness theme.

With Chapter 26 as a transitional text, the book of Numbers is divided into two periods reflecting two communities of faith.[29] The situation for the people of Israel changes from death sentence placed upon the old generation to that of hope for the next generation. In addition to the shift from the mood of despair to hope, the new generation is also characterized in sharp contrast to the first generation of the exodus. Numbers 27–36 describe the loyalty and perseverance of the new generation. The reward for their faithfulness, for example, is that Israel sustains no loss of life in the conflict with the Midianites (Num. 31). Certainly for the book of Numbers, the wilderness traditions can be set apart from the traditions that follow by observing the change in the state of affairs for the new generation of Israelites. The change is brought about primarily by the judgment of Yahweh against the people who rebelled in the wilderness. The great distinction between the Wilderness Traditions and the transjordan traditions is that judgment. Numbers 26 would be the next logical step in the movement of the traditions from the exodus, Sinai, and the wilderness, toward the setting for the conquest tradition.

Numbers 26–36 reveals the appropriation of the wilderness traditions for the new generation.[30] The appropriation of the wilderness traditions in Numbers 26-36 can contribute to the task of identifying the wilderness traditions, as well as their scope and content. In Numbers 26–36 the generation and events of the wilderness period are referred to in an illustrative manner by referring back to the experiences of the generation of the exodus as people who lived in the past. The census of Numbers 26, for example, begins with a reference to Dathan, Abiram, and Korah (Num. 26:9–11, also 27:3). Dathan, Abiram, and Korah died in the wilderness because they "contended against the Lord" (Num. 26:9). This particular event apparently proved to be of great significance for the wilderness traditions since it is the only event mentioned specifically within the detailed list of families.

After accounting for the tribes that will possess their portions of the promised land, the Levites are numbered in the latter part of the census (Num. 26:57–62). The Sons of Aaron, Nadab and Abihu, are the only family members mentioned who are associated with an incident in the past (Num. 26:61). The account of the sin of Nadab and Abihu falls within the Sinai material (Lev. 10:1–3). The family of Moses and Aaron, which include Nadab and Abihu, is listed initially within the pre-Sinaic material in Exodus 6:19–23. Nadab and Abihu are also associated with Moses and Aaron in the performance of leadership roles during the Sinai experience (Exod. 24:1,9). In Exodus 24:9, Moses, Aaron, Nadab, and Abihu take part in the receiving of the book of the Covenant. The sin of Nadab and Abihu, in particular, is "offering unholy fire" (וַיַּקְרִבוּ לִפְנֵי יְהוָה אֵשׁ זָרָה [Lev. 10:1]), which is recorded by the Priestly Writer to stress the need for compliance with the ritual laws.[31]

In Numbers 26:64–65, the allusion is most assuredly to the spy narrative of Numbers 13–14. The Priestly Writer refers to the two families of Caleb and Joshua as the only surviving members of the first generation, a crucial statement in the census, since the census stresses the fulfillment of the judgment of Numbers 14:26–35 (P) with the passing away of those who rebelled. In Numbers 26:65, what is surprising is the absence of reference to the forty years of wandering in the wilderness as part of the judgment. The forty years of wandering must be understood since the census is focused primarily upon the transition to the next period through the motif of death in the wilderness (Num. 26:65a).

In brief, the census in Numbers 26 lists the families in a straightforward manner, but when commentary is used in the census, two traditions are reflected, Sinai and the wilderness traditions. Apart from the fact that the families listed in the census were those who came from Egypt in the exodus (Num. 26:4), events reflecting the period prior to the Sinai experience are not mentioned.

Further appropriation of the Wilderness Traditions in Numbers 26–36 is taken from the events recorded in Numbers 10:12–25:18. Major references to the wilderness traditions include the waters of Meribah (Num. 27:12–23), the Baal Peor incident (31:13–20), and the spy narrative of Numbers 13–14 (Num. 32). No explicit reference is made in Numbers 27–36 to the wilderness narratives in the book of Exodus. In Numbers 27:12–23 the incident at Meribah (Num.

20:2–13) is recalled from tradition not only to explain why Moses did not enter the land but to introduce Joshua as the successor to Moses. The Baal Peor incident of Numbers 25 is recalled by Moses in Numbers 31:13–20 in an effort to prevent the repeat of the sin at Baal Peor in the present context. In Numbers 32 the spy incident of Numbers 13–14 is restated in order to compare the potential consequences, should the sons of Reuben and the sons of Gad refuse to participate in the conquest, with the consequences of the previous generation's refusal to enter the land.

The illustrative use of the various stories suggests a shift in the situation from a wilderness setting to another setting characterized with anticipation of and preparation for entrance into the land of Canaan. In Numbers 26–36 the traditions of the wilderness are utilized for the first time as a means for addressing new situations encountered by the new generation. The primary concern in each recollection and appropriation is disobedience by the community and its consequences which would result in a common fate to that of the wilderness generation.[32]

Within Numbers 26-36, Chapter 33 contains the itinerary of Israel's journey from Rameses in Egypt to the plains of Moab at Abel-shittim. The itinerary reflects an advanced literary stage in utilizing the traditions of the journey.[33] The chapter emphasizes the goal of the journey as the inheritance of the land of Canaan (Num. 33:50–56). The development of the itinerary in the books of Exodus and Numbers closely parallels and relates to the same late redaction process that produced the itinerary in Numbers 33.[34] The list of stations in the Numbers 33 itinerary is brief, displaying a rhythmic text with few comments.

The itinerary commentary, though scarce indeed, can provide information regarding the scope of the wilderness traditions. The death of Aaron, for example, is mentioned in connection with the station at Mount Hor (Num. 33:38–39). The incident of Aaron's death is linked by implication to Numbers 20:2–13. In Numbers 33:8, however, the event at the sea is not described in detail as a miraculous deliverance (וַיַּעַבְרוּ בְתוֹךְ־הַיָּם, cf. Exod. 14:29), though the imagery is an allusion to the Reed Sea tradition. Kallai suggests that Numbers 33 is a stylized summary of the journey, and some of the important stations and events in the wilderness journey are not included.[35] The stations at Kadesh, for example, are not included except in passing. Further, the Sinai experience is not mentioned in the journey from Egypt to Moab.

One reference is made in Numbers 33:14 to waters of Rephidim (Exod. 17:1), a prominent station located in the Wilderness of Sin. The traditions of the waters of Massah-Meribah (Exod. 17:1–7) and the war with the Amalekites (17:8–16), two traditions in the wilderness traditions associated with the location, are not mentioned. Numbers 33, however, represents an itinerary tradition and not an appropriation of the wilderness traditions as such. Compared to other occurrences of individual traditions in Numbers 26–36, Numbers 33 does not follow the same tradition structure, but can be understood as a separate tradition accounting for a structured journey from Egypt to Moab and standing alongside the content of the wilderness narratives. The itinerary recapitulates the movements of the Israelites with limited use of the content of the wilderness narratives. Though a reference is made to Rephidim in Numbers 33, the wilderness traditions primarily reflect those represented in the Book of Numbers.

As the events from the wilderness period are appropriated or recalled in Numbers 26–36, when situations arise within the community of faith, the primary text from which the narratives are drawn is the book of Numbers. The book of Numbers, of course, presents the traditions following the Sinai experience, while the Priestly Writer draws upon the priestly traditions of Exodus and Leviticus, as indicated in Numbers 26 and 33. This point lends further credence to the notion that the wilderness traditions in the book of Exodus are linked primarily to the exodus and the journey to Sinai.

The Wilderness Itinerary

The wilderness itinerary is another recurring element in the narratives of Exodus and Numbers that can assist in identifying the wilderness traditions. The wilderness narratives are structured in such a manner so as to place emphasis upon the journey from Egypt to the transjordan.[36] The account of Israel's time spent in the wilderness begins with the exit from Rameses (Exodus 12:37), including the Reed Sea event, and continues until the people arrive at the plains of Moab (Numbers 22:1). The last itinerary, which occurs in Numbers 22:1, connects the Balaam narratives and the Baal Peor incident with the wilderness theme.[37] The itinerary serves as a unifying element in the wilderness narratives and emphasizes the point that the wilderness period ends without the wilderness community entering the land of Canaan.[38]

Itinerary notes occur with smooth succession from the exodus to the arrival in the Wilderness of Sinai (Exod. 12:37–19:1). The next itinerary after the Sinai material is Numbers 10:12. During the period of the Wilderness of Paran (Numbers 10:12–19:22), the itinerary is virtually absent. Yet within this portion of narratives are found some of the major stories of the wilderness traditions.

In regard to the structure of Exodus through Numbers, three major breaks occur in the itinerary. The first break in the itinerary occurs in Exodus 19:1. Exodus 19:1–2 serves as an introduction to what follows at Sinai and marks a departure from the previous historical narration. The Sinai experience represents a massive block of material that links the Exodus wilderness narratives with the narratives of the wilderness traditions in Numbers (Exod. 19:1–Num. 10:11). In Numbers 10:12 the Israelites depart from the wilderness of Sinai and travel to Hazeroth (Num. 11:35).

The second major break in the itinerary is Numbers 12:16, which has the Israelites arriving at the Wilderness of Paran (Num. 12:16), a place already mentioned in Numbers 10:12. Another great block of material follows Numbers 12:16 and extends further to events at Mount Hor (Num. 20:22). The itinerary that follows the bronze serpent narrative (Num. 21:4–9) is given in rapid sequence (Num. 21:10–35) and concludes with the arrival at the plains of Moab recorded in Numbers 22:1, the last major break in the itinerary.

Even in its complicated structure, the itinerary reveals two stations in the journey. One principal station is the Wilderness of Sinai (Exod. 19:1–2), and a second station is found at Kadesh (Num. 20:1).[39] If we follow Coats' suggestion that references to the Wilderness of Paran and the Wilderness of Zin represent the same location, then the wilderness traditions in Numbers would have one setting prior to Numbers 22:1.[40] As some scholars suggest, the wilderness traditions would have developed around the station at Kadesh (Num. 20:1, 13:26).

Perhaps the primary contribution made by the itinerary is that it helps provide unity for the various traditions in the books of Exodus and Numbers. The itinerary marks the beginning and/or closing of major narrative events, but may not always relate closely to the development of the narration.[41] The wilderness itinerary, then, cannot be used conclusively to determine the scope of the wilderness traditions since the period represented by the itinerary might not necessarily coincide with the wilderness period.

The scope and content of the wilderness traditions may be summarized through an analysis of the two blocks of material that occur in Exodus and Numbers. The individual narratives are interrelated by common itinerary or stations in the itinerary. Table 3 (see below) is a chart of those relationships. The pairing of the narratives is created by a common station in the itinerary which links the narratives in sequence. The narratives of the first pairing (Part I) are primarily concerned with the ordinance of the passover and the consecration of the first born, both human and cattle. The Reed Sea narrative (Part II) stands alone because it shares a unifying setting with the stations in the exodus narratives but does not share an itinerary station with another narrative. The third pairing (Part III) contains stories depicting the life situation during the journey to Sinai. The fourth pairing has a common station at Rephidim for smooth transition to the Sinai narratives.

The first and second pairings are connected by the common setting at the Reed Sea. The transition from the Reed Sea narrative to the wilderness narratives (Part II to III) is the only occurrence in which two settings are joined in the itinerary (Exod. 15:22). According to the unifying setting in Numbers 15:22, a transition is made from the Reed Sea tradition to the wilderness traditions. The third and fourth pairings have a common setting in the Wilderness of Sin. For the whole journey from Succoth to Sinai no continuous chain of stations is evident. Three settings, however, occur in the Book of Exodus that bind the narratives into one sequential whole; The Reed Sea, the Wilderness of Shur, and the Wilderness of Sin.

One wilderness narrative remains that needs to be placed within the traditions. The commonality of the Jethro narrative in Chapter 18 with the surrounding narratives is not apparent. Numbers 18:5 only states that Moses was in the wilderness, and the link with the Wilderness of Sin must be implied. A setting has not been established that would allow the Jethro narrative to fall within the logical progression of the traditions.

Among the numerous points of discussion and debate over the Jethro narrative, some scholars suggest that the narrative is chronologically out of order within the narratives of the book of Exodus and probably belongs to the period of the journey after Sinai.[42] The station for the Jethro narrative should be Rephidim since the Massah-Meribah narrative (Exod. 17:1–7), the war with the Amalekites (17:8-16), and the arrival at Mount Sinai (Exod. 19:2) are linked by this common station. Further ambiguity is evident in the vague reference to הַר הָאֱלֹהִים in Exodus 18:5 and הָהָר in Exodus 19:2, indicating in the former that Moses was in the vicinity of their destination Sinai while the latter suggests the people had just entered the wilderness of Sinai where the holy mountain is located.

The unity of the wilderness narratives in the book of Exodus is undeniable. The structure of the narratives that reflect the journey from Succoth to Sinai is smooth and well-organized. The Jethro narrative is distinct from the balance of the wilderness traditions in the book of Exodus and may not be a primary contributor to the wilderness traditions. In regard to the structure of the wilderness narratives in the book of Exodus, a journey is presented unhindered by anything along the way, a clear contrast from the wilderness journey in the book of Numbers (Table 4 below).

Table 3

THE WILDERNESS ITINERARY AND NARRATIVES IN EXODUS

Texts	*Itinerary*
PART I	
12:37–51 Passover ordinance	Succoth (Exod. 12:37)
13:1–22 Consecration of first born	Succoth (Exod. 13:20)
Unifying Setting	Reed Sea
PART II	
14:1–15:21 Reed Sea narrative	Pihahiroth (Exod. 14:2)
Unifying Setting	Reed Sea/Wilderness of Shur
PART III	
15:22–27 The Marah narrative	Elim (Exod. 15:27)
16:1–36 The Quails/Manna narrative	Elim (Exod. 16:1)
Unifying Setting	Wilderness of Sin
PART IV	
17:1–7 Massah-Meribah event	Rephidim (Exod. 16:1)
17:8-16 War with Amalek	Rephidim (Exod. 17:8)
18:1–27 Jethro narrative	(No itinerary)
19:1–Num. 10:11 The Sinai narrative	Rephidim (Exod. 19:2)

Though the journey presented in the book of Numbers is not as smooth and refined as the journey portrayed in Exodus, the structure of the wilderness traditions and the itinerary in the book of Numbers is very similar to the book of Exodus. The departures in both blocks of wilderness narratives contain various incidental events of lesser magnitude (Part I). The Exodus itinerary does not link more than two stations to one setting, but the settings do provide continuity for the journey from Succoth to Sinai.

Table 4

THE WILDERNESS ITINERARY AND NARRATIVES IN NUMBERS

Texts	*Itinerary*
Exod. 19:1–Num. 10:10	The Sinai event
Unifying Setting	Wilderness of Sinai
PART I	
10:11–11:35 Departure/Craving	Hazeroth (Num. 11:35)
12:1–16 Aaron/Miriam controversy	Hazeroth (Num. 12:16)
Unifying Setting	Wilderness of Paran
PART II	
13–14 The Spy narrative	Kadesh (Num. 13:26)
16–17 Korah, Dathan, Abiram Rebellion	No Itinerary
18–19 Levite election/purity laws	No Itinerary
Unifying Setting	Wilderness of Zin
PART III	
20:1–21 Meribah event/Edom conflict	Kadesh (Num. 20:1)
20:22–29 Death of Aaron	Kadesh/Mt. Hor (Num. 20:22)
21:1–10 Arad Conflict/Bronze Serpent	Mount Hor (Num. 21:4)
Unifying Setting	Moab (?)
PART IV	
21:10–35 Oboth to the plains of Moab	Various itineraries
22–25 Balaam/Baal Peor	Plains of Moab (Num. 22:1)

In the wilderness narratives of Numbers, by contrast, the station at Kadesh links two settings, the Wilderness of Paran and the Wilderness of Zin, and these two settings unite the whole of the traditions.[43] The transition from one narrative to the next is also not as smooth as those found in the book of Exodus. The itinerary is closely linked to the surrounding narratives at the point when the Israelites leave the Wilderness of Sinai (Table 4), but, within the period of the setting in the Wilderness of Paran, the narratives acquire an independence from any prescribed journey. Apart from the station at Kadesh, the itinerary, for example, is virtually absent in the setting of the Wilderness of Paran. The setting in the Wilderness of Zin, Part II to Part III, reflects a period of movement from Kadesh to Mount

Hor. The location of the concluding setting that unites Part III with Part IV is unclear since there is a break in the journey sequence from Mount Hor (Num. 21:4), as well as the uncertainty of the location of Oboth (Num. 21:10). The itinerary reflects a journey toward the plains of Moab and away from Edom and the wilderness below. The final setting in the itinerary is clearly in Moab (Num. 22:1).

A summary observation might suggest at this point that the narratives in the wilderness traditions do not correspond completely to the journey outlined by the wilderness itinerary. The narratives reflecting the wilderness period appear at times to be independent from the itinerary. Further, the stations in the itinerary at the beginning and the end are not necessarily in the wilderness.[44] The scope and content of the wilderness traditions may not include the Reed Sea event at the beginning nor the Balaam narratives and Numbers 25 at the end simply because they fall within the scope of the itineraries.[45] The itinerary may have a wider function and purpose than to claim the actual stations in the wilderness, and such an investigation is beyond the scope of the present discussion.

In conclusion, the wilderness narratives in the book of Numbers are very complex, including sundry accounts of the early traditions of Israel. The narratives in Numbers 10:11–25:18 appear to be less polished and less unified than the traditions of the journey from Succoth to Sinai in the book of Exodus (Exod. 13:17–18:27). The narratives of the wilderness period between the exodus and Sinai, on the other hand, are shaped to fit smoothly within the overall theme of the book of Exodus. The wilderness narratives in the book of Exodus would therefore better serve the exodus theme than to be viewed as separate literature representing another setting and tradition.

The itinerary of the wilderness traditions is more structured in the book of Exodus, giving the appearance of a unified theme for Exodus 1–18. The individual narratives are connected by carefully placed itinerary notes that direct the narratives along a journey which ends at Exodus 19:1. The apparent intrusion of the Sinai material has virtually subdued the wilderness narratives to serve that event by uniting the exodus and the Sinai traditions. This point is further suggested through the appropriation of the traditions in Numbers 26–36 in which the events in the book of Exodus are not recalled. Instead, for the book of Numbers, the wilderness traditions appear to be located in a group of narratives from the Sinai material to Numbers 22:10. Numbers 33:14 is the only reference to the traditions in Exodus, and the commentary on Rephidim is given within the itinerary genre of Numbers 33 (cf. Exod. 17:1).

The scope and content of the wilderness traditions may be attributed in part to the itinerary. The wilderness itinerary provides unity for the journey from Egypt to Moab.[46] Numbers 26–36 provide a working model for the appropriation of the wilderness traditions. Through this appropriation, one can identify the scope of the wilderness traditions that proved to be important for the writer of the book of Numbers. Two blocks of texts can now be attributed to the wilderness traditions. The first block is located in the book of Exodus, Exodus 15:22–18:27. The present study will not consider the Reed Sea narrative as part of the wilderness traditions. Evidence suggests that, first, the itinerary does not necessarily reflect a framework for the wilderness traditions, though a journey is the design of the itinerary. Second, the Reed Sea event is a self-contained narrative without a station in the itinerary linked to another station. Instead, Moses leads the people away from the vicinity of the Reed Sea. The use of two itinerary settings in Exodus 15:22 (Reed Sea and the Wilderness of Shur) indicates that a new block of material has begun. The second block of material extends from the Sinai narratives to the narratives reflecting Israel's arrival at the plains of Moab (Num. 10:11–21:10). With their arrival on the plains of Moab, the people of Israel depart from the wilderness setting.

Tradition Duplication

The narratives of Exodus 15:22–18:27 contain stories with similar content and motifs, which indicate duplicate accounts of the same event, thus suggesting the possibility of more than one stream of similar traditions. Each apparent duplication, listed below, involves similar narratives or traditions found in the book of Exodus, prior to the Sinai material, and following the material in the book of Numbers.

Water at Marah (Exod. 15:22–27)
Massah and Meribah (Exod. 17:1–7)
Water of Meribah (Numbers 20:1–13)
Quail/Manna (Exod. 16)
Quail/Manna (Num. 11:4–35)
Jethro/Moses (Exod. 18)
Hobab/Moses (Num. 10:29–32)

Exodus 15:22–27, 17:1–7, and Numbers 20:1–13 may represent similar accounts from the same tradition that were associated with a similar location in the wilderness. Since Deuteronomy 33:8, for example, uses Massah and Meribah in parallel, the two stories in

Exodus and Numbers, by their use of the same place names, may therefore represent the same water tradition (See Ps. 78:15–31 and 95:8–9, cf. Ps. 81:7).[47] The Marah story in Exodus 15:22–27 is linked to a possible tradition duplication because the story contains a play on the word Massah, thus indicating perhaps a connection with Exodus 17:1–7.[48] The water miracle in Exodus 17, however, is located at Massah-Meribah, implying a duplicate name for one place.

Deuteronomy 6:16 and 9:22 refer to the testing and provocation of God by the people in which the name Massah is mentioned alone, thus indicating that Massah and Meribah could refer to two distinct places, not to mention the fact that the water story in Numbers 20:1–13 is located at Meribah with no reference to Massah. Evidence indicates, though not conclusively, that in the present canonical shape of the wilderness traditions, two accounts of the same or similar tradition appear before the Sinai event and one following it.

The traditions of the quails and manna in Exodus and Numbers can be understood in a similar way to that of the water stories. In Exodus 16 the shape and content of the quails\manna story are influenced by the cultic and religious concerns of the Priestly Writer.[49] The narrative in Exodus 16 has been shaped to place emphasis upon obedience to God through the observance of the Sabbath. The miraculous provision of the manna maintains the dominant role in the narrative while the role of the quails is overshadowed.

The quails/manna story in Numbers 11:4–35 differs from Exodus 16 in that the miraculous provision of the quails holds the dominant role in the story. The manna, which has been provided already, is mentioned only briefly to emphasize the negative attitude of the people (11:6–9). The people have grown tired of a manna diet, and they long for fresh meat. The aid of Yahweh in the wilderness, demonstrated through the miraculous provision of food, is a common theme in both the Exodus and Numbers narratives, but Numbers 11:4–35 contains the additional judgment motif of Yahweh.

The logical progression in both the Exodus narratives and the Numbers narrative is complex and broken. An abrupt intrusion occurs in the Exodus account by the emphasis on Sabbath observance, and, in a similar manner, the Numbers account contains Moses' dispute with God over his unbearable task as their leader. In Exodus 16 the murmuring motif provides the context for the miraculous provision of manna which, in turn, provides the context for the writer's stress on Sabbath observance. In Numbers 11 the miraculous provision of quails is merged with the murmuring theme, and the divine judgment of the plague is given along with the miraculous provision of quail in response to the people's craving for meat. The two stories in Exodus 16 and Numbers 11, though appearing similar in content due to the duplicate references to manna and quails, are utilized for different purposes within the same wilderness traditions.

Though duplicate traditions are not present as in the water and quails/manna narratives, the role of the Amalekites in Exodus 17:8–16 and the spy narratives of Numbers 13–14 reveal the great contrast between the situation experienced by the Israelites before Sinai and after. In Exodus 17:8–16, the Amalekites are defeated through a miraculous display of Moses' power as leader of the Israelite people. In contrast to the victorious memorial in Exodus 17:8–16, Numbers 13:29 portrays Israel as a people who fear the Amalekites as well as the other nations. The story of the Amalekites' defeat in Exodus 17 appears to have been overlooked completely or forgotten by the people in the spy narrative of Numbers 13–14, and the presence of the Amalekites and the other nations obstructs Israel's entrance into the land of Canaan (Num. 13:27–29). The victorious affirmations of Exodus 17 now must be seen in contrast to Israel's defeat at the hands of the Amalekites and the Canaanites (Num. 14:39–45).

The great shift in the presentation of the Israelite and Amalekite situation is the result of the disobedience of the Israelites. Israel's encounter with the Amalekites in Exodus represents success through the miraculous aid of Yahweh and Israel's obedience to Yahweh through the leadership of Moses. Israel's encounter with the Amalekites in Numbers occurs in conjunction with Israel's rebellious disobedience to God. The defeat of the Israelites in Numbers 14 is presented as part of the failures of Israel in the wilderness which, in this particular illustration, demonstrates their failure to accept and trust the leadership of Yahweh and the chosen leaders.

Another possible duplicate account of traditions is the meeting between Moses and Jethro. In addition to Exodus 18 where Moses meets with Jethro, Numbers 10:29–32 contains a story of a brief encounter between Moses and Hobab. Hobab is identified in Numbers 10:29 as the son of Reuel, the father-in-law of Moses. He is familiar with the territory through which Moses and the Israelites wish to pass, though the text is not clear as to where Hobab actually went following the encounter.[50]

Important studies have been conducted in an attempt to establish the identity of Jethro, an issue that is beyond the goals of the present study.[51] Scholars also suggest that Moses' encounter with Jethro in Exodus 18 has been placed prematurely in the narratives of the Exodus wilderness narratives. Prior to Sinai, as the arguments suggest, Moses did not know the statutes of God (Exod. 18:20), and the tabernacle or altar for sacrifice had not yet been created (18:12).[52] In Exodus 15:22–27, however, other statutes and ordinances apparently were given for observance by Moses and the people. The claim that the law and other legal guidelines were given only at Sinai is difficult to maintain due to the various emphases on divine commandments prior to the experience at Sinai.

An analysis of the content and context of the narratives in Exodus 18 and Numbers 10:29–32 reveals similar situations. Both narratives include statements about Jethro/Hobab returning to Midian (Exod. 18:27, 10:30–33). Numbers 10:29–32 appears at first to be an isolated record of the conversation between Moses and Hobab. The encounter precedes a situation similar to that in Exodus 18, the motif of the difficulties of Moses' difficult leadership role (Num. 11:10–30). Jethro's timely advice in Exodus 18 alleviates the problems confronting Moses. In the book of Numbers, the leadership problem is contained within the Manna/Quails story that follows in Numbers 11.

The solution to the problem of Moses' leadership task, the choosing of additional leaders to assist in counseling the Israelites, is the same in both narratives, but the method of choosing the additional advisors is different in each account. In Exodus 18 Moses himself chooses leaders from among the Israelites while, in Numbers 11:10–30, God anointed seventy men with a portion of Moses' spirit. Exodus 18 and Numbers 10:29–11:35, therefore, appear to be duplicate accounts of the meeting of Jethro or Hobab, different names apparently referring to the same individual, and the problems confronting Moses in his leadership role. The content and setting of the two traditions suggest this conclusion.

The wilderness narratives of Exodus 15:22–18:27 are characterized in particular by their apparent duplication of other traditions appearing in the book of Numbers. None of the narratives stands alone as an independent tradition without some question as to its relationship with other events or narratives in the wilderness traditions of Numbers. Due to the apparent duplicate nature of the traditions in Exodus 15:22–18:27, the kerygmatic interpretation should be focused on the message of the final shape of the wilderness traditions, rather than upon the traditio-historical arguments.

The evidence thus far suggests that the narratives of Exodus present a particular message in a pre-Sinai setting and the Numbers narratives, though containing similar elements from traditions, present their own message in a post-Sinai context. Brevard Childs identified a distinguishing feature in the two blocks of wilderness narratives in

Exodus and Numbers which can contribute to a better understanding of the message. He credits Paul Hanson with the identification of two patterns in the wilderness narratives, one occurring in the material prior to the Sinai material and the other pattern evident in the wilderness narratives after Sinai.[53]

In the book of Exodus the wilderness narratives contain similar themes and motifs, such as the murmuring motif, as the narratives in Numbers, but the distinction between the two blocks of narratives is the response of Yahweh to the murmuring of the people. The first pattern represents the positive accounts of the situations confronted by the people during the wilderness journey to Sinai. The basic pattern of the positive accounts include a statement of an initial need that stimulates a complaint by the people. Moses then intercedes before Yahweh on behalf of the people. The narrative concludes with a miraculous intervention by Yahweh in a positive manner, and the problem is resolved by a miraculous act thus providing for the expressed need. In the narratives of the second pattern, which are found predominately in Numbers, the divine response changes. The basic pattern of the murmuring narratives includes an initial complaint by the people which causes a display of Yahweh's anger followed by punishment. Moses intercedes in a similar manner as before, and Yahweh relieves the people from the punishment.

The water narratives in Exodus 15:22–29, 17:1–7, and Numbers 20:2–13 remain positive in nature, with emphasis on God providing for the needs of the people. Numbers 20:2–13, however, is used in the negative sense to explain why Moses and Aaron did not enter the promised land (Num. 20:12, 24; Deut. 32:48–52). The Meribah narrative is the only event recorded in the wilderness traditions of the book of Numbers that does not include a show of anger from Yahweh toward the people by some form of punishment, but rather it is Moses and Aaron who receive the punishment. In the narratives of the second pattern, illustrated by Numbers 11:1–3, 17:5–15, and 21:4–9, the response by Yahweh includes punishment. Other stories, such as Numbers 12 and 16, do not describe the murmuring or rebellion as originating from the community of Israelites as a whole but from a segment or portion of the people. Thus a distinction is therefore made between the wilderness traditions of Exodus and Numbers.

The narratives in Exodus 15:22–18:27 represent the miraculous preservation of Israel in the wilderness. The stories in Numbers 10:11–21:9 also represent the miraculous preservation of Israel in the wilderness, but, on the other hand, they stress the disobedience of Israel during the wilderness period. The positive pattern is grounded in a basic need by the people. The negative pattern includes a series of complaints directed against the leadership, Moses, Aaron, and Yahweh, that have arisen apparently in conjunction with an expressed genuine need, but not necessarily reflecting a genuine need alone.

The narratives of the second pattern, which include elements from traditions similar to those found in the pre-Sinai material, have come to assume the more significant role in the wilderness traditions, thus contributing to the negative picture of Israel in the wilderness. Moses functions as mediator for the people in both blocks of wilderness narratives. He intervenes on behalf of the people in times of basic need (Exod. 17:1–7), as well as in times of divine punishment (Num. 11:1–3). Moses successfully mediates for the people in Exodus 15:22–17:16, though the anger of Yahweh is expressed (Exod. 17:28). In the narratives of the book of Numbers, the response of Yahweh to the murmuring is not always relieved, even though Moses mediates as before (14:20–35). According to the shape of the wilderness traditions, the Sinai experience created a difference between the two periods reflected in the Exodus and Numbers narratives. One view suggests that after Sinai the conditions had changed and Israel's relationship to her leadership became formalized.[54]

Themes and Motifs

Martin Noth has identified five themes that represent the periods before the Israelites became a state: "guidance out of Egypt," "guidance into the arable land," "promise to the patriarchs," "guidance in the wilderness," and "revelation at Sinai."[55] The themes are listed in a definite order according to their traditio-historical priority or degree of importance. Noth suggests that the themes were joined together step-by-step in a particular sequence that can still be determined with some accuracy. The wilderness traditions are a later addition to the exodus and guidance into the arable land traditions with the Sinai material added last. The guidance in the wilderness and Sinai traditions are less significant to Israel's sacred history than are the first three themes.[56] The dominant themes are guidance out of Egypt and guidance into the arable land. The narratives of the wilderness traditions lack the formal unity compared to that of the exodus and conquest traditions.[57]

The presence of the apparent duplicate accounts of events in the wilderness, such as the water and food narratives and references to Jethro, reflect a complex history of tradition and literary development. Perhaps in their early development traditio-historically, the wilderness traditions were less significant compared to the other events remembered in tradition, but in the process of canonical structuring, the wilderness traditions eventually came to be utilized among the more popular illustrative subjects for preaching and teaching by later generations (cf. Ezek. 20; Ps. 106; Neh. 9). The wilderness traditions provide the example *par excellence* for each generation's trials and hope for survival.[58]

Gerhard von Rad stresses the presence in biblical literature of the short "credo" as a theological statement or confession that influenced the formation of early Israelite traditions.[59] According to the view of von Rad, the credo is understood to be the theological motive underlying the structuring of the Hexateuch. The two themes proposed by Noth, "guidance out of Egypt" and "guidance into the arable land," are also the two major acts of salvation expressed in credal confessions of early Israel. The credo identified by von Rad in Deuteronomy 26:5–9, and other so-called credo texts, does not include a reference to the Sinai experience, nor are the wilderness traditions explicitly mentioned nor fully developed. A solution to this apparent oversight is to suggest that the wilderness traditions are implied within the exodus tradition.[60] Furthermore, the complex nature of the various stories of the wilderness traditions may indicate that the wilderness narratives were incorporated within the development of the fundamental themes which run throughout the Pentateuch.[61] The wilderness traditions in the books of Exodus and Numbers are nevertheless characterized by certain basic themes. Some are common to other traditions, such as the guidance theme in the exodus tradition, while others occur only in association with the wilderness traditions, such as the theme of death in the wilderness.

Evidence of the rebellion or murmuring motif extends from the Reed Sea event (Exod. 13:17–14:31) to the last episode of rebellion recorded in Numbers 25:1–9, prior to the transition texts in Numbers 26. The murmuring motif, then, occurs primarily, but not exclusively, in those narratives that fall within the wilderness motif (Exod. 13:17–Num. 21:9). The recognition of the murmuring motif in the narratives of Exodus and Numbers can be attributed mainly to the work of George W. Coats.[62] The rebellion motif is characterized by Israel's rebellion against the leadership of Moses stimulated by the conditions of life in the wilderness and within the community itself.[63] The murmuring motif, as understood by Coats, does not reflect the notion of complaining or murmuring by the people as much as an action of outright rebellion against Moses and Aaron, and Yahweh.[64]

From a traditio-historical analysis of the wilderness narratives, Coats proposes that the murmuring motif originated in the Jerusalem cult, with evidence in Psalm 78 so indicating an anti–Northern Kingdom polemic.[65] The polemic was an attempt to undermine the claims of the Northern Kingdom to their right to be in the land.[66] According to this view, the rebellion motif as a polemic is based on the idea that since the first generation of Israelites died in the desert because of their rebellion against Moses and Yahweh, the tribes of the Northern Kingdom, who held fast to the traditions of the fathers who came out of Egypt and settled in the land, could not claim the right under the basic tenets of election. The polemic against the Northern Kingdom is made in support of the Davidic covenant at Jerusalem (Ps. 78:67–72) which replaced the old covenant that died with the fathers in the desert.[67] Thus, the kerygma of the Yahwist, the primary source for the wilderness traditions, is pro–Davidic.

The murmuring or rebellion motif has broadened during the tradition process beyond its initial polemic to include virtually all of the narratives that reflect the period that the first generation spent in the wilderness. According to Coats' investigations, the primary traditions about the wilderness were originally positive in nature, and then were united to the confession of God's aid to Israel. The murmuring or rebellion motif became a part of the early traditions associated with Israel's beginnings. With the union of the various motifs, the murmuring motif came to be viewed as an unjustified complaint by the Israelites that shaped the image of Israel as an unfaithful and disobedient generation in the wilderness.[68] Such an interpretation is perhaps based on the judgment of Ezekiel (Chapters 16, 20, 23), which claims that Israel was stubborn and rebellious from their beginnings in Egypt.[69] Ezekiel 20:30, for example, compares the idolatrous nature of Ezekiel's present generation to that of their fathers, indicating that the fathers have become negative archetypes.[70]

Having focalized the wilderness motif at this point in our discussion, within those narratives from Exodus 15:22 to Numbers 21:9, does the murmuring motif occur outside the wilderness narratives? The golden calf episode in Exodus 32, for example, contains the rebellion motif, but the narrative does not contain the same elements normally found in other murmuring episodes. A personal challenge against Moses does not occur, though the community loses patience with Moses, because of his extended period of time on the mountain. The people also do not express a desire to return to Egypt, a common element in other narratives containing the murmuring motif, but they do challenge the validity of the exodus as a divine act (Exod. 32:4), which may be understood as a negation of the Sinai covenant.[71]

Additional views suggest that the murmuring motif begins as early as Exodus 2:14 where the people reject Moses in Egypt. The motif is also found in the Nadab and Abihu incident (Lev. 10:1–5) and the Baal Peor incident (Num. 25), the latter incident falling outside the scope of the wilderness traditions.[72] Further, though the murmuring motif occurs in many of the wilderness narratives, not all narratives of the wilderness traditions contain the murmuring motif (cf. Exodus 17:8–16, 18, Numbers 10:11–28, 10:29–34, 12, 15, 17, 18, 19, 20:14–21, 21:1–3). The account of the death of Aaron (Numbers 20:22–29), however, is narrated in connection with the rebellion at the waters of Meribah (Numbers 20:1–13), though the motif does not occur.

In conclusion, the murmuring motif is helpful, though not completely useful, in determining the scope of the wilderness traditions. The murmuring motif, according to the above discussion, is basically restricted to those narratives extending from the Reed Sea event to the Bronze Serpent story in Numbers 21:4–9. Only in a few cases do the wilderness narratives in the books of Exodus and Numbers appear to be independent from the influence of the murmuring motif. Both the murmuring motif and the traditions of the wilderness period appear to end at the same juncture in Israel's journey to Canaan.

One of the dominant themes in the wilderness traditions in the books of Exodus and Numbers is the guidance of Yahweh. Harrelson suggests that the theme of divine guidance and presence constitutes the fundamental biblical traditions which pre-date the wilderness traditions. Belief in Yahweh is what initiated the basic traditions.[73] The leadership of Yahweh or the guidance theme is a major unifying element that runs throughout the wilderness traditions.[74] According to Coats, the guidance theme, which reflects the positive traditions of the wilderness period, is introduced in Exodus 13:21–22, a summary or exposition of the entire scope of the wilderness theme.[75] The traditions within the wilderness theme include narratives about the miraculous aid of God, Israel's murmuring, the Sinai narratives, the Balaam cycle, military conflicts, and various legal material scattered throughout the wilderness traditions.

The guidance theme is not exclusively associated with, but occurs outside, the parameters of the wilderness traditions.[76] Although the texts appear before the account of the Reed Sea crossing, the basic contents point to the guidance theme of the wilderness traditions as a whole. Yahweh leads (נָחָה) the community in the correct way (דֶּרֶךְ) in which they should go, by a pillar of cloud (בְּעַמּוּד עָנָן) and a pillar of fire (בְּעַמּוּד אֵשׁ) (see Num. 14:14). These elements recur frequently during the narration of the wilderness journey as well as other references to the wilderness traditions in the Pentateuch and various texts of the Hebrew Bible. In the wilderness traditions following the Sinai experience, the cloud comes to be associated with the tent of meeting which, according to the Priestly Writer, became the central place for the community in the wilderness where Moses received his divine instructions in the governance of the community.[77]

The positive theme of Yahweh's guidance reveals that Yahweh is in control and has a purpose which validates that leadership (Num. 14:1–12, cf. Num. 13:39–45). Of considerable significance to the kerygmatic nature of the theme is the fact that the Israelites are guided by Yahweh and receive the aid of Yahweh in spite of their persistent rebellion and acts of unfaithfulness. Zimmerli compares the wilderness period to primeval history in which mankind, now more focused on Israel, is subjected to death by mankind's own guilt, a condition of hopelessness, yet sustained by Yahweh.[78]

The theme of death in the wilderness is the result of a final shaping of the wilderness traditions that reflects a disobedient generation of Israelites in the wilderness. The theme occurs for the first time in the Reed Sea narrative: "Is it because there are no graves in Egypt that you have taken us away to die in the wilderness? . . . For it would have been better for us to serve the Egyptians than to die in the wilderness" (Exod. 14:11–12). The theme, then, is contained within the traditions about Israel's rebellion in the wilderness. The murmuring in Exodus 14:11–12 expresses the desire of the Israelites to return to Egypt so as to escape the threat from the conditions encountered in the wilderness. A complaint of this nature is stated repeatedly in various forms throughout the wilderness traditions (e.g., Exod. 16:3, 17:3; Num. 14:2).

Within the narratives of Exodus 15:22–18:27, the theme of death in the wilderness is presented as a threat to the exodus generation, though none of the Israelites dies in the Exodus accounts of the wilderness journey. Nevertheless, death is a threat from both the living conditions in the desert and the potential judgment of Yahweh (Exod. 15:26). In Exodus 16, for example, the Israelites who kept the manna longer than the instructed time (Exod. 16:20) did not actually die for their disobedience; instead, all that is noted is that the manna spoiled. The story of Massah and Meribah (Exod. 17) pictures Moses faithful in the performance of his duties similar to his functions later in Numbers 20:2–13. In the Numbers account his actions result in his eventual death as punishment for his disobedience.

In the book of Numbers the threat of death becomes a reality. In the wilderness narratives of Numbers, the theme of death in the wilderness appears in relation to the judgment of God. Because of their sins, the Israelites are condemned to live as well as to die in the wilderness, and they were not permitted to return to Egypt nor leave the desert. The threat of death in Numbers 10:11–21:10 is at its highest mark in the spy narrative in Numbers 13–14 and the Korah rebellion in Numbers 16–17. The shape and the content of the spy narrative in Numbers 13–14 establish the overarching theme for the book of Numbers and constitutes a turning point in the wilderness traditions.[79] Through the judgment of Yahweh, the people of the first generation who came out of Egypt are condemned to die in the wilderness. In the pattern of the rebellion narratives, when Moses intercedes in the judgments against Israel in the wilderness the judgment is usually terminated. In the judgment of Numbers 13–14, Moses' intercession does not relieve the judgment entirely, but he is successful in part since Yahweh pardoned the sins and did not disinherit the people altogether (Num. 14:12, 20).

In the Korah rebellion, those who rebelled were also sentenced to death. In this particular episode, the theme of death in the wilderness is associated with the leadership of Moses. The theme is used to validate the leadership of Moses by using the death of those who rebelled as a sign or proof that God sent Moses (Num. 16:29). If the rebels lived to die a natural death, then Moses would be discredited. Their death was uncommon, however, since they died in the divinely orchestrated earthquake (Num. 16:31–33). The theme of death in the wilderness does not end with the resolution of the Korah rebellion but continues in Numbers 16:49 (Hebrew 17:14) where fourteen thousand also die by the plague as punishment for their further rebellion. Aaron's rod is kept as a testimony to the deadly rebellion.

Another illustration of the theme is found in the appropriation of the wilderness traditions in Numbers 27:1–11. In this incident the daughters of Zelophehad seek to be reinstated as heir to their father's inheritance. The argument for the daughters' rightful place as heirs is based on the claim that their father did not participate in the Korah rebellion (Num. 16). Apparently those participating in the rebellion lost their claims to the normal family inheritance.[80] Although their father did not participate in the rebellion, he still did not die of natural causes for he died in the wilderness, along with the rest of his rebellious generation, because of "his own sins" (Num. 27:3).

The above examples illustrate that, in the wilderness, death is an unnatural element in the life of the wilderness community. The tragic fate of the first generation was not an integral part of the divine plan for the community, which included the deliverance from bondage in Egypt to a new life in the promised land. Death as a dominant theme in the wilderness period is inseparably linked to sin and disobedience. Death of an individual by natural and physical causes is not recorded in the wilderness traditions. The one possible exception is the account of Miriam's death at Kadesh in Numbers 20:1. The brief account of Miriam's death may be linked to her rebellion and punishment in Numbers 12, thus placing her fate within the theme of death in the wilderness.[81]

In a closely related view to the previous theme, Dennis Olson proposes that the theme for the book of Numbers as a whole is "the death of the old and the birth of the new."[82] The census lists in Numbers 1 and 26 "play a pivotal role in providing the primary and overarching structure for the book of Numbers in its present form."[83] The two census lists provide the unifying framework both literarily and theologically. The judgment of the plague in Numbers 25 indicates that the last of the first generation has died leaving a new surviving generation of Israelites. The beginning of the census in Numbers 26 affirms this interpretation by stating "After the plague," thus referring to the rebellious Israelites who died in that incident, while the new generation represent the candidates who are included in the census.[84]

The shift from one generation to the next is further evident in the Priestly Writer's account of the instruction to Moses and Eleazar in Numbers 26:2, where the age requirement of twenty years old and older follows the details of the judgment in Numbers 14:29. In other words, the instructions for the taking of the census assumes that the judgment of Numbers 14:26-35 (P), in which all those who rebelled from twenty years old and older were doomed to die in the wilderness, has been fulfilled by the passing of that generation. The transition from the old generation to the new generation in the book of Numbers is significant since the transition focalizes the theme of death in the wilderness with the first generation exclusively.

In Numbers 26–36, the new generation now stands at the entrance to the promised land, and the theme of death in the wilderness ends. In contrast to Numbers 1–25, Numbers 26–36 does not record the death of any Israelite. Potential crises do not develop into rebellions but are successfully negotiated (27:1–11, 31:14–15, 32:1–42). Numbers 32 reflects the situation in Numbers 13–14 and illustrates a potential conflict involving the tribes of Reuben and Gad who desire to remain in the transjordan. The recollection of a similar experience recorded in Numbers 13–14 that proved to be tragic for the community helps to solve the community's present problem which, when viewed as a potential rebellion, could threaten the survival of the community. The crisis is resolved when Reuben and Gad agree to participate with the rest of Israel in the taking of the land. The responses of Reuben and Gad, which preserved the life of the community, are considerably different from the negative reaction of the people in Numbers 13–14 that caused death in the wilderness. In this situation, the wilderness traditions were successfully used to solve potential problems and avoid the fate of the previous generation.

In conclusion, the wilderness traditions in the books of Exodus and Numbers contain many themes, none of which function in isolation from another. The presentation of the community in the wilderness is extremely negative, due to the rebellions of Israel which permeate the wilderness journey from Egypt to Moab. The theme of the guidance of Yahweh provides the contrast whereby the community in the wilderness owes its survival to God's fidelity to them in spite of their rebellion. Rebellion by the people, the guidance of Yahweh, death in the wilderness, and divine judgment for sin are themes and motifs that are primarily confined to the wilderness period.

Literary Analysis of the Wilderness Traditions

The literary composition of the wilderness traditions is complex and detailed, with numerous views proposed by Biblical scholars. Fohrer, for example, suggests that Exodus 15:22–29 and 17:8–14 are from the N source, a source older than the Yahwist or the Elohist, which represents the nomadic period prior to the settlement in Canaan.[85] In a similar manner, Eissfeldt assigns Exodus 17:8–14 to the laity source (L).[86] An extensive literary analysis could be included in the present discussion, but the complex nature of such an effort is beyond the confines of the present study. The following analysis, instead, will address the roles of the prominent literary sources of the Yahwist and the Priestly Writer in the narrative structure of the wilderness traditions in the books of Exodus and Numbers.

By electing to concentrate the literary analysis upon these two primary literary strands, the present survey proceeds with the knowledge and recognition of the presence of other literary sources in the wilderness traditions, such as those mentioned above. When references are made to the Yahwist literary source, for example, the literary relationship between the Yahwist and the Elohist is assumed.[87] The present work will refer to the priestly influence in the Pentateuch as the Priestly Writer, acknowledging that various terms may refer to a similar literary source, such as the Priestly Document, the priestly source, the priestly writings, or Priestly Code, not to overlook the fact that more than one "Writer" may be implied through the use of the singular term.

Exodus 15:22–27

Exodus 15:22–27 is the first narrative depicting the life of the Israelite community in the wilderness following their miraculous deliverance from the Egyptian bondage. The two priestly itinerary notes in 15:22a and 15:27 enclose the story.[88] According to the Priestly Writer, the first stopping place in the wilderness is Elim. An earlier source could have had an itinerary as well (v. 22), since the construction that refers to מִיַּם־סוּף in the itinerary statement is unusual for the Priestly Writer.[89] Verses 25b–26, which some scholars attribute to the Deuteronomist, emphasize obedience to the statute and commandment of Yahweh.[90]

The supposed Deuteronomistic addition apparently means that only if Israel observes the "statute and ordinance," and so pass the test which Yahweh has imposed upon the community, then Yahweh will help the people in the future as he has done in the past. By making such a demand upon the community, the narrative also affirms that Yahweh alone is their provider and healer.[91] This initial narrative establishes the parameters within which the community must exist in order to live and avoid the fate of the Egyptians who died of the plagues. The contrast between death and life is clearly evident.

Other elements in the narrative include the "testing" (נִסָּה vs. 26) of the Israelites, murmuring against the conditions of the wilderness, and the reference to Yahweh as the healer (vs. 26b). Elements in the narrative are strikingly similar to Numbers 21:4–9, though the motif of testing is not explicit in the latter. In both narratives the progression from the initial complaint to the resolution of their problem is the same.[92] Both narratives are basically positive with Numbers 21:4–9 containing the additional element of divine judgment given in response to the murmuring. In each incident, the situation that creates the murmuring is resolved through the mediation of Moses before Yahweh on behalf of the people. The resolutions to the problems in the final statements of the two stories are without guarantee, even though Moses petitions Yahweh for them and a divine response relieves them of their unbearable situation. The following structural comparison reveals the conventional shape of the two narratives.

	Exodus 15:22–27	Numbers 21:4–9
1. Itinerary	Reed Sea (v. 22)	Reed Sea (v. 4)
2. Situation	No water (v. 23a)	No food and water (v. 5)
	Bad water (v. 23b)	Worthless food (v. 5b)
3. Murmuring	וַיִּלֹּנוּ הָעָם (v. 24)	וַיְדַבֵּר הָעָם (v. 5)
3a. Punishment		Serpents (v. 6)
3b. Repentance		"We have sinned" (v. 7)
4. Petition	Moses cried (v. 25a)	Moses prayed (v. 7b)
5. Instrument	Tree (v. 25a)	Fiery serpent (v. 8)
6. Resolution	Became sweet (v. 25a)	Healing (v. 8b)
7. Conditions	חק וּמִשְׁפָּט (v. 25b–26)	When he sees it (v. 8b)
8. Confession	Your healer (v. 26b)	Provider of life (v. 9)

The actions by Yahweh provide the occasion for a demand for decision and obedience from the community. The potential for future healing in Exodus 15:22–27 is conditional, just as the healing in Numbers 21:4–9 is dependent upon trust in Yahweh. Both concluding statements are set within the conditional אִם (15:26, cf. 21:9). Exodus 15:26 specifically makes a confession that Yahweh is their healer, compared to the confessional in Numbers 21:9 that Yahweh is the sustainer of life, understood in the statement, "If a serpent bit any man, he could look at the bronze serpent and live."

Future orientation is central to the Marah narrative, and the Priestly Writer's interest in the narrative is not surprising, because the narrative, though short and fragmented, speaks directly to the subsequent fate of the first generation. The writer utilizes the plague imagery of the exodus tradition to invoke the seriousness of the potential transgressions and the consequences.[93] The sins of the community may also be linked to the spread of disease among the people.[94] What had happened to Egypt reveals God's purposes which are not to be forgotten because the fate of Egypt can also come upon those who disobey and hinder God's divine will. Among the judgments of God in the exodus and wilderness traditions, the plague is used in many narratives as punishment against the disobedient.[95] The wilderness traditions therefore assume that where there is sin there is the undeniable threat of punishment by plague. The warning of a coming judgment by plague is not always mentioned explicitly. In Numbers 25:9, for example, the plague is mentioned without an introduction and is understood as divine punishment.

In conclusion, the pedagogical intention of the story is revealed by its kerygma or that which is proclaimed. The great truth to be learned is that instruction and guidance come from Yahweh from whom the community will find its source of life.[96] The miracle of the water directs the community to that realization. The narrative verbally links the event at Marah with Israel's deliverance from Egypt. A consistent pattern evolves that reveals the prescribed nature of the relationship between Yahweh and the people. The pattern is one of obedience and faith, a prefiguring of the Leviticus Holiness Code (Lev. 26:21) which stipulates the requirements for continued existence under the watchful care of Yahweh. Those who fail the test of faith will answer directly to Yahweh, who will "smite" (מַכָּה) them with plagues. The future conditions within which the community enjoys a relationship to Yahweh are solemnly established with no doubt as to the possible consequences should that relationship be aggravated by the sin of disobedience.

Exodus 16:1–35

The narrative as a whole is basically attributed to the Priestly Writer, with only a few elements assigned to the Yahwist.[97] The Priestly Writer characteristically refers to the visible presence of Yahweh as the כְּבוֹד יְהוָה "glory of the LORD," (v. 7). The expression is among the supernatural images used to describe Yahweh's being, an image that is symbolized by the cloud that comes down before the people (v. 10 [P]).[98] For the Yahwist, the image of the cloud is used in association with the pillar of fire (Exod. 13:21–22; Num. 14:14). Both images represent the dynamic presence of Yahweh with the community as they journey toward the promised land. Within the priestly writings of the wilderness traditions, Yahweh's כָּבוֹד, appearing in the image of the cloud, almost always occurs in conjunction with the tabernacle following the Sinai event. Appearing together with the tabernacle for the first time in Exodus 40:34f, Yahweh's כָּבוֹד came to represent the guiding presence of Yahweh in the midst of the community. The Priestly Writer is not the only writer who apparently linked the presence of Yahweh with the tabernacle. Both the Priestly Writer and the Yahwist associate the cloud of Yahweh's presence with the tent of meeting (Num. 11:25 [J]), since the three (JEP) were accustomed to including the tent as part of the cultic structure during the wilderness period.

Emphasis on Sabbath observance occurs early in Exodus 16 (v. 5) with the full implications of the importance of the Sabbath unfolded in vv. 22–30, followed by further commentary in vv. 31–35 of a cultic orientation. Has the role of Sabbath observance in Exodus 16 been stressed prematurely since the narrative occurs prior to the Sinai experience? As some scholars suggest, the command not to gather manna on the Sabbath does not necessarily presuppose knowledge of the Sabbath in the fullest sense, at least in accordance with Sinai law. Such a view might conclude that Exodus 16 could be understood as an event anticipating Exodus 31:12–17."[99] Understood in this manner, the Priestly Writer places the origin of the Sabbath not at Genesis 1 but within the traditions of Israel's wilderness experience.[100]

Regardless of the argument concerning its origin, the emphasis in Exodus 16 is unmistakably centered upon the relationship between the manna and Sabbath observance. The Priestly Writer fashions the tradition of the manna into a lengthy exposition dealing with the proper observance of the Sabbath. The event of the miraculous feeding is remembered as Yahweh's aid to Israel in her time of need and recorded as a memorial for future generations, functioning perhaps as an etiology of a future religious practice or observance.[101]

Though present in Exodus 16, the rebellion motif is not developed by the Yahwist nor the Priestly Writer in the fullest sense but is used to establish the context for other motifs to develop.[102] The murmuring motif is attributed to the Priestly Writer (vv. 1–3) where specific attention is placed on the whole congregation who are guilty of murmuring against Moses and Aaron (v. 2). The occurrence of the murmuring is rather significant since the incident is at the beginning of the wilderness period in which Yahweh is accused of evil intentions in bringing the people into the wilderness.

Within the murmuring motif, a comparison is made between the land of Egypt and the community's present situation. The people find the threat of death in Egypt (מִֽי־יִתֵּ֨ן מוּתֵ֤נוּ בְיַד־יְהוָה֙ בְּאֶ֣רֶץ מִצְרַ֔יִם, v. 3a [P]) more appealing than their death in the wilderness. Such comparison implies the community's regret that the exodus has occurred (see Num. 20:3). The substance of the rebellion, then, lies in the problem caused by the community's departure from Egypt and the uncertainty of their present situation. The complaint has virtually no connection with the need for food, and the problem of hunger and the need for food simply provides the setting for the murmuring.[103] The murmuring reflects the amazing indifference of the people toward the phenomenal deliverance of Israel from their slavery under the Egyptians. The basic content of their complaint reflects the community's complete misunderstanding of why they departed from Egypt. In effect, the people challenge the notion that the exodus was a divine act. The problem is therefore more related to the community's knowledge and understanding of the exodus than the need for food.[104]

Since the validity of the exodus itself is brought into question, the intention of the Priestly Writer in the wilderness traditions can be understood in part as the progressive revelation of Yahweh as the one who delivered them from the hands of the Egyptians. The Priestly Writer utilizes the murmuring motif to introduce the theme of the revelation of Yahweh to the people. The kerygma of Exodus 16 is therefore revealed in the response by Yahweh in verses 6–7.

> So Moses and Aaron said to all the people of Israel, "At evening you shall know that it was the LORD who brought you out of the land of Egypt, and in the morning you shall see the glory of the LORD, because he has heard your murmurings against the LORD. For what are we that you murmur against us?"

The emphasis is upon "knowing" that Yahweh was the one who delivered them from the Egyptian bondage (וִידַעְתֶּם כִּי יְהוָה, 16:6b הוֹצִיא אֶתְכֶם מֵאֶרֶץ מִצְרָיִם).[105] The miraculous provision of manna is intended to prove that the exodus was a divine act. The language of the text, shaped by its teaching function, portrays them as listeners who may not have been in Egypt to experience the deliverance. The Priestly Writer is careful to point out that the complaining against the leaders is the same as complaining against Yahweh. Not only do the quails and the manna appear as miraculous provisions that prove to the people that Yahweh was the one who delivered them from Egypt but also that Yahweh is their provider during the wilderness period. Again, the stress is placed explicitly on the pedagogical purpose of the narrative (וִידַעְתֶּם כִּי אֲנִי יְהוָה אֱלֹהֵיכֶם, v. 12).

The Priestly Writer calls the community, and the future generations of Israelites, to recognize and confess the saving deeds of Yahweh, which may be understood in relation to Israel's ancient credo. The purpose of these recollections in the book of Exodus (14:4; 16:6, 12; 18:12; 29:46) is that the people will know and understand their relationship to their God who brought them out of the land of Egypt. The emphasis on "knowing" involves the full revelation that Yahweh was the one who delivered the Israelites from bondage. The response to the murmuring, then, is to establish the fact that Moses and Aaron were not responsible for the exodus, and they were not the ones to whom the complaints should be addressed. The incident in Exodus 16 reveals more than the community's experience of discomfort and disappointment with the wilderness: the community is being taught a lesson in self-identity as the people of God.

The language of the Priestly Writer in 16:6–7 is reminiscent of the exodus tradition. In Exodus 16 Yahweh's actions are referred to as God's revealed glory. With the complaint which reveals a rebellious attitude on the part of the people, the setting in verse 10 is excellent for the judgment of God to come upon the people. Yet, instead of judgment, the emphasis shifts from the problem of a food shortage, thus causing a rebellion, to the revelation of the glory of God through the miraculous. In Exodus 16:6–7, 10–12, the language and imagery of the revelation of Yahweh to the community are similar to the revelation of Yahweh to the Egyptians (Exod. 7:5, 17; 13:3–10; 14:30–31 [to Israel]). The revelation of Yahweh to the Egyptians functions to effect the exodus from Egypt, and, now, the revelation of Yahweh is focused on the doubting Israelites. The function of the experience of God's revelation is, then, to teach the Egyptians and, most especially, the Israelites the truth of Yahweh's relationship with the community.

Such a relationship between the Israelites as a community and Yahweh, which had not existed prior to Egypt, is initiated through the miraculous deliverance. The miracle of the feeding in the wilderness is not simply connected with the theme "guidance in the wilderness," as Noth suggests, but, for the priestly concern, the manna is used symbolically in direct association with the exodus in that the teaching function is the revelation of Yahweh as the one who delivered them.[106] To remember the manna is also to recall the great event where the people became a community under the leadership and care of Yahweh.

The Yahwist's opening line in Exodus 16 refers to Moses alone as the one addressed by Yahweh in response to the murmuring (Exod. 16:4ab). The balance of the verse, given in Deuteronomistic style, reflects the purpose of the narrative, "that I may prove them, whether they will walk in my law or not." In 16:5 Yahweh's provisions on the sixth day are later associated with the Sabbath (16:26 [P]).[107] The Yahwist stresses in characteristic fashion the guidance and aid of Yahweh for the Israelites in the wilderness through the miraculous acts of provision such as the manna which was provided during the community's time of need (v. 32b). The miraculous in the narrative is incorporated within the priestly emphasis on the observance of the Sabbath. The Yahwist's main interest, nevertheless, lies in the feeding itself as a miraculous act by Yahweh (cf. Num. 14:21–22 [J]).

The manner in which the Yahwist maintains a close relationship between the exodus and the wilderness journey as a continuous act of deliverance by Yahweh (Exod. 16:32b) is significant for distinguishing between the kerygma of the Priestly Writer and that of the Yahwist. Even for the Yahwist, the exodus and the wilderness are inseparably linked as a divine act of guidance and care. The Yahwist's final word stresses that Israel survived the wilderness through Yahweh's miraculous provisions, "They ate manna, till they came to the border of the land of Canaan" (16:35b).

The narrative shifts in verses 14–27a from the initial murmuring to emphasize the sanctity of the Sabbath as a day of rest (22–26) for the community during the wilderness period. Yahweh's response in 16:27–28 illustrates the teachings regarding consumption of the manna which carries with it certain stipulations for its use.[108] The manna is not to be kept overnight nor is it provided by Yahweh on the Sabbath, though some of the people do not trust this stipulation (v. 20, 27). Yahweh's question of frustration, עַד־אָנָה מֵאַנְתֶּם לִשְׁמֹר מִצְוֹתַי וְתוֹרֹתָי "How long do you refuse to keep my commandments and my laws?" (v. 28), suggests that the proper observance of the Sabbath, demonstrated by the proper use and consumption of the manna, is in compliance with the commandments and laws of Yahweh. The testing of the obedience of the people by Yahweh is joined by the two motifs of the guidance of Yahweh, illustrated by the miraculous provision of manna, and the observance of law through the teachings on Sabbath observance.[109] The role of the laws and commandments is, of course, more explicit in Exodus 16 than where they are introduced briefly in Exodus 15:26.

The etiological intention of the narrative is shared by both the Yahwist and the Priestly Writer. The primary theme of the Yahwist material incorporated within the dominant priestly narrative in Exodus 16 is the guidance of Yahweh. The kerygma of the Yahwist proclaims that Yahweh fed the Israelites with the bread, thus sustaining them in the wilderness (v. 35).

The Priestly Writer introduces two unusual elements in its etiological point. First, the manna was placed "before the Lord" and "before the testimony" (vv. 33–34). The anachronism regarding the "testimony" reflects a later knowledge of the tabernacle established at Sinai and not prior to that event.[110] The Yahwist, concerned only with the confession that Yahweh had fed them in the wilderness, does not indicate where the omer of manna was to be kept. The narrative, nevertheless, suggests that both the manna and the tablets or testimony belong together before God. The manna has come to be viewed as a sign of divine grace demonstrated in the wilderness preceding the giving of the law at Sinai.[111] Second, the forty years wandering foreshadows Numbers 14:33–34, where Israel's forty years in the wilderness is associated with God's judgment against Israel for her disobedience. The priestly confession states that Israel was provided manna until the community came into the promised land (v. 35a), but, for the Yahwist, the manna sustained them until they came to the "border of Canaan" (v. 35b). The fact that the Yahwist does not have Israel entering the land is not insignificant considering the incident of Numbers 13–14 (cf. Josh. 5:11–12). The duration of the manna (v. 35) represents the period of the sustaining power and grace of Yahweh while they were yet outside the land.

In conclusion, the role of the manna, for the Priestly Writer, can be understood also as food for the body with no deeper meaning lying behind it. Such a view is seen in contrast to Deuteronomy 8:3 where the experience of the miraculous provision of manna is spiritualized.[112] The function of the manna, however, has not remained in its simple or basic beginnings. The manna has evolved from its role as miraculous food for survival in the wilderness to become a primary influence upon the shape of the kerygma of the story. For the Yahwist, the etiological statement in 16:35 proclaims what Yahweh has done for the community. The community owes its survival to their God. In light of the Priestly Writer's wider concern for cultic matters, a basic physical view of the manna must be understood in association with the stress on the sanctification of the Sabbath. The Priestly Writer's confession that the community ate manna while they were forty years in the wilderness further validates the role of the cult throughout the full scope of the wilderness period. Since the miraculous provision of the manna is given in accordance to the sanctity of the Sabbath, the theme of the miraculous aid of Yahweh is inseparably linked to God's holy laws and commandments.

The establishment of the relationship between Israel and Yahweh is accomplished through miraculous acts of provision used to teach them the fundamental principles in that relationship: Yahweh is the God of Israel their provider who delivered them from Egypt; the community of Israel is not alone in the wilderness, for Yahweh is with them; and obedience to Yahweh includes the observance of Yahweh's statutes and commandments.

Exodus 17:1–7

Unlike Exodus 16, which shows major priestly narrative work, the only text assigned to the Priestly Writer in Exodus 17:1–7 is the short itinerary note in 17:1a while the Elohist is limited to 17:3.[113] The Yahwist is understood to be the major recognizable literary strand in the Massah and Meribah narrative. The narrative of the water miracle at Massah–Meribah is commonly understood to represent a place etiology associated with a local tradition since the narrative concludes with an etiological statement associating the place name Massah and Meribah with the murmuring of the people.[114] Whatever its initial relevance might have been, the etiological intention of the story has been reworked during the tradition process to speak directly to its confessional intention. Gerhard von Rad proposes that the two names, whose origin reflects the notion of contention (רִיב) and testing (מְרִיבָה), point to a social setting where the community functioned in a sophisticated system much similar to higher developed communities of later times in Israelite history.[115] The formation of a community with a developed complex structure at this early stage in the wilderness experience is perhaps unlikely, and some scholars suggest that both water stories (Exod. 16:1–17:7) probably should be given a setting that reflects a time following Sinai.[116] Exodus 18 appears to be the first attempt by Biblical writers to present a community struggling with a more functional socio-political system. The incident in Exodus 17:1–7, to be sure, is shaped to reflect an evolving relationship between Yahweh and the community of Israelites during the early stages of the wilderness period. The contention and testing do not reflect problems existing within the Israelite community alone, which appears to be more characteristic of Exodus 18, but also problems associated with the community and its relationship with Yahweh. The initial stories in the wilderness traditions are interrelated in part by the common contention and testing motif (Exod. 15:25; 16:4; 17:2, 7).[117] Consideration of the kerygmatic function of these stories should be considered in light of this unity.

The concluding statement in the narrative (v. 7) portrays the "fault-finding" nature of the people, presented in an etiological framework. The etiological statement reveals one of the basic problems experienced by the community during the early stages in the wilderness period, that is, the question regarding the presence of God. The kerygmatic function of the narrative is found in this important issue, and the text proclaims the presence of Yahweh in its final etiological point (אִם־אָיִן הֲיֵשׁ יְהוָה בְּקִרְבֵּנוּ). Davies suggests that Exodus 17:1–7 could be a pivotal text and even the clue to the meaning of the book of Exodus. Davies writes of the task set before Moses:

> In short, Moses has imparted to them the belief, gained by himself at his call (3:12, etc.), that the meaning of his own life, his apostolic mission among them, and their deliverance from Egypt, is to be found in the faith that the Presence of God is among them.[118]

The narrative concludes by creating a tremendous gap in the information. In the murmuring motif (17:2–3), the community challenges the validity of the exodus as a divinely ordained event, an element also occurring in Exodus 16. The seriousness of the offenses by the community implies that someone should have been punished.[119] In Numbers 20:1–13, a supposedly parallel incident, punishment of the people is also withheld and exacted against Moses and Aaron only. The wilderness period associated with the station at Kadesh following the Sinai experience depicts the Israelites as rebellious and contentious among themselves and even toward the leadership. When an etiological statement concludes a narrative in the wilderness traditions of the book of Numbers, divine judgment occurs to some degree against either the community as a whole (Num. 11:34; 21:9) or against individuals (Num. 20:13). Traditions such as those in Exodus 15:22–17:7 reveal that divine justice was administered in legal debates within the wilderness community but without explicit reference to divine judgments against the community. The narratives in the book of Exodus remain positive in nature, though conflict is present. The post-Sinai wilderness narratives primarily emphasize the negative nature of the first generation and consequences of its rebellious disposition. In its canonical shape, even though conflict is central to the narrative's purpose, Exodus 17:1–7 retains a positive impression.

One can perhaps state that the traditions of the Yahwist focus on the miraculous in a secular sense; whereas, the Priestly Writer, whose presence in Exodus 17:1–7 is limited, leans more toward the cultic context of the miraculous which is virtually absent in the present narrative. The focal point for the kerygma of the story stresses the presence of God through the miraculous provision of water for his people in their time of desperate need.[120] The basic needs of the people, which do not reflect a religious institutional nature, are met by a basic miracle which is similar to the other miracles in the exodus tradition. The signs performed during the exodus and the journey to Sinai are inseparably linked to the purpose of the narrative, the building of faith and trust in Yahweh (cf. Num. 14:21–22). Belief in what Yahweh has done for the community during this period would become the measure by which the first generation of Israelites would be allowed eventually to enter the promised land.

Regarding the book of Exodus, the following conclusion appears in order. Exodus 17:1–7 is similar to Exodus 15:22–27 and 16:1–36, since the three stories share a common concern: the developing relationship between the community and Yahweh that began in Egypt.[121] The key words that express the difficulties encountered in that relationship are רִיב and נִסָּה; words which are rather complex from a form critical and tradition historical perspective.[122] The water stories (Exod. 15:22–27, 17:1–7, Num. 20:1–13) reflect positive traditions of the wilderness period and do not exhibit the motif of the punishment of the community, though not all the stories occur prior to the Sinai experience. In the beginnings of the wilderness journey, the growth in relationship for the Yahwist is basic, a community/Yahweh pattern (Exod. 15:22–27; 17:1–7). For the Priestly Writer the relationship is characterized by a community/cult/Yahweh pattern (Exod. 16).

The wilderness narratives in the book of Exodus are incorporated within the overall theme of the exodus from Egypt. The complaints and the responses to the people's murmurings even reflect the language of the exodus (Exod. 16:8). For the traditions reflecting Israel's origins, the exodus from Egypt represents one stage in the revelation of Yahweh to the community. The Yahwistic account of divine actions is developed in relation to both the exodus and the wilderness. As the narration proceeds in the pre-Sinai narratives under the umbrella of the exodus theme, the exodus itself may be understood as not having been completed in the fullest sense until the Israelites believe and come to understand that Yahweh is the God of the Israelites, who brought them out of Egypt, and now journeys with them in the wilderness as their provider and healer. The people put Yahweh to the test saying, "Is Yahweh among us or not?" (Exod. 17:7). Yahweh also puts the people to the test to determine whether they will be obedient (Exod. 15:25b, 16:28). Yahweh's essential being is gradually made known to the community through the progress and development of the relationship between the people and their God.[123]

Since the chronological order of the narratives in relation to the Sinai episode, for example, the Exodus 18 and other apparent tradition duplications, is not logical according to some scholarly conclusions, then, the redactional intent of the final shape of the traditions in Exodus 15:22–17:7 must be addressed. The final shape of the traditions is where the teaching purpose prevails.[124] Understood in this regard, the essence of the early narratives in the wilderness traditions is therefore the revelation of Yahweh as the God of the community.

For the Priestly Writer, the community's growth in the knowledge and understanding of its relationship to Yahweh is of considerable importance.[125] The focus is not so much the murmuring nor the miraculous provisions but the establishment of the relationship. The Priestly Writer stresses that the historical act of deliverance from Egypt is understood only when Israel comprehends through that act that Yahweh intends to be the God of Israel and for Israel to be his people.[126] The difficulties confronting the developing relationship between Yahweh and his chosen people do not originate with the wilderness traditions. The initiation of the relationship is Moses' encounter with Yahweh, when Yahweh instructs Moses to encourage the people to believe in Yahweh and depart from Egypt under the leadership of Moses (Exod. 3:7–20 [J]).

The revelation of Yahweh to the Israelites through Moses in Egypt appears to be more than the disclosure of the divine name (3:14), though the disclosure is obviously significant. The revelation of Yahweh to Moses and the community includes the knowledge of the power and presence of God. The power and presence of God is revealed subsequently in the exodus and the Reed Sea miracle as well as through the miraculous provisions in the wilderness and the defeat of Israel's enemies (17:8–16).

The climax to the exodus event occurs when the confession by Jethro (Exod. 18:10–11) is voiced after hearing the testimony of Moses (Exod. 18:8). The confession by Jethro עַתָּה יָדַעְתִּי (18:11a) is given in great contrast to the failure of the community to achieve such an understanding.[127] Exodus 18 may not indicate that Moses was speaking on behalf of the community in his words of praise, but, on the other hand, Exodus 17:1–7 indicates that Moses attempted to impart to the people the knowledge that God was present with them while they were in Egypt and remains with them in the wilderness. If this is to be understood, then Moses' confession in Exodus 18:8 might imply that the people have been taught the fundamentals in Israel's confession of faith.[128] The wilderness narratives of Exodus 15:22–18:27, however, do not provide any response by the people other than one of dissension.

Due to the prominent role that the knowing motif maintains in the early narratives of the wilderness traditions, noting the absence of the element of divine judgment, the revelation of knowledge to the new community in the wilderness has displaced punishment as a teaching paradigm. Such a displacement is not as apparent in the wilderness traditions of the book of Numbers where the punishment motif is prominent.

Numbers 11–12

The texts of Numbers 11–12 contain four separate stories, the Taberah murmurings (11:1–3), the craving for meat (11:4–35), the prophetic story of the seventy elders (contained also in 11:4–35), and Miriam and Aaron murmuring against Moses (12:1–15).[129] The dominance of the style, motives, and ideas of the Yahwist and Elohist indicates that the two chapters are from JE.[130] The story of the manna in Exodus 16 can be assigned predominately to the Priestly Writer while Numbers 11 can perhaps be considered the Yahwist's counterpart to the manna story. By the time of the incident recorded in Numbers 11, the manna has become an accepted provision for the community in the wilderness and is now detested by the people thus creating a motive for complaint.

The murmuring motif is an element occurring in the story of Exodus 16 and now in Numbers 11. The task of determining the identity of those who murmured in Numbers 11:33–34 is rather complex. The instigators of the murmuring could be non-Israelites who joined the community during the exodus from Egypt.[131] The phrase וְהָאסַפְסֻף אֲשֶׁר בְּקִרְבּוֹ can be translated as "a mixed company of strangers" who had joined the community.[132] Two groups of rebels may be indicated in the punishment statements of 11:33–34. The punishment for the craving appears to be different for the Israelites who die of the plague (v. 33). The instigators, on the other hand, may be the subject of the etiological point (v. 34).[133] Both groups, nevertheless, die for their craving of meat. In regard to the kerygma of this Yahwist narrative, the foreign element in the narrative may prove significant. Wolff proposes that the foreigner is important to the kerygma of the Yahwist.[134] If rebellion against Yahweh is instigated by the foreigner, then both the Israelite and the foreigner, by not obeying the will of Yahweh, place themselves in jeopardy of not receiving the promise of blessing. Both parties are guilty of disobedience and overt rejection of Yahweh. Numbers 25:1–5 reveals the same consequences to the joint act of disobedience, which in the context of the Baal Peor incident is judged as apostasy.

The progression of the murmuring motif in the narration includes the problem of the role of Moses as the leader of the community. The murmuring motif and the role of Moses as leader transcend both Numbers 11 and Numbers 12, and both chapters can be understood in regard to the overall problem of leadership with Moses as the key subject. As the narratives of Numbers 11 proceed, the murmuring shifts from the community, who voice their displeasure, to Moses as the one who complains (v. 10). Thus, Numbers 11:4–35 contain two separate murmuring incidents with two separate parties to the murmuring. Reference to the problem of the exodus is a common element in both murmuring accounts. The people, on the one hand, refer to Egypt as a more desirable place to live (v. 5), while Moses, on the other, defends himself before Yahweh against the apparent claim that it was he, and not God, who masterminded the exodus (v. 12). Because of the shift in the person who murmurs, the murmuring incident departs from the usual sequence of events in which Moses functions as an intercessor for the people. He does not intercede on behalf of the people to alleviate the problem, but Moses, instead, intercedes on his own behalf. The narrative progresses to the resolution of both the initial problem of food expressed by the community (v. 31) and the problem of Moses' leadership responsibilities, a resolution similar to the leadership problem of Exodus 18.[135]

Numbers 12 is another example of mixed motifs evolving out of a murmuring scene. The motive for the murmuring against Moses by Miriam and Aaron is similar to that revealed in the Korah rebellion (Num. 16) which challenges the authority of Moses as leader of the community. The reason for their approach against Moses at first appears to center around an issue relating to Moses' marriage to the Cushite (12:1); however, the narrative develops further without any reference to the initial explanation for the unrest. The murmuring centers around the struggle between the authority of Moses as opposed to the authority of Miriam and Aaron. Such a challenge is similar to the problem encountered later by Moses and Aaron in Numbers 16. Moses does not respond in his own defense, but he is defended by Yahweh who responds to the murmuring with divine punishment which, in essence, validates Moses' authority as their divinely appointed leader. The claim on the part of Miriam and Aaron to possess a direct relationship with Yahweh is not invalidated necessarily by the response of Yahweh. Rather, the response establishes the authority of Moses as the true representative of God, a relationship that is distinguished from that of the prophet (12:6–8). The venerated role of Moses is stressed further by the fact that Aaron intercedes on behalf of Miriam (12:11), and it is Moses, not Yahweh, to whom Aaron makes intercession. The guidance of Yahweh theme has now taken on an additional emphasis since Sinai with the role of Moses as the divinely appointed leader whose authority must not be challenged (12:8).

The wilderness traditions in the book of Numbers maintain important roles for two individuals. Though the murmuring motif is one of the common elements in Numbers 11 and 12, the role of Moses is the important issue that unites the two chapters. In the final shape of the two chapters, Moses is given a primary place in the wilderness traditions (12:6–8), and an understanding of the kerygma of the two chapters must take into consideration the role of Moses within the wilderness community. Numbers 16:1–20:13 maintains Aaron (with Moses) as the principal subject.

NUMBERS 13–14

The narratives of Numbers 13–14 represent the pinnacle of the wilderness traditions in the book of Numbers, whose influence upon the wilderness traditions as a whole is without question, as the literary analysis and the interpretation of the kerygma will reveal. Numbers 13:1–14:45 is a complex narrative containing the two traditional literary sources of the Yahwist and the Priestly Writer.[136] The initial instructions to Moses in Numbers 13:1–17 are attributed to the Priestly Writer. Twelve leaders are chosen from the twelve tribes who are to be sent on the scouting expedition into the land.[137] The Priestly Writer is quite explicit in stating that the whole of Israel was involved in the scouting expedition.

Considering the complex relationship between the Priestly Writer and elements of the Yahwist, Numbers 13:17b–20 can be assigned to the Yahwist. Specific instructions are given to the scouts in regard to obtaining a detailed description of the land and the inhabitants. The description of the land, given in terms of "good" or "bad," is absent in the priestly portions of the narrative. In 13:23–24, for example, the Yahwist presents an etiological statement that stresses the goodness and the prosperity of the land.[138] The last distinctive text assigned to the Yahwist in Numbers 13 is the spy report (vv. 27–28), which fulfills the initial instructions given in verses 17b–20 in which the spies are told to enter the Negeb and to go into the hill country of Canaan.[139] In the report of the spies, the land is described in Yahwistic language as "the land flowing with milk and honey."[140]

At this point in the narrative, the hesitancy of the spies to encourage entrance into the land (v. 28) does not reflect the notion of rebellion in the fullest sense.[141] The statement made by the spies in verse 28 is not a strong negative but a qualifier that could be expressed by "but" as well as "yet:" "*But* the people who dwell in the land are strong . . ." (v. 28a). For the Yahwist, the report initially contains a mood of hesitancy that is directly related to the inhabitants, and the people do not speak harshly of the land, which is a characterization of the land more common to the work of the Priestly Writer. The land is not so much the problem in the Yahwist's account of the spy mission. The land is good; the inhabitants of the land are the problem. The Yahwist states in a rather detailed manner the reasons that the people should not enter the land. The reasons include the presence of Anak (see v. 33 from P), and the well-known enemies of Israel, the Amalekites, the Hittites, the Jebusites, and the Amorites (13:29). The Yahwist's greater concern, then, is the people's inability to succeed against their enemies. As the scene develops, the effort by Caleb to "quiet" (וַיַּהַס 13:30) the people before Moses depicts a scene of increasing concern.[142] The full expression of the murmuring occurs later in Numbers 14.

In regard to the Priestly Writer, specific itinerary notes are included that reveal a particular concern for the location from which the scouts were sent to spy out the land (13:3, 21). The particular destination of the spies is attributed not to the priestly material but to the Yahwist (13:22–24). Elements of the priestly version of the reporting by the scouts are only brief. The scouts indicate the primary danger in the land to be the giants (v. 33), thus reflecting a fear of entering the land because of the people in the land. In a similar comparative manner to their present wilderness situation, the land is described as a land that "devours" its inhabitants. The acquiring of the "habitable land" (אֶל־אֶרֶץ נוֹשָׁבֶת) is linked to the divine promise (Exod. 16:35), but here the evil report portrays the land as a dangerous place to live.[143] The Priestly Writer, who does not mention the inhabitants by name with the exception of the Nephilim, stresses the extreme difference between how the people of the land appear in comparison to the meager strength of the Israelites (13:33). The whole of Israel, therefore, rebelled against the thought of entering the promised land. Because of their unwarranted fear, they viewed the land as a threat to life, and the land was no more appealing than the wilderness (vv. 32–33).

If we accept Noth's view that only 14:1aβa and 14:4 are attributed to the Yahwist, the balance of the murmuring segment in Numbers 14:1–10 would be assigned to the Priestly Writer.[144] The repetition of the crying out of the people indicates the presence of two sources in verse 1, while in verse 4 the motif of choosing a new leader in order to return to Egypt is characteristic of the Yahwist.[145] The initial complaint in 14:2–3 implies that the people are already in the land (אֶל־הָאָרֶץ הַזֹּאת 14:3). If this setting is indicated, then a significant gap is created between the events of Numbers 13 and the situation revealed in Chapter 14. In Numbers 13 the threat which causes hesitation lies before them; however, in Numbers 14 the threat has become a present reality as though the community has entered the land only to discover the threat before them. In the priestly account, the Israelites complain that it is more desirable to die in any place other than where they are at the present. In other words, death in Egypt or even in the wilderness would be better than in the land.[146]

Up to this point in their journey, oppression and discomfort, as well as more serious experiences such as the divine judgment of plague (Num. 11:33), were threats associated with the wilderness. The complaint in Numbers 14:2–3, with its heightened concern for survival, foreshadows ironically the reality of the entire experience of the wilderness period. The threat of death in a wilderness setting was to be remembered through tradition as a reality epitomizing the experiences of the first generation that came out of Egypt.

As the murmuring unfolds, the people express the belief that Moses has brought them into the land to die by the sword of the enemy. The threat of death in Numbers 14:3 is heightened through the language and imagery of war. The impending danger is to the women and children who will become "booty" (בַּז) for the enemy so indicating a fear of the military power of the inhabitants.[147] Similar language occurs in Numbers 31. In the Midianite war, בַּז is translated as "prey," "booty," in reference to the spoils of war (31:25–41). Further, in Numbers 14:31 Yahweh responds to the murmuring by defending Yahweh's ability to conquer the enemy who would prevent the people from entering the land. Additional language that is associated with war or the conquest includes the use of עָבַר, "pass over, through," (14:7).[148] The spy narrative even begins with the language of war and conquest through the instruction given the spies by the use of the term תּוּר, "seek out, spy out, explore" (Num. 13:2). The rejection of the notion of entering the land due to the imposing threat is accompanied by an alternative proposition that would have the community return to Egypt. Such an option is certainly implied in other complaints during the wilderness period, but now the suggestion is voiced openly.

Numbers 14:6–9 (P) is a confessional praising the goodness of the land given by Joshua and Caleb in response to those who reject the notion of entering the land. The murmuring is not only directed at the exodus, which has been a recurring motif in other events containing the rebellion motif, but now the complaint is related to the conquest and, in essence, the possession of the land.[149] Considering the significance of the land in relation to the promise made at the exodus (Exod. 6:6–8), the confessional of Joshua and Caleb is a timely corrective to the wavering faith of the people. The priestly confessional venerating the land (14:6–9) encapsulates chapter 14 by reflecting the mood of the judgment in 14:34. The statement "If the Lord *delights in us*, he will bring us into this and give it to us" (v. 8) is implied by the stated purpose of the judgment, "you shall know *my displeasure*" (v. 34b). The rebellion, which reveals a contrary attitude toward the land, causes divine displeasure, and the judgment prevents those who rebelled from entering and taking possession of the land which would fulfill the promises made in Egypt. The complaint in 14:2–3 and the land confessional in 14:6–9, then, bring together the theological issues of the exodus and the conquest in one narrative. With the merging of the two motifs into one incident of rebellion, the first generation is characterized as guilty of challenging both the exodus and the conquest, two major confessional elements in Israel's religious heritage.

Numbers 14:11–45 concludes the spy narrative by announcing the divine judgment upon the community. The Yahwist's account (14:11–24) and the Priestly Writer's account (14:26–35) of the judgment upon Israel may reveal kerygmatic elements at work in the redaction of these two important chapters.[150] A conclusion may be stated, hopefully not prematurely, that the two judgment texts of the Yahwist and the Priestly Writer stand at the pinnacle of the wilderness traditions.[151] The impact of the judgment in Numbers 14 is unquestionable since the negative picture of Israel's formative period has overshadowed many positive elements of the early traditions.

The judgment section of the Yahwist (Num. 14:11–25) begins with a lament of Yahweh (v. 11) which establishes the brief motif of the people's despite for Yahweh as an important element in the judgment.[152] Following the initial lament, the intercessory text of Numbers 14:13–20 stresses the mercy of Yahweh (cf. Exodus 34:6f.) as the primary reason for the future survival of the nation. Because of their persistent refusal to believe, Yahweh desires to disinherit Israel whereby Moses would be allowed to replace them as heir to the promises of Yahweh. Exodus 32:7–14 also emphasizes a similar intention of Yahweh to establish a nation through Moses instead of Israel.

The covenant with the patriarchs plays a central role in Exodus 32:7–14 as the determining factor that persuaded Yahweh to stay the punishment of the Israelites following their great apostasy in the golden calf incident (Exod. 32–34). Yahweh's intentions in Exodus 32:7–14 and the confession in 34:6–9 spoken by Yahweh are presented in relation to the covenant and the promises. Exodus 34:6–9 focuses upon Yahweh's mercy in much the same manner as the confessional's counterpart in the dialogue between Moses and Yahweh in Numbers 14:18–19, which, in the later context, is voiced by Moses as a reminder to Yahweh of the previous affirmation of divine mercy toward the community.[153] The apostasy at Sinai can be understood to be a summary of Israel's fate since Sinai in which the community's survival grew even more dependent upon the mercy and commitment of Yahweh.

The pattern of appeal for forgiveness is established in Exodus 34:9, which recurs in Numbers 14:17–19.[154] In Numbers 14 Moses appeals to Yahweh's mercy by informing Yahweh that divine action at this stage in the journey, witnessed by Egypt and the nations, could be an embarrassment to Yahweh. The threat of divine punishment by pestilence and disinheritance that was pronounced earlier (v. 12) is clarified as death in the wilderness (vv. 15–16); and abandonment in the wilderness, which would inevitably result in death to the community, is viewed as a threat to the integrity of Yahweh. The motive for Moses' intervention on behalf of the people is therefore influenced by the promises made to the patriarchs and the significance of the nations in the divine plan. Contrary to Wolff's view that the Yahwist had limited interest in the nations within the Sinai and wilderness traditions, the kerygma of the Yahwist in the spy narrative depends fully on the role of the nations.[155] The nations that stand before them in the land create fear and resistance within the community, yet the witness of God's actions before the nations, represented by Egypt in 14:13–20, is the reason for Yahweh's extended mercy rather than divine wrath. Numbers 14:21, then, summarizes the motive for the show of mercy by Yahweh toward the disobedient community with the nations in consideration, ". . . the earth shall be filled with the glory of the LORD."

The intercession of Moses in Numbers 14:13–19 should therefore be interpreted in light of the role that covenant and promise take in the Yahwist's narrative. The promises in Exodus 3:7–8 (J) stress two confessional elements, the deliverance from Egypt and entrance into the land. One of the primary issues facing the community in the wilderness was confessional in nature. On the one hand, a problem that arose within the community, which is addressed in Numbers 14:15–16, implies that Yahweh was not able to fulfill the promises (מִבִּלְתִּי יְכֹלֶת v. 16a). On the other hand, the sins of the people also impeded the fulfillment of the promises due to the divine response to their murmuring. Depending on the magnitude of the judgment imposed by Yahweh, the actions of Yahweh could likewise hinder the fulfillment of the promises, and anything short of entrance into the land could reflect the inability of Yahweh to fulfill the promises. Both the confessions of the exodus and entrance into the land affirm that Yahweh is able to accomplish the requirements of the covenant. The community is judged, in part, by their actions that reveal their inability to express and proclaim such a confession.

In the judgment passage of 14:21–23, the Yahwist appears at first to present the judgment in the mood of a present indictment with little opportunity for appeal. The certainty of the fate of the rebellious people, whether death or life, has been determined by the expression of their faith and trust in Yahweh. In the final shape of the spy narrative, however, the absolute nature of the Yahwist indictment, which could imply the cancellation of the patriarchal promises, is broadened to a resolution that would allow the whole of Israel the hope for a future.[156] Coats adds that 14:22 may indicate exceptions in the judgment which would allow for the survival of others in the community besides Caleb.[157] The uncertainty of the expected circumstances is expressed through the frequent use of conditional particles in the spy narrative.[158] The entire episode, to include both the Yahwist and the Priestly Writer, is presented in this conditional mode.[159] The prominent emphasis on future generations by the Priestly Writer, in narrative and the legal material alike, also overshadows the absolute nature of the Yahwist's judgment. If the judgment in 14:21–23 is to be understood as absolute, this would indicate that none of the Israelites would enter the land except for Caleb. Verses 22–23 can be understood, nevertheless, as an absolute judgment from the standpoint of the oath proclaimed by Yahweh whereby Yahweh will accomplish what is sworn.

The judgment texts of the Yahwist are sandwiched by the motive for the judgment, the people's despite for Yahweh (יְנַאֲצֻנִי, 14:11a, and מְנַאֲצַי, 14:23b).[160] The motive for judgment occurs later in Numbers 16:30 where the judgment is given in response to the people's despite for the Lord (כִּי נִאֲצוּ הָאֲנָשִׁים הָאֵלֶּה אֶת־יְהוָה). The punishment in Numbers 14 is directed against those who have experienced the miraculous events of the exodus and the wilderness, referred to as the Lord's signs and glory (v. 21), yet they put the Lord to the test and refuse to listen to Yahweh (v. 22). One of the motives for the rebellion is found in the word יָכֹל, a term used to contrast between the emphatic positive attitude of Caleb (Num. 13:30) and the weak unsure response of the people (Num. 13:31–32). The emphasis is not so much on the land in these passages as on the powerlessness of the people that originates from their lack of insight into the presence of Yahweh as the source of that power.[161] The fear of their inability to succeed reflects their belief that Yahweh is likewise unable. According to the Yahwist's presentation of the rebellion, such actions by the community are understood as despite for Yahweh (14:23b).[162]

The Yahwist account of the punishment, accordingly, has no exclusive dependence on the spy mission nor the land as such, except that the murmuring in the spy narrative provides the setting for the divine response. The motive for the punishment reflects their entire experience and relationship with Yahweh from their beginnings in Egypt to their present situation prior to entrance into the land. The pronouncement of judgment upon the Israelites in Numbers 14:21–23 appears to be a summary statement made by the Yahwist in an attempt to explain the nature of the judgment that resulted in the death of the first generation of Israelites during the wilderness period. The judgment, like that of the priestly version to be discussed below, prevented them from entering the land, but the reason for the judgment reflects the whole period of the wilderness experience and not simply the spy episode.

The Yahwist's version of the murmuring is related to the condition of the people and their immature relationship with Yahweh. The land is not an obstacle when compared to the later military exploits of Joshua. The persistent obstacle that has been present during the entire journey from Egypt is the people themselves. Israel's rebellion in the spy narrative is incorporated into Israel's past history of rebellion and disbelief, and contributes to the presentation of Israel as a rebellious community who refuse to become molded into a community of faith during the wilderness period. The ultimate sin according to the Yahwist is that of despising the God who has delivered them from bondage in fulfillment of previous promises.

The murmuring episode in Numbers 14:1–10 is recorded primarily by the Priestly Writer. The murmurings of the people entail their fear of death at the hands of the enemy who are in the land. This expressed fear is linked also to the nature of their punishment, as though they voice their own judgment: they shall die in the wilderness (Num. 14:32). The Priestly Writer's account of the judgment (14:26–35) refers to the whole of Israel as the wicked congregation (לְכָל־הָעֵדָה הָרָעָה) who unite against the Lord (v. 35, cf. v. 27). The community's usual hostile despite for the wilderness is carried forward to include the land as the place they equally despise. The priestly influence places considerable importance on the role that the land takes in the spy narrative and, quite specifically, the response of the community toward the land itself.

Caleb and Joshua, who appear together in Numbers 14:6–7 for the first time in the priestly writings, play an important role in providing a further contrast to the people's negative response to the entrance into the land.[163] Since the two share and confirm the good news of the land of Canaan, they will be permitted to enter the promised land (14:30). Caleb's report in the Yahwist account counters the people's fear of failure in taking the land (Num. 13:30) while, in the priestly writings, Joshua and Caleb proclaim the goodness of the land (Num. 14:7). Both reports are equally emphatic; the emphasis is simply different:

וַיֹּאמֶר עָלֹה נַעֲלֶה	And he said, "Let us go up at once
וְיָרַשְׁנוּ אֹתָהּ	and let us take possession of it
כִּי־יָכוֹל נוּכַל לָהּ	for we are well able to do it" (Num. 13:30b [J])
טוֹבָה הָאָרֶץ מְאֹד מְאֹד	the land is exceedingly good (Num. 14:7b [P])

Joshua and Caleb say nothing about the defenses nor the difficulty in taking the land. In the final shape of the narrative, the land appears to be the important concern for the priestly kerygma, not so much the conquest of it since the responsibility of the spies in the priestly view is not militarily significant. Considering the manner of their response which focused primarily on the land itself (14:7–8), the spies were most likely instructed to obtain knowledge about the promised land and confirm its goodness.[164] The priestly account of the judgment in Numbers 14:26–35 can be understood primarily in association with the people's attitude toward the land, which is clearly an attitude of "despite" or "rejection" (מְאַסְתֶּם) of the land (v. 31b).

In conclusion, the major distinctions between the Yahwist's and the Priestly Writer's accounts of the judgment are relatively clear. Though the spy episode established the context for divine judgment, the Yahwist does not specifically restrict the judgment in reaction to the actions of the people associated with the spy mission alone. The traditions of the exodus, the wilderness journey, and entrance into the land (or taking of the land) represent the many acts of Yahweh in the formative period of the community. The Yahwist assumes the people have experienced first-hand the power of God in deliverance and guidance (14:22). Disbelief in these events as divine acts is the reason for judgment. In the Yahwist account, the great sin of the first generation is the people's despite or rejection of Yahweh.[165] In the priestly account, the judgment of the Israelites is dependent on the spy tradition insofar as it links the forty years the Israelites were to remain in the wilderness to the number of days of the spy expedition (v. 34).[166] The judgment of forty years in the wilderness correlates with the death of the first generation during that period in which the rebellious and disbelieving generation is not allowed to enter and possess the promised land. In the priestly account the land is therefore the object of the people's despite and represents the most serious stage in the rebellion of the community (v. 31).

NUMBERS 16–17

Numbers 16:1–17:13 (Hebrew 16:1–17:28) is composed of two literary sources in general, the Yahwist and the Priestly Writer.[167] The two literary sources are, for the most part, clearly distinguishable in these chapters, and each source presents a full account of a rebellion. The Yahwist material is found primarily in the initial murmuring episode of chapter 16. The Priestly Writer, on the other hand, has developed the Korah tradition alongside the Dathan/Abiram tradition and extends the narrative beyond the initial murmuring traditions in chapter 16 to include additional events beginning in 16:36 that concern issues related to the cult. In the rebellion narrative of Numbers 16, the Yahwist account is commonly associated with Dathan and Abiram while the rebellion of Korah is associated with the Priestly Writer. In essence, the narrative in its canonical shape contains two features characteristic of each literary source. One feature indicative of the Dathan/Abiram rebellion is its basic socio-economic setting with limited religious institutional features.[168] In the Priestly Writer's account of the Korah rebellion and the extended narrative the religious application dominates, and the rebellion becomes relevant only in its relationship to the cult.[169]

When we borrow Jacob Milgrom's outline of Numbers 16, the various units reveal the conflict between the community and its leadership.[170]

1. Korah, Dathan and Abiram, chieftains (נְשִׂיאֵי עֵדָה) versus Moses and Aaron (vv. 1–4 [J,P])
2. Dathan and Abiram versus Moses (vv. 12–15 [J])
3. Korah and his company (עֵדָה) versus Aaron (vv. 5–7, 16–18 [P])
4. Korah and the congregation (עֵדָה) versus Moses and Aaron (vv. 19–22 [P])
5. The whole congregation (עֵדָה) versus Moses and Aaron (vv. 41–50 [P])
6. The leaders of the tribes versus Aaron (17:1–13 [P])

In the introductory section (vv. 1–4), the Yahwist and the priestly sources merge into a complex unit. Section two contains primarily the Yahwist's account of the confrontation. The balance of the sections is assigned to the Priestly Writer. The most striking distinction is the role and presence of Aaron. In contrast to Dathan and Abiram, who were from the tribe of Reuben, the Priestly Writer's account of the rebellion involves Korah who was from the priestly tribe of Levi, also a relative to Moses and Aaron.[171]

The language of the rebellion in Numbers 16:1b–2a utilizes the term קוּם, "rise up," suggesting that the people rose up in the hostile sense or in revolt. Determining the literary source from which the statement originated is questionable, but, for the final shape of the narrative, the term suggests a similar motive for both rebellion traditions. The opening statement could be simply a redactional prologue to the narrative permitting the two accounts of the rebellion to be united in one narrative. In the murmuring motif of the Yahwist, Moses is accused of exerting himself to a higher position of authority over the people. The term שָׂרַר "act as prince" (v. 13, in the Hithpael) does not indicate religious authority, but the similar accusation that occurs in 16:3 is a priestly narration in which Moses is accused of lifting himself above the assembly or congregation of Yahweh.[172] Both traditions associated with the Yahwist and the Priestly Writer build upon the claim by the community that Moses (and Aaron) try to place himself (themselves) in authority over the community.[173] The traditions will attempt to dispel the accusation that Moses assumes authority at his own initiative by connecting the authority of Moses and Aaron to the divine will of Yahweh for the community (See Num. 12:1–16). Herein lies the distinction between the rebellion of Numbers 16–17 and other narratives depicting a journey filled with conflict. In Numbers 16–17 the problems faced by the people are no longer related solely to the survival of the community in the life-threatening conditions of the wilderness. The problems encountered by the people are now associated with internal matters within the community and its leadership.[174]

In Numbers 16:12–15 the anti-exodus and the the anti-Moses motifs appear within the rebellion theme. The anti-exodus motif is common to the Yahwist material throughout the wilderness narratives, though not exclusive to the Yahwist (cf. Num. 14:2–3 [P]). In the present narrative, the motif is revealed when the promised land and Egypt are described in stereotyped language as "a land flowing with milk and honey." The mood is that of regret for leaving Egypt, expressing explicitly for the first time the notion that expectations are unfulfilled in regard to the promises made by Yahweh to Israel in Egypt (Exod. 3:8, 17). In the anti-Moses motif, the community accuses Moses of being responsible for all that has happened from the very beginning when Israel was yet in Egypt.[175] The nature of the murmuring incident suggests at first that Yahweh is not the defendant since the accusations are directed against Moses alone. The response by Dathan and Abiram, "we will not come up," can also be understood to say, "we will no longer obey your orders," and such a response indicates a conflict between the community and Moses' leadership in which there is an open break with Moses' authority.[176]

The response by Yahweh to the rebellion in the Yahwist passages excludes the emphasis on the land as the motive for punishment. The apparent derogatory comparison of the promised land with Egypt as "a land flowing with milk and honey" should also be understood in relation to the people's frustration with Moses. The complaint in 16:13–14 reflects the people's anxiety over not reaching the promised land and the fear of their inevitable death in the wilderness. The actions by the community are interpreted by the Yahwist as despite for the Lord (16:30), and, as discovered previously in the spy narrative of Numbers 13–14, the land is not the primary issue that motivates Yahweh to punish those who rebel. The judgment that relegated the community to a life of wandering and death in the wilderness (Num. 14:29 [P], Num. 14:22–23 [J]) is assumed perhaps to be known by the people in 16:12–14 since their expressed anger involves the apparent certainty of their death in the wilderness.[177] In the final shape of the traditions, one might reach this conclusion, but if the judgment of forty years wandering in the wilderness originates from traditions other than the Yahwist, in particular the Priestly Writer, then we might assume that the community's expressed fear of death in the wilderness in Numbers 16:13–14 (J) reflects a knowledge of the judgment in Numbers 14:22–23. Numbers 32:6–15, which acknowledges and appropriates the tradition of the judgment in Numbers 14, does not provide a clear answer to the question regarding the connection between Numbers 16:13–14 and Numbers 14. According to Gray, Numbers 32 is a freely composed section, written by a later writer who utilized JEP in the Reuben and Gad narrative, though others such as Eissfeldt and Fohrer attribute Numbers 32 to a combination of the Yahwist and the Elohist.[178] Considering the motive for the punishment, despite for Yahweh (16:30 [J]), which is a theme consistent with the Yahwistic judgment in Numbers 14, Numbers 16:12–14 can probably be understood to reflect a knowledge of the Yahwist's judgment in Numbers 14.

The judgment section in Numbers 16:31–35 is shared by both the Yahwist and the Priestly Writer, thus making the distinction between the two difficult, if not impossible, to determine (vv. 31–34).[179]

Korah is the only offender punished (16:32) while Dathan and Abiram are assumed to have suffered the same fate (Num. 26:9–10). Both the Priestly Writer and the Yahwist include similar arguments that seek to validate Moses' position in the community. Recognizing the complex nature of the judgment narrative, Numbers 16:25–34 is the last section attributed to the Yahwist, though verse 32 may be an exception. In verse 28, the Yahwist expresses a concern for the people to "know." The motif of increased knowledge and understanding is not easily assigned to any single tradition such as the Yahwist or the Priestly Writer. Prior to Sinai the emphasis on knowing has been almost entirely associated with the revelation of Yahweh through the exodus, yet, in the wilderness narratives of Numbers, the spy narrative (Num. 13–14) and the Korah/Dathan/Abiram rebellion (Num. 16–17) are likewise influenced by this motif. In the spy narrative the priestly concern is the displeasure of Yahweh and appreciation for the land which dominate the knowing motif: "you shall bear your iniquity forty years, and you shall know my displeasure" (Num. 14:34b) and "your little ones . . . they shall know the land which you despised" (Num. 14:31 [P]). The revelation of the exodus, which was a dominant teaching motive prior to Sinai, has been displaced in Numbers 13–14 by the concern for the land. Furthermore, in Numbers 16–17 an additional motif of knowing includes the community's growth in understanding of Yahweh's divine will for Moses as their leader. Moses proclaims in the Yahwist texts, "Hereby you shall know that the LORD has sent me to do all these works . . ." (16:28a [J]), thus maintaining a focus on the acts of Yahweh which are here linked to Moses as Yahweh's appointed leader (cf. Num. 14:22).

The Yahwist is consistent in expressing the sin of those who rebel as despite for Yahweh; whereas, the expression of Yahweh's displeasure by the Priestly Writer, previously seen in relationship to the community's contempt for the promised land (Num. 14:34), is now caused by the community's contempt for Moses and Aaron, and both literary traditions focus now upon the relationship between the community and its leadership. The contest in verse 29, which is intended to validate the authority of Moses, centers upon the manner by which the rebels die. A common death, or death through natural human process, would prove that Moses is a fraud. In other words, if nothing happens to the rebels, then Moses, and Yahweh as well, no longer will be the force leading the community. Of course, the contest is similar to other testings of Yahweh whereby Yahweh's power and divine will dominate the event. What distinguishes the present contest from other similar events is that, whereas other contests involve natural elements, the contest in Numbers 16 is between the community itself and Yahweh (cf. Exod. 15:22–27; 16:1–35; 17:1–7; Num. 11:4–35; 20:1–13). The miraculous earthquake scene is described as the divine judgment of the rebels, and the fate of the rebels enhances the overall view that death in the wilderness is an unnatural process. The authority of Moses and his standing in the community as Yahweh's designated leader is proven by the unnatural death of those who oppose him.

In summary, the focal point of the Yahwist account is the authority of Moses as the leader of the wilderness community. Unlike other wilderness narratives that relate the problems encountered by the community to the conditions of life in the desert, the specific needs of the community in Numbers 16 are not mentioned. The focal point is the community's dissatisfaction with Moses, presented within the context of the anti-exodus motif which expresses their regret for leaving Egypt and their hatred for the wilderness. The implications in verses 13–14 suggest that Moses has not fulfilled the promises made to the people that persuaded them to leave Egypt and journey to a new land under the leadership of Moses. The Dathan/Abiram story further illustrates the unruly nature of the community. The murmuring is directed entirely against Moses, and the community does not mention, nor do they imply, that Yahweh is responsible for their problems. Yahweh does not speak in the Yahwist account, though the narrative finally refers to Yahweh in 16:28. Only the words spoken by Moses bring the event to pass, further indicating the authority of Moses as true representative of Yahweh for the community (16:28–30). In the traditions of Israel's deliverance, the exodus from Egypt and the Sinai experience are to be understood as the signs which prove that Yahweh has sent Moses to lead the people (Exodus 3:11–12).[180] Since the community has challenged the significance of the exodus and other acts of Yahweh, an attack upon Yahweh's divinely appointed leaders is not surprising.

The Priestly Writer establishes an important priestly concern early in the narrative by addressing the issue of who is made holy by Yahweh and who is permitted to enter the presence of Yahweh (vv. 2–7). The basic theme of the Korah narrative is the threat of the gradual reproach upon the priesthood and the sanctuary. The narrative concludes with an apparent isolated cry of despair, "Are we all to perish?" (הַאִם תַּמְנוּ לִגְוֹעַ 17:13b).[181] The cry of despair reflects the fear of the community in committing wrongful acts with the tabernacle, thus causing further punishment by death.[182] The role of the Aaronite priesthood is further enhanced in the assumption of the responsibility of preventing sins against Yahweh through the wrongful use of the tabernacle. Aaron's responsibilities also include making atonement for the sins of the people (Num. 16:41–50).

The narration in Numbers 16:36–40 (H. 17:1–5) provides a concluding aftermath to the Korah, Dathan, and Abiram rebellion. As a cultic etiology, Numbers 16:36–40 focuses on the use of the melted down censers on the altar in the tabernacle, and the narrative is clearly associated, through the role of the censers, with the priestly concerns in the previous story.[183] The melted censers provide not only a covering for the altar but also a memorial of the Korah rebellion for future generations (v. 40). In the full scope of the rebellion, which comes to a logical conclusion for the Yahwist with 16:34, the narrative continues with its point of emphasis moving away from Moses to the role of Aaron and the Aaronite priesthood.

Numbers 16:41–50 (H. 17:6–15) contains a distinctly different murmuring episode that sets this new incident apart from the past events of Numbers 16. The judgment in 16:32, which resulted in the death of many individuals from the community, provides the connection between 16:41–50 and the Korah rebellion. The present murmuring is motivated by the death of those who were previously punished for their assault upon Moses and Aaron (16:1–35). The response to murmuring is given not through the vehicle of the miraculous, which has been common to other divine responses in rebellion narratives, but through priestly functions in which Aaron performs an act of atonement on behalf of the community. Aaron functions, at the instructions of Moses, as a mediator to relieve the potential destruction of the people (vv. 46–48) and his actions cause the plague to stop. A new twist to the rebellion narratives finds both Moses and Aaron working on behalf of the people to ease Yahweh's unrelenting anger. In this second rebellion, the community owes its survival to Aaron and the performance of his duties. The irony of the Korah rebellion is found in the contrast between the initial complaint against Aaron and Moses that challenged their self-appointed authority over the people (16:3, 11) and the fact that they perform their duty as authoritative leaders to save the people.

In the final episode (17:1–13; Heb. 17:16–28), which exhibits its own characteristics as an independent narrative, the murmurings are directed against Aaron alone (17:5). Another contest is performed similar to the previous contest narrated by the Yahwist in the Dathan and Abiram rebellion at which time the office of Moses is validated (16:28–31). In Numbers 17:1–11 the miraculous blossoming of Aaron's rod clinches the contest in favor of the priestly family of

Levi. The murmuring episode concludes with a cultic etiological statement used as a reminder to future generations warning that to challenge the priestly office of Aaron is the same as rebelling against Yahweh.[184]

In conclusion, the situation in the Yahwist account almost always reflects the desire on the part of the community to leave the wilderness, and the direction is always to Egypt, uncommonly epitomized as "the land flowing with milk and honey." The situation in the life of the community involves conflicts between the community and its leadership which specifically includes Aaron along with Moses, and the murmurings directed against Moses and Aaron are eventually linked to their relationship with Yahweh. The revolt of Korah in the priestly writings has basically nothing to do with the wilderness traditions as such, except to provide the setting for the narratives. The context of the rebellion in the priestly account is the cultic community while the Yahwist presents the Dathan and Abiram account in a socio-political arena. For the Yahwist the rebellion is linked to the wilderness setting through the emphases on the exodus and the threat of death in the wilderness (16:12–14).

The incidents of Numbers 16–17 represent a process within the community of Israel where the cult itself is the divinely ordained instrument of Yahweh. The cult functions to fulfill the promises of God by providing a means for receiving Yahweh into the midst of the community. The challenge to the authority and function of the cult, given in the context of rebellion against the leadership, is successfully overcome with the cult carrying on its functions with purpose and authority. Numbers 16:3 is a statement filled with irony in which the problems existing between the community and the cultic community are revealed in the claim "You have gone too far! For all the congregation are holy, every one of them, and the LORD is among them; why then do you exalt yourselves above the assembly of the LORD?" The murmuring explicitly states, 1) the cult has extended its role beyond community expectations, 2) the community claims to experience the presence of Yahweh, thus challenging the need for the cult and its leaders, and 3) the community rejects the attempts of the cultic leaders to exert any control over them. In the final shape of the traditions, the story reflects a community struggling with the evolving role of the cult. The religious significance of the confrontation has become the primary force with the redaction of Numbers 16–17. The confrontation is between those who oppose and fail to cooperate with the divinely sanctioned religious institution and its leadership. Even with the Yahwist's account where the cult influence is limited, the conflict is between the community and its leaders. In the final analysis, it is the shape of the community that has been challenged.

NUMBERS 20:1–29

With the Meribah story (Num. 20:1–13) and the account of Aaron's death (20:22–29), the Aaron narratives conclude (Num. 16:1–20:29), thus bringing the wilderness traditions to a close with the death of Aaron (20:22–29).[185] In what is called the Aaron narratives of Numbers 16:1–20:29, Aaron is given an increased standing in the wilderness traditions almost equal to that of Moses, particularly in Numbers 17 and the murmuring segment of Numbers 20:1–13.

The text of Numbers 20:1–13 is predominately from the Priestly Writer with limited literary dependence on the Yahwist.[186] The murmuring for water followed by the miraculous provision of water from the rock is united with the cultic etiology, and the latter element in the narrative explains the name of Meribah while the murmuring motif provides the context that reveals the reason why Moses and Aaron did not enter Canaan. The theme of the aid of Yahweh, which is developed in the miraculous provision of water, is integrated into the Priestly Writer's overall concern. The murmuring motif shifts its focus away from the community to that of the leadership, Moses and Aaron, who are accused of having a contrary attitude toward Yahweh that is characterized by rebellion and disbelief (Num. 27:14), a sin usually associated with the community. Furthermore, Moses' and Aaron's sin is related to their leadership roles in the wilderness.[187] Numbers 16:1–20:29 is directly related to the problem of holiness within the community, and the consequence of Moses' and Aaron's transgression, likewise, is judged by the Priestly Writer to be their inability to sanctify Yahweh (לְהַקְדִּישֵׁנִי לְעֵינֵי בְּנֵי יִשְׂרָאֵל, v. 12a).

The conclusion of the wilderness traditions is indicated in Numbers 20 by the emphasis on the death of three significant persons in Israel's wilderness traditions, Miriam, Moses, and Aaron. Miriam dies first at Kadesh (Num. 20:1) and Aaron dies on Mount Hor (20:28) with the eventual death of Moses being delayed and carried forward to Deuteronomy 34.[188] The language used in Numbers 20:1–29 to describe the threat to the life of the community (20:3–4), as well as the account of the death of Aaron (20:29), directly links the narrative to Numbers 16–17.[189] Numbers 20:3b, which refers to the persons who had died in the Korah rebellion because of the judgment of Yahweh, establishes the connection through the use of the term גָּוַע, "he perished, died." The Priestly Writer presents the threat to the community as death in the wilderness (וְלוּ גָוַעְנוּ בִּגְוַע אַחֵינוּ לִפְנֵי יְהוָה, 20:3b). In other narratives the Priestly Writer uses מוּת, "to die," to express the death of individuals (לוּ־מַתְנוּ בְּאֶרֶץ מִצְרַיִם אוֹ בַּמִּדְבָּר הַזֶּה לוּ־מָתְנוּ, Num. 14:2b).

The notion of perishing or death occurs also in Numbers 20:1–29 through the priestly poetic term גָּוַע, "he expired, perished, died." The expressive use of גָּוַע does not occur in the narratives of Exodus, and the only other use of the term in the wilderness traditions is Numbers 17:12–13 (Heb. 17:27–28). In Numbers 17:12–13 the people cry in fear of their lives because they have come under the judgment of Yahweh for their abuse of the tabernacle, but their fear of death appears to imply more than the fear of death expressed in other narratives in the wilderness. In this particular instance, גָּוַע probably denotes the fear for the community's survival. Thus, the dreadful cry of Numbers 17:13, הַאִם תַּמְנוּ לִגְוֹעַ "Are we all completely to perish?" captures this fear. In Genesis 6:17 and 7:21, גָּוַע is used to stress that all of mankind perished in the flood. The other occurrences of גָּוַע in the book of Genesis are associated with the deaths of Abraham (Gen. 25:8), Ishmael (25:17), Isaac (35:29), and Jacob (49:33). Each death appears to represent the passing of an era in the ancient Israelite traditions and, of course, the beginning of a new period. Each death represents a generation that passes away while another continues, and in Numbers 20:29 the reference to Aaron's death could be understood in the same manner.[190]

The fear of the people expressed in their cry of despair (Num. 17:13) and murmuring (Num. 20:3) must, then, be understood in a rhetorical manner, that would suggest a response of "No!" to the question similarly stated in Numbers 17:13 and restated in 20:3. Used and understood in this manner, the Priestly Writer's use of גָּוַע would not imply the total destruction of the people during the wilderness period, but simply the transition from one generation to the future generation. Understood from its kerygmatic function, Numbers 20:22–29 should be included within the wilderness narratives because of its message of hope.

NUMBERS 21:4–9

Numbers 21:4–9 is a highly polished narrative attributed primarily to the Yahwist and represents the last narrative depicting the experiences of the Israelite community during the wilderness period.[191] With Numbers 20 the period of the wilderness is basically concluded, and the serpent story of Numbers 21 can be understood as a remnant from the wilderness traditions. Noth is cautious in assigning an etiological function to the narrative that would link the story of the creation of the bronze serpent to the cultic object housed in the temple at Jerusalem at the time of the reign of Hezekiah (2 Kgs. 18:4).[192] The ultimate goal of the story is, nevertheless, the creation of the bronze serpent by Moses at the instruction of Yahweh.[193] The strong emphasis on the creation of the bronze serpent suggests that there was some apparent etiological concern on the part of the compilers of tradition who viewed its creation as significant among the vast stories depicting the experiences of the community during the wilderness period.[194]

The narrative is introduced by the wilderness itinerary which records the Israelites traveling southward from Mount Hor, and this location links Numbers 21:4–9 with the incident of Aaron's death in Numbers 20:22–29. The murmuring motif plays an important role in the narrative, but the motif acquires a distinct character compared to its previous occurrences in the wilderness traditions. The phrase נֶפֶשׁ־הָעָם "the soul of the people" (21:4b, 5) occurs only here in reference to those who grew impatient during the journey from Mount Hor. Reference to the food by the adjective הַקְּלֹקֵל, "worthless," is also unusual. The murmuring is directed against Moses and Yahweh, and such murmuring which includes Yahweh openly as the recipient of the complaints occurs for the first time in Numbers 21:4–9. The murmuring motif in Numbers 11:1–3 refers only to Yahweh, insofar as Yahweh hears their words, but the recipient of the murmuring is Moses. In Numbers 21:4–9 the narrative is quite explicit in acknowledging the presence of Yahweh, and the response of the people, following the crisis with the desert serpents, further indicates their awareness that Yahweh, along with Moses, had been the recipient of their murmuring (21:7). In this final narrative from the wilderness traditions, the acknowledgment by the community of the presence of Yahweh and the recognition of the consequences of the community's rebellious attitude are very explicit. Previous narratives from the wilderness traditions emphasize that rebellion against Moses is also rebellion against Yahweh. The present concern on the part of the writer is not so much the problems related to Moses' leadership as with the community's survival in the wilderness.

The narrative introduces the living creatures of the wilderness as a new threat to the community, and the wilderness is remembered by the Deuteronomist as an arid habitat for serpents and scorpions (Deut. 8:15). Unlike Numbers 11:1–3, the narrative does not provide an immediate resolution to the problem of food and water since the problem is not addressed beyond the initial murmuring. Instead, the murmuring creates an additional crisis for the community. The threat from the snakes, that were sent among the people as punishment for their murmuring, is not resolved in the same manner as the crises of other situations. In other narratives the problem is at times resolved by the reversal of the situation, such as in Numbers 11:1–3 when Yahweh stopped the fire. The snakes, however, are not removed, though a means is established whereby anyone who is bitten could be cured and live. Numbers 21:4–9 contains a magical element with the creation of the serpent on the pole, much like the tree in Exodus 15:22-27. In both narratives the miraculous is not directly initiated by Yahweh personally but the aid of Yahweh is transmitted through an object.

In the Ancient Near East, the serpent was associated with the restoration of life and came to be identified with fertility cults.[195] As a fertility symbol, the role of the serpent may go back to a pre-Israelite time in which the serpent was understood to possess healing and protective properties, and these properties, which are no longer associated with fertility as such, are stressed in Numbers 21:4–9 in association with Moses and the guidance of Yahweh in the wilderness.[196] The primary message in Numbers 21:4–9, as it is understood from a kerygmatic perspective, is that Yahweh is the source and sustainer of life during the journey through the wilderness, or, in fact, during any crisis. Sailhamer is correct to link the bronze serpent of Numbers 21 with the earlier occurrence of a serpent in Exodus 4:3 where the miraculous appearance of the serpent is used as a sign to convince the people that Yahweh did in fact call Moses to lead them from Egypt.[197] In both events when the serpent is used, the people are called upon to trust in Yahweh and thereby receive life through deliverance from their present crises. The basic distinction between the two incidents concerns the traditions associated with the narratives: one relates to receiving life through the exodus while the other serves as a means for overcoming the judgment of Yahweh which, in essence, provides a way for the community to survive the hazards imposed upon them during the wilderness period. Both events point to the revelation of the truth that Yahweh is the provider of life.

The threat of death is replaced with the chance for life, and Numbers 21:4–9 asserts in a fresh new way the proposition that the wilderness is not necessarily equated with doom and death, even though the threat most assuredly exists. Considering this to be a very significant point, the narrative may be in conflict with the judgment texts of the spy narrative (Num. 14:20–35) where the fate of the community, whose disposition is judged as rebellious, has been sealed.

However, if judgment of Numbers 14 allows faithful individuals from the community to enter the land in addition to Joshua and Caleb, then, the kerygma of the narrative of the bronze serpent would correlate with the message of the wilderness traditions as a whole. One aspect of the kerygma is the encouragement of hope through obedience in which the community can still enjoy a future, and such a focus places the narrative within the positive traditions that are reflected primarily in the pre-Sinai period of the Exodus wilderness traditions. On the other hand, if the structure of the book of Numbers is truly focusing on the transition from the old generation to the new, then what value would a word of hope have for an ill-fated community? The function of the narrative, then, must be found within its future orientation and its consideration of the communities of the future which might experience similar hardships.

The Kerygma of the Wilderness Traditions in Exodus and Numbers

The wilderness traditions in the book of Exodus function within the overall theme of the exodus from Egypt. The wilderness narratives in Exodus 15:22–18:27 do not assume an independence from the surrounding materials in the book of Exodus since they do not appear as a free-standing set of narratives contained within a particular tradition.[198] Functioning with the exodus tradition, the narratives of the wilderness traditions in the book of Exodus serve a highly concentrated purpose. That purpose can be identified through the redactor's repeated emphasis on "knowing," though יָדַע is not the only indicator of the notion; for example, רָאָה appears frequently as a means whereby the actions of Yahweh become known (Exod. 16:10–12). The wilderness narratives repeatedly attempt to remind and to teach the community that the exodus from Egypt was a divine act of Yahweh, accomplished on behalf of the community and occurring within Yahweh's ultimate purpose for the world. The disclosure of Yahweh through these divine actions is a primary kerygmatic function for the exodus and the wilderness narratives in the book of Exodus (Exod. 6:6–8–Exod. 18:12). In opposition to this divine disclosure, and almost appearing as opponents to God's purposes, the exodus community responds to the exodus by constantly looking back to their hardship in Egypt in euphoric fantasy, simply because they cannot understand the relationship between their experiences and God's purposes for the community.

The pedagogical schema of the Exodus wilderness narratives calls the community to look to its past in order to understand why they were delivered and to whom they should be grateful. Yahweh called Israel out of Egypt under a new plan for the community to be revealed in the desert, a calling that was the source of their identity and purpose as the people of God.[199] Moses is the divinely appointed leader, but he is not responsible for the community's salvation. The role that Moses takes in the traditions of the exodus and the wilderness period serves the broad theme of the creation of the Israelite community with a special relationship to Yahweh.[200] If Israel's identity and self-understanding are rooted in the wilderness period, a time prior to the monarchy and statehood, then, the role and image of the community should be central to the interpretation of the wilderness traditions.[201] The wilderness traditions of the book of Exodus reveal not only the early stages in the establishment of the people as a community under God's will, a goal of the exodus consummated at Sinai, but also disclose the trials, temptations, and development of the faith of the new community.

The wilderness traditions in the book of Exodus contain the primary trilogy of Exodus 15:22–27, 16:1–35, and 17:1–7, followed by the Amalekite (Exod. 17:8–16) and Jethro narratives (Exod. 18). One of the functions of the short narrative in Exodus 15:22–27 is to establish the conditions for the developing relationship between Yahweh and the community, conditions set forth by the demands of Yahweh for obedience and faith. Important to the Yahwist in this initial narrative is the disclosure of the miraculous aid and guidance of Yahweh that remains a prominent theme for the entire wilderness journey. Exodus 15:22–27 stresses that Yahweh will guide the community through the journey so long as they rise above the faithless actions of the Egyptians; otherwise, the fate of the Egyptians will be theirs as well. The contrast between the community's Egyptian experience and their wilderness experience is a feature repeated throughout the wilderness traditions of Exodus and Numbers.

For the Priestly Writer in Exodus 16:1–35, and normally for the Yahwist as well, the exodus continues to be the prerequisite to understanding the manna narrative. The leadership of Yahweh motif, demonstrated in the miraculous provision of manna, is incorporated into the Priestly Writer's concern for the sanctification and observance of the holy Sabbath. The manna is therefore to be remembered as a sign of Yahweh's presence and guidance during the forty years in the wilderness, which is also freely given according to the graciousness of God and the manner of its consumption is in keeping with the commandments and laws of Yahweh. Whether the community failed or succeeded in obeying the mandates of Yahweh is yet another issue since a contrary attitude develops among the people in the form of constant murmuring. The reason for the miraculous provision of the manna, which is given in response to the murmuring and in association with observance of the Sabbath, then, is to proclaim the truth of the exodus (16:6b) in such a manner as to teach the fundamental principles of the community's relationship with Yahweh.

Exodus 17:1–7 may show signs of a developed, organized community whose experiences center around a site in the wilderness called Massah-Meribah. The frequent use of רִיב, "to contend," and נִסָּה, "he tested," indicate that the narrative could be historically connected to a setting somewhere in the wilderness which is probably near Kadesh.[202] But in its final shape within the Exodus narratives, one of the functions of the Massah-Meribah narrative is confessional in nature and bears witness to the exodus event. Not unrelated to the witness to the exodus event is the revelation of the presence of Yahweh in the midst of the community during the wilderness period. The people's challenge to the validity of the exodus as a divine event is also interpreted as a challenge to the presence and reality of Yahweh as the God of the community, and the miraculous provision of water is testimony to the truth of Yahweh's relationship to the community.

When the people entered the wilderness, their faith exhibited signs of immaturity, intrinsic to the stage in the development of the newly formed community of the exodus. The narratives of the wilderness traditions in the book of Exodus do not infer that Israel acknowledged or confessed the exodus as a divine event, which also would be a proclamation that Yahweh is their redeemer. The fact that the community left Egypt is nevertheless an indication of an act of faith to some degree, which is suggested by the confession in Exodus 15:1–21. The term used most frequently throughout the wilderness traditions by the Priestly Writer to denote the community of Israelites as a worshiping community is עֵדָה, "congregation."[203] Biblical tradition portrays the Israelites as leaving Egypt under the hope and expectation of God's new plan for their future; however, a great contrast exists between the ancient song in Exodus 15:1–21, where the "people of Israel" (וּבְנֵי יִשְׂרָאֵל) and Moses sang praises to Yahweh for their deliverance at the יַם־סוּף, and the community's subsequent actions in the wilderness. The song of praise in Exodus 15:1–21 is the climax to the exodus tradition and is, in fact, the last word of praise voiced by the exodus generation.

Exodus 15:22–17:13 leave the confessional stance of the community open and ambiguous. Within the murmuring motif one could possibly identify the notion of covenant expectations, wherein the community expressed disappointment in the unfulfilled promises (Exod. 3:7–8).[204] In the book of Exodus, the community is not condemned for their reluctance to acknowledge the exodus as a divine event nor are they judged harshly for their failure to confess Yahweh as their God. The pedagogical schema of the traditions takes full advantage of this apparent deficiency in the character of the community. In the face of the community's rebellion and unfaithfulness, the wilderness traditions nevertheless affirm the truth of the exodus and the community's election as God's own people. The kerygma of the wilderness traditions in Exodus finds expression in the witness, which was voiced at the beginning (Exod. 15:1–21), that Yahweh is the God who delivered them from bondage, dwells in the midst of the Israelites, and leads the community through the wilderness. This confession is established as a permanent theological affirmation regardless of the reaction of the community.

In the wilderness traditions in the book of Numbers the setting for the wilderness community and nature of the community change. In the book of Exodus the purpose of the wilderness traditions must be understood in association with the miraculous acts of God beginning in Egypt and continuing until Sinai. At the community's beginnings, the wilderness traditions are shaped to serve the confessional of Israel's birth from Egypt. In the book of Numbers, the community, whose nature and structure have become more complex, has suddenly become accountable for its actions that, on the surface, appear not unlike its actions prior to Sinai. The kerygmatic intention of the wilderness narratives in Numbers should be understood in relation to this change. The kerygma departs from the primary concern with the exodus event, though the motif remains an integral part of the narratives, and becomes embodied within the future orientation of the priestly emphases in the traditions.

The kerygmatic intention of Numbers 11–12 is perhaps the most difficult to determine. The theme of the guidance of Yahweh is central to Numbers 11, and in Numbers 12 the role of Moses becomes interrelated with Yahweh's guidance. Numbers 11 clearly states that Moses is not eager for his role as leader, due to the difficulties faced, anymore than the community is willing for Moses to lead them (Num. 11:10–15). Moses is Yahweh's divinely appointed leader whose presence within the community represents Yahweh's presence as well (Num. 12:7–8). In Numbers 11–12 the situations experienced by the community and the response of Yahweh to the community's murmurings are indications of the divine program for life in the wilderness. But the critical issue established in the relationship between Yahweh and the community is that Yahweh commands and wills the Mosaic leadership in a similar manner as Yahweh had previously commanded obedience to the laws and statutes. Moses' authority as the leader of the wilderness community is validated through the events in Numbers 11–12. The context within which the task of Moses' leadership is performed is different for the Yahwist and the Priestly Writer (Num. 16–17). The Yahwist traditions portray Moses and the community in a more socio-political context. The Priestly Writer incorporates the Yahwist material within a more developed religious program for a religious community with Moses and Aaron as their religious leaders. Since Exodus 16 and Numbers 11 are similar in their murmuring motifs, the sandwiched interludes that interrupt the flow of the basic murmuring texts perhaps reveal their distinctiveness. In the priestly dominated narrative of Exodus 16, the abrupt interlude (16:13–30) connects the miraculous aid motif with the priestly concern for sanctification of the Sabbath. The interlude in the Yahwistic narrative of Numbers 11 (11:10–30) is primarily related to Moses and the leadership of the community.[205] As a whole, for the Priestly Writer, the wilderness narratives in Numbers 10:11–21:9 focus more on the leadership of the community as a religious community and the problems associated with that leadership than do the traditions in Exodus 15:22–17:13.

Numbers 13–14 hold a crucial position in the wilderness traditions. The Yahwist presents the people in a negative light as a community who rebels against Yahweh thus causing the judgment of death to all who reject Yahweh. The Priestly Writer records a judgment characterized by grace, though the wilderness generation is condemned to live in the wilderness and eventually to die therein. Joshua and Caleb represent the faithful in the community, but even their faith does not stand above the hope that Yahweh will allow all future generations who are faithful and obedient to enter the land. According to the nature of the judgment pronounced in Numbers 14:26–35, which stresses the age limitation thus restricting the older members of the community who rebelled from entering the land, the Priestly Writer is responsible for this unusual exception to the judgment which sealed the dreadful fate of the first generation. Such a show of mercy engenders hope for future generations, and the kerygmatic stance of Numbers 13–14 must be considered within this future orientation.

Following the Sinai experience the kerygma of the wilderness traditions has shifted to place specific emphasis on the land. The kerygma of the Priestly Writer is completely immersed with the promise of entrance into the land, and such preoccupation with the land dominates to the extent that the priestly program of the cult maintains a limited role in the spy narrative.[206] Within the spy narrative two elements merge that are confessional in nature. The confession that Yahweh delivered the community from Egypt and guided them in the wilderness, thus implying that Yahweh is the God of Israel, is joined with the confession of the land. The opposing attitude of the community does not overshadow the show of divine mercy when Yahweh delivered them out of bondage nor does their sin completely destroy the prospect that Israel will enter the land. The three-fold promises of Yahweh underlie the more fully developed kerygma in Numbers 13–14, deliverance, land, and divine presence (cf. Lev. 26:38).

Numbers 16:1-20:29 (excluding 20:14-21) is shaped primarily by the priestly influence. In Numbers 16-17 the role of the Aaronite priesthood is validated through a series of contests that attempt to resolve conflicts between the leadership and members of the community. Groups of individuals within the community challenge the role and standing of the cultic leaders within the community structure, and such a challenge may be interpreted as an effort on the part of those who rebel to function independently of Yahweh's divinely ordained cult. The cult, and its leadership, is inseparably linked to the presence of Yahweh among the people during the wilderness experience. Though the murmurers in the community claim to be religiously acceptable in their beliefs and actions, their confessional stance and views toward the cult fall short of the requirements for holiness. A point of distinction can be made between the priestly influence and the Yahwist in which the Yahwist presents the revelation of Yahweh through personal guidance and supernatural aid.

Three primary confessional elements are revealed in the wilderness traditions that are included in the promises of God, which also provide a basis for Israel's existence: the nationhood of Abraham's descendants, the possession of the land of Canaan, and the divine presence in Israel.[207] When we look beyond the confines of the wilderness traditions in the books of Exodus and Numbers, these three elements become critical for the community following the great tragedy of 586 B.C.E. when fragmentation becomes a threat to the survival of the community. The community finds itself once again in a wilderness setting, figuratively speaking, during the period of the exile.[208] Confession of the ancient religious heritage, seen in light of this threat, has the potential of producing and also preserving the community of faith. Confession of one's religious faith and heritage is therefore related to the constitutive function of the early Israelite traditions.[209] The Pentateuch, or more specifically, the Torah, is a constitutive force in the establishment and preservation of the community of faith only when the community claims the traditions of the Torah as their own and confesses its witness to the acts of God in Israel's sacred history.[210] The kerygma of the wilderness traditions appeals to the community to embrace the sacred heritage of Israel by portraying a community in a wilderness situation whose structure and character are fragmented or at least divided by various problems and individual concerns. As a consequence to this fragile situation, the community resists the development and maintenance of a confessional stance in the early period of the community's existence as a united people recently freed from their Egyptian bondage.

One of the concerns facing the community during the exilic period is the danger of assimilation into the cultures of the Ancient Near East and the eventual loss of their identity. Within the priestly institution, highlighted by circumcision and observance of the Sabbath, traced to Israel's beginnings, the Israelites could find their identity as a peculiar people of God.[211] Though the wilderness period should not be viewed as an allegory of the exilic period, as some scholars would suggest, both periods exhibit similar problems of religious interest.[212] From a common context of crisis and threat to their survival as a community the traditions of the wilderness period in the Hebrew Bible make a plea for the restoration of faith which affects the future survival of the community. The three elements in the confessional that prove to be crucial for the exilic community are challenged if not denied at times by the first generation in the wilderness. The rejection of their election, the refusal to accept the land, and the doubting of God's presence are characteristic of the contrary attitude and actions of the community in the wilderness traditions. The confession of Exodus 15:1–21 indicates that Israel is a confessing community who praises God for their deliverance at the Reed Sea. When the community enters the wilderness, evidence suggests they depart from their confessional awareness of God's activities. The first generation, then, can be described as a non-confessional community because they do not constitute a mature community in terms of an obedient faith, regardless of whether the Israelites were conscious of their distinctness from other people as early as their Egyptian bondage (Exod. 2:10–15).[213] The sacred traditions that reveal God's steadfast relationship to the community are challenged repeatedly by those who rebelled in the wilderness.

The three-fold confession of Leviticus 25:38 is also contained in the statement made to Moses in Exodus 3:7–8, and the three elements become the essential theological issues addressed by the wilderness traditions. The elements of the three-fold confession that occur in the wilderness traditions are the exodus (Exod. 15:22–18:11), the land of promise (Num. 13–14, also 15:2), and God's presence (Exod. 17:1–7; 40:34–38, Num. 10:11–36; 16–17). From Exodus 15:22 through Numbers 21:9 the community fails to acknowledge faithfully these sacred beliefs. When the confessional or any portion of it is voiced, the confession usually is spoken by Moses or another individual (Num. 14:6–9).

In the Exodus narratives of the wilderness traditions, the exodus event is challenged by the community, and instead of expressing joy for their deliverance, they regret leaving Egypt and do not understand the full implications of its occurrence. At the conclusion of their journey from the יַם־סוּף to Rephidim (17:1; 19:2) at the "Mountain of God" (18:5) near Sinai, a confession of the miraculous acts of Yahweh is voiced by Moses to Jethro (Exod. 18:8).[214] Are we to assume that Moses is speaking on behalf of a community who share the same faith and joy?[215] From a kerygmatic point of view, the text of Exodus 18 provides a confession that functions as a witness or testimony to the great acts of Yahweh in Egypt and the wilderness (Exod. 18:10–11). Moses' contact with Jethro and the Midianites in Exodus 4:18 and Exodus 18 appears to represent inclusive events. Lying between the two are the exodus event and the traditions confessing the event. The meeting between Moses and Jethro is of central importance to the exodus tradition because in the sharing of the news of Israel's recent experiences a confession is spoken regarding the fulfillment of the promises made to Moses.[216] The confession of Jethro, a non-Israelite, in Exodus 18:10–11 can be recognized in contrast to the community's persistent disbelief and disobedience.

Numbers 16:3 represents an attempt on the part of a portion of the community to confess that which is not acceptable according to Yahweh's plan for the community in the wilderness. The community claims that each individual is holy because Yahweh dwells with them.[217] The confession is used in their attack against Moses and Aaron. Of course, the consequences of their actions reveal that the claim and, therefore, their confession are invalid. At this juncture in the wilderness traditions, the non-confessional stance of the community comes full circle with its previous challenges to the exodus, the land,

and now the role of the cult and its leaders who provide the means for Yahweh's presence in the community. The Priestly Writer promotes the notion that Israel's true existence is only possible when the glory of Yahweh is dwelling in its midst.[218] Thus, the rebellions of Israel after Sinai must be interpreted in light of the creation of the tabernacle in the wilderness which symbolizes the presence of Yahweh. Complaints that question or even presume the presence of God are direct slanders against the very nature and meaning of Sinai.

Numbers 20:14–21 is a final episode in the wilderness traditions within which a confessional statement is expressed. The proclamation of the saving acts of Yahweh is given by the messengers of Moses to the king of Edom in an effort to achieve for the community passage through the Edomite territory. The power of the confession fails to create a response from the king of Edom in the same manner expressed by Jethro (Exod. 18:8). Such an affirmation like Jethro's must await that of Balaam, a non-Israelite, who voices a confession of Yahweh's deity while also acknowledging God's relationship to Israel (Num. 22–24). The Balaam narratives stress the contrast between the faithfulness of God in continuing the promises to the people and the unfaithfulness of the people.[219] Due to the rebellious nature of the community, what party could be used in the wilderness traditions to affirm God's plan for the community and provide the contrast? The two confessions in Exodus 18:8–11 and Numbers 22–24 are expressed by a non-Israelite, prompted by the power of Yahweh in providing understanding of Yahweh's divine plan. Both incidents follow a distinct journey in which the experiences of the community are used for pedagogical reasons. Exodus 18:8–11 provide the important affirmation of Israel's origin as a community while Numbers 22–24 provides the confession of Yahweh's blessing on the people as a great nation among the nations.

In closing, Walter Brueggemann makes a connection between the appropriation of tradition and the education function of tradition.[220] Obviously since this relationship exists, then, the kerygma of Biblical traditions can serve a similar function. Seen in this perspective, the ancient Israelite credo or confession of faith serves an educational function. The appropriation of traditions is the use of past traditions to inform future experiences. Therefore, the relationship between the Biblical traditions and the community provides the traditions with their *raison d'être*. In the wilderness traditions the actions of the first generation function as an example of what not to do in a community of faith. The first generation is the example of a community, who in times of chaos, danger, and confusion, become disobedient, rebellious, and ignorant of the presence and power of God. Each subsequent generation of Israelites throughout history has the tendencies of the first generation. The challenge is in the form of a warning to all future generations to overcome the tendencies of the first generation. The kerygma of the wilderness traditions makes its appeal to faithfulness by demonstrating through Israel's ancient traditions how a community fails to become molded into a community of faith. The wilderness traditions also affirm the success of God's divine plan, even when confronted with failure on the part of the community itself.[221] The kerygma of the wilderness traditions functions in this regard to encourage each new generation of Israelites in the renewal of faith in Yahweh, thereby assuring the future of the community of faith.

Notes

[1]George Buchanan Gray, *A Critical and Exegetical Commentary on Numbers* (Edinburgh: T. & T. Clark, 1903), p. xxiv.

[2]Brevard S. Childs, *Introduction to the Old Testament as Scripture* (Philadelphia: Fortress Press, 1979), p. 170; Martin Noth, *Exodus* (Philadelphia: Westminster Press, 1968), p. 127. With J. Philip Hyatt, *Exodus* (Grand Rapids: Wm. B. Eerdmans Publishing Co., 1971), p. 17, and others, the common reference to the wilderness traditions in the book of Exodus is found in 15:22–18:27.

[3]Joseph Blenkinsopp, *The Pentateuch: An Introduction to the First Five Books of the Bible* (New York: Doubleday, 1992), p. 157.

[4]See "The Reed Sea Tradition" below for a discussion of the arguments for the placement of the Reed Sea narratives in the wilderness traditions.

[5]J. de Vaulx, *Les Nombres*, (Paris: J. Babalda, 1972), pp. 12–13.

[6]Volkmar Fritz, *Israel in der Wüst, Traditions-geschichtliche Untersuchung der Wüstenüberlieferung des Jahwisten* (Marburg: N. G. Elwert Verlag, 1970), p. 33.

[7]Jacob Milgrom, *The JPS Torah Commentary: Numbers* (Philadelphia: The Jewish Publication Society, 1990), p. xiv; Gunther W. Plaut, *The Torah* (New York: Union of American Hebrew Congregations, 1981), p. 1016.

[8]Shemaryahu Talmon, "The 'Desert Motif' in the Bible and in Qumran Literature," in *Biblical Motifs: Origins and Transformations*, ed. Alexander Altmann (Cambridge: Harvard University Press, 1966), pp. 31–63.

[9]See below *Exodus 32 and Numbers 25* for further discussion of the role of these two passages in the presentation of the wilderness traditions.

[10]Milgrom, *Numbers*, p. xiii.

[11]Ibid., p. xix. Milgrom concludes that the Korah rebellion is a composite of several rebellions. Also, Jacob Silver, "Korah, Dathan and Abiram," in *Scripta Hierosolymitana*, ed. Chaim Rabin (Jerusalem: The Magnes Press, 1961), pp. 189–217.

[12]Martin Noth, *Exodus: A Commentary*, trans. J. S. Bowden (Philadelphia: Westminster Press, 1962), p. 105.

[13]Nahum Sarna, *Exploring Exodus: The Heritage of Biblical Israel* (New York: Schocken Books, 1986), p. 103.

[14]George W. Coats, "The Traditio-Historical Character of the Reed Sea Motif," *Vetus Testamentum*, 17 (1967), 253–265. Also, in "An Exposition for the Wilderness Traditions," p. 289, he states that Exodus 13:17–22 is not only an introduction to the Reed Sea event but the introduction to the larger collection of wilderness narratives.

[15]Coats, "The Traditio-Historical Character of the Reed Sea Motif," p. 254.

[16]Ibid., p. 256. Also, in George W. Coats, "A Structural Transition in Exodus," *Vetus Testamentum*, 22 (1972), 129–142, he further states that Exodus 12 marks the conclusion of the exodus for both J and P: "The conclusion to the exodus theme places the Sea tradition in the wilderness."

[17]Brevard S. Childs, "The Traditio-Historical Study of the Reed Sea Tradition," *Vetus Testamentum*, 20 (1970), 406–418.

[18]Ibid., p. 418.

[19]Ibid., p. 409.

[20]George W. Coats, "The Sea Tradition in the Wilderness Theme: A Review," *Journal for the Study of The Old Testament*, 12 (1979), 2–8.

[21]Davies, "The Wilderness Itineraries and the Composition of the Pentateuch," p. 10.

[22]*BDB*, p. 892.

[23]Childs, *Exodus*, p. 217, briefly summarizes these various attempts at translation.

[24]Noth, *Exodus*, p. 108, adds that the name Etham could be a Hebraizing of an Egyptian place name that can no longer be determined thus leaving the name Etham completely unknown. See G. I. Davies, *The Way of the Wilderness* (Cambridge: Cambridge University Press, 1979), p. 79.

[25]Milgrom, *Numbers*, p. 99.

[26]*BHS* notes the confusion over the term בְּרָע. LXX has τὸ ὃρμημα, "impulse," or "impetuosity." The term reflects perhaps a tendency on the part of the community toward violence and impulsive behavior. The recurrence of singular pronouns further complicates the translation. The translation of verse 33b, for example, which contains the singular pronoun הוּא, could be "for *this people* is set on evil." LXX has τοῦ λαοῦ τούτου, "this people."

[27]Milgrom, *Numbers*, p. 211.

[28]Dennis T. Olson, *The Death of the Old and the Birth of the New: The Framework of the Book of Numbers and the Pentateuch* (Chico: Scholars Press, 1985), p. 179.

[29]Ibid., p. 180. Olson states that Numbers 25 is the last act of rebellion for the old generation.

[30]See Olson, *The Death of the Old and the Birth of the New*, p. 183, for discussion of traditions in general that are appropriated by each new generation. The book of Numbers establishes a paradigm for that purpose.

[31]Baruch A. Levine, *The JPS Torah Commentary: Leviticus* (Philadelphia: The Jewish Publication Society, 1989), p. 58.

[32]Olson, *The Death of the Old and the Birth of the New*, p. 183.

[33]Z. Kallai, "The Wandering-Traditions from Kadesh-Barnea to Canaan: A Study in Biblical Historiography," *Journal for Jewish Studies*, 33 (1982), 175–184.

[34]Coats, "The Wilderness Itinerary," p. 145. Noth, *A History of Pentateuchal Traditions*, p. 221, states the itinerary in Numbers 33 is "authentic itinerary," i.e., a list of stations along a route which serves no other function than to establish the route. "Secondary itinerary" originates by virtue of the local centers to which the individual narratives were attached. Noth is not clear as to which stations or settings relate to each type.

[35]Kallai, "The Wandering Traditions from Kadesh-Barnea to Canaan," p. 182.

[36]G. I. Davies, "The Wilderness Itineraries and the Composition of the Pentateuch," *Vetus Testamentum*, 33 (1983), 1–13.

[37]George W. Coats, "The Wilderness Itinerary," *Catholic Biblical Quarterly*, 34 (1972), 135–152, states that as far as the itinerary is concerned Numbers 22–25 belong to the wilderness theme. Since the Baal Peor event involved the whole of Israel in rebellion, it belongs at some level in the wilderness.

[38]Ibid., p. 142.

[39]Jerome T. Walsh, "From Egypt to Moab," *Catholic Biblical Quarterly* 39 (1977), 20–33.

[40]Coats, "The Wilderness Itinerary," p. 140, states that since the itinerary in Numbers 33 does not mention the Wilderness of Paran but places Kadesh in the Wilderness of Zin (Num. 20:1) then Paran and Zin must refer to the same wilderness. The Septuagint has the Wilderness of Paran in Numbers 33:36 instead of the Wilderness of Zin. In the Septuagint, Kadesh is identified with the Wilderness of Paran. See J. L. Mihelic, "Paran," *The Interpreter's Dictionary of the Bible*, vol. 3, ed. George A. Buttrick (Nashville: Abingdon Press, 1962), p. 657.

[41]Coats, "The Wilderness Itinerary," p. 143.

[42]Childs, *Exodus*, pp. 321–336.

[43]Coats, "The Wilderness Itinerary," p. 140.

[44]G. I. Davies, "The Wilderness Itineraries: A Comparative Study," *Tyndale Bulletin*, 25 (1977), 46–81.

[45]Ibid., p. 47.

[46]Ibid.

[47]Milgrom, *Numbers*, p. xvi.

[48]Childs, *Exodus*, p. 264.

[49]Noth, *Exodus*, p. 131.

[50]Gray, *Numbers*, p. 94. Hobab may have been persuaded to go with the Israelites (vv. 31–32). The verb in Numbers 10:33 (מֵהַר יְהוָה וַיִּסְעוּ) has no subject, making it difficult to determine its antecedent. Noth, *Numbers*, p. 98, adds that Judges 4:11 suggests that Hobab did go with Moses since there were Hobabites present in the land following the Conquest.

[51]The scope of the present study does not permit a complete analysis of the debate over the identity of Jethro nor the Kenite theory. A brief summary is found in Childs, *Exodus*, pp. 322–326. In relation to the apparent duplicate reference to Jethro in Exodus 18 and Numbers 10:29–32, see W. F. Albright, "Jethro, Hobab and Reuel in Early Hebrew Tradition," *The Catholic Biblical Quarterly*, 25 (1963), 1–11, who concludes that the text in Numbers 10:29 can be emended to refer to Hobab as the son-in-law of Moses, the Midianite. However, see Noth, *Numbers*, p. 77, who suggests that a tradition is found in Judges 4:11 of a person by the name of Hobab who was Moses' father-in-law and belonged to the tribe of the Kenites. The tradition in the Judges passage (see 1:16), however, does not agree with the Jethro traditions of Exodus which portray him as a priest of Midian. The present study is concerned with the role and function of the narratives in Exodus and Numbers that contain the apparent duplicate tradition surrounding the person of Jethro or Hobab.

[52]Childs, *Exodus*, pp. 321–322, presents a brief discussion on the arguments for placing Exodus after the Sinai event.

[53]Ibid., p. 258. George Mendenhall, "Covenant," *The Interpreter's Dictionary of the Bible*, vol. 1, ed. George A. Buttrick (Nashville: Abingdon Press, 1962), pp. 719–720, identifies the difference between the narratives in Exodus before Sinai and those following the Sinai event. Milgrom, *Numbers*, p. xvi, states that for the redactor of the Pentateuch, Sinai is the critical event. The covenant event makes the difference in God's reaction to Israel. In Milgrom's theological-literary structure of the Hexateuch (p. xviii) Mount Sinai, specifically the theophany (Exod. 33), is the great divide of the Pentateuch. The Israelites are delivered from slavery to this event, and from Sinai they are delivered to freedom in the land.

[54]Jay A. Wilcoxen, "Some Anthropocentric Aspects of Israel's Sacred History," *The Journal of Religion*, 48 (1968), 333–350.

[55]Noth, *A History of Pentateuchal Traditions*, pp. 46–62.

[56]Ibid., p. 58.

[57]Childs, *Exodus*, p. 254. Also, Noth, *Numbers*, p. 1–3, suggests a lack of unity with no discernible pattern in its construction.

[58]Andrew C. Tunyogi, "The Rebellions of Israel," *Journal of Biblical Literature*, 81 (1962), 385–390, states that the fathers in the wilderness have become negative archetypes in the *exemplar history* (using a term from M. Eliade's *Patterns in Comparative Religion*, trans. Rosemary Sheed [New York: New American Library, 1958], p. 32ff.) of Israel's beginning when everything meaningful to Israel originated.

[59]Gerhard von Rad, *The Problem of the Hexateuch and Other Essays*, trans. E. W. Truemann Dicken (London: SCM Press, Ltd., 1966), pp. 1–78.

[60]Gerhard von Rad, *Old Testament Theology*, vol. 1, trans. D. G. M. Stalker (New York: Harper & Row, Publishers, 1962), p. 281.

[61]Walter Harrelson, "Guidance in the Wilderness: The Theology of Numbers," *Interpretation*, 13 (1959), 24–36.

[62]The major work of George Coats, in regard to the rebellion motif in the wilderness traditions, is his Yale University dissertation published under the title *Rebellion in the Wilderness: The Murmuring Motif in the Wilderness Traditions of the Old Testament* (Nashville: Abingdon Press, 1968).

[63]Coats, *Rebellion in the Wilderness*, p. 249.

[64]Ibid., p. 28.

[65]Ibid., p. 251.

[66]Simon J. de Vries, "The Origin of the Murmuring Tradition," *Journal of Biblical Literature*, 87 (1968), 51–58, disagrees with Coats and suggests that the murmuring motif was intended to reconcile the southern conquest tradition with the tradition of the central amphictyony. Noth, *A History of Pentateuchal Traditions*, p. 124, suggested the origin to be found in the Manna/Quails story (Num. 11:4–35), from an etiological intention, and from there the motif spread to other stories and became embedded in the "guidance in the wilderness" motif.

[67]Coats, *Rebellion in the Wilderness*, p. 251.

[68]Ibid., p. 252.

[69]Harrelson, "Guidance in the Wilderness," p. 25.

[70]Tunyogi, "The Rebellions of Israel," p. 388.

[71]Coats, *Rebellion in the Wilderness*, p. 188.

[72]Tunyogi, "The Rebellions of Israel," p. 386.

[73]Walter Harrelson, "Life, Faith, and the Emergence of Tradition," in *Tradition and Theology in the Old Testament*, ed. Douglas A. Knight (Philadelphia: Fortress Press, 1977), pp. 11–46.

[74]George W. Coats, "An Exposition for the Wilderness Traditions," *Vetus Testamentum*, 22 (1972), 288–295.

[75]Ibid, pp. 289–290.

[76]Ibid., p. 292; Coats, *Rebellion in the Wilderness*, p. 250.

[77]Blenkinsopp, *The Pentateuch*, p. 168.

[78]Walter Zimmerli, *Man and His Hope in the Old Testament* (London: SCM Press Ltd., 1971), p. 48.

[79]Olson, *The Death of the Old and the Birth of the New*, pp. 88–91.

[80]John Sturdy, *Numbers* (Cambridge: Cambridge University Press, 1976), p. 194.

[81]Noth, *Numbers*, p. 145, states that Numbers 20:1 could have been a report of a tradition that had Miriam buried at Kadesh and there is no connection with Numbers 12. In reference to the purification practices in Numbers 12, see Milgrom, *Numbers*, p. 98, who indicates that the healing of Miriam is uncertain due to the short quarantine. Miriam's exclusion could be due to shame and not to illness, thus implying that she was cured.

[82]Olson, *Death of the Old and the Birth of the New*, p. 91.

[83]Ibid., p. 125.

[84]Ibid., p. 84.

[85]Georg Fohrer, *Introduction to the Old Testament*, trans. David E. Green (Nashville: Abingdon Press, 1965), p. 161, notes that Exodus 17:8–14 and Numbers 21:1–3 are the only narratives in the wilderness traditions whose relationship with the traditional sources JEP are usually questionable.

[86]Otto Eissfeldt, *The Old Testament: An Introduction*, trans. Peter R. Ackroyd (New York: Harper and Row, Publishers, 1965), p. 195.

[87]Scholars such as Eissfeldt, Fohrer, Noth, and others, recognize that other sources are present that cannot be definitively assigned to the Yahwist, the Elohist or the Priestly Writer. For a detailed discussion on the literary developments in Pentateuchal studies see Fohrer, *Introduction*, pp. 103–196.

[88]Coats, *Rebellion in the Wilderness*, p. 49, identifies three sources: J (22b), 23–25a; P (22a), 27; Dtr., 25b–26.

[89]Childs, *Exodus*, p. 266. Noth, *Exodus*, p. 128.

[90]Coats *Rebellion in the Wilderness*, p. 49. Noth, *Exodus*, p. 129, and J. P. Hyatt, *Exodus*, The New Century Commentary (Grand Rapids: Wm. B. Eerdmans, 1971), p. 172, judge vv. 25–26 to be clearly from a Deuteronomic hand in its present form.

[91]Noth, *Exodus*, p. 129; S. R. Driver, *Exodus* (Cambridge: Cambridge University Press, 1911), p. 143.

[92]Exodus 15:24 contains a rhetorical question indicated by the presence of מַה. Bruce K. Waltke and Michael P. O'Connor, *An Introduction to Biblical Hebrew Syntax*

(Winona Lake: Eisenbrauns, 1990), p. 327, suggest that the form expresses the expectation of a strongly negative response. "What are we to drink?" may read "we have nothing to drink!" Therefore, the combination of the murmuring motif and this strong rhetorical question indicates a strong outright confrontation. Cf. Childs, *Exodus*, p. 268, who disagrees by stating that the rebellion is but an expression of discontent.

[93]U. Cassuto, *A Commentary on the Book of Exodus*, trans. Israel Abrahams (Jerusalem: The Magnes Press, 1967), p. 184, makes a further connection with the exodus event: the condition of the water compares to the first plague in Egypt.

[94]Von Rad, *Old Testament Theology*, vol. 1, p. 275.

[95]Various terms are used to refer to the disease of the plague in the wilderness traditions. נֶגֶף, "blow," "striking" is used by the Priestly Writer to refer primarily to judgment (*BDB*, p. 620 [Exod. 12:13]). The plague is associated with sin, for example, in Numbers 8:19 where the Levites are given the duty to make atonement for the sins of the people so that there will not be any plague among them, unless the people come near the tent of meeting and defile its holiness (see Numbers 17:12–13 [Heb. 17:27–28]). In Numbers 14:37 (P) death by plague (מַגֵּפָה) is the divine judgment against those who brought an evil report about the promised land. Further references to divine judgment by plague are related to נֶגַע, used predominantly in Leviticus, and מַכָּה, "to slaughter with plague," (*BDB*, p. 646) Also, in Num. 11:33 (JE) plague is the judgment for the craving by the people.

[96]Cassuto, *Exodus*, p. 184.

[97]Coats, *Rebellion in the Wilderness*, p. 87, identifies the literary structure of Exodus 16:1–35, along with Noth's assessment, as follows: The Yahwist, 4ab, 5, 29–32, 35b; The Priestly Writer, 1, 2–3, 6–7 (8), 9–13, 14–26, 33–35a; The Deuteronomist, 4bβ, 27–28. See Noth, *A History of Pentateuchal Traditions*, p. 31.

[98]Von Rad, *Old Testament Theology*, vol. 1, p. 240. G. Henton Davies, "Glory," *The Interpreter's Dictionary of the Bible*, vol. 2, ed. George A. Buttrick (Nashville: Abingdon Press, 1962), p. 401, adds that the glory of Yahweh appears also as a fiery presence associated with Sinai (Exod. 14:4, 17–18; 24:16–18; 34:29–35).

[99]Joseph Blenkinsopp, "The Structure of P," *The Catholic Biblical Quarterly*, 38 (1976), 275–292.

[100]Ibid., p. 281.

[101]Noth, *Exodus*, p. 137, writes that the manna testimony is an indication of a future cult practice intended for a time when there would be a local place for "the law" or testimony housed in the holy ark.

[102]Coats, *Rebellion in the Wilderness*, p. 88.

[103]Ibid., p. 90.

[104]Ibid., p. 91.

[105]Peter R. Ackroyd, *Exile and Restoration* (Philadelphia: Westminster Press, 1968), p. 234, speaks of "knowing" to be an important idea present throughout the wilderness period, and in the legal material as well. Of the narratives in the wilderness traditions, in Chapters 16 and 18 of Exodus and Chapters 14 and 16 of Numbers, the idea occurs most explicitly.

[106]Noth, *A History of Pentateuchal Traditions*, p. 119.

[107]The difficulty lies in not assigning verse 5 to the Priestly Writer, where the sixth day is mentioned. Noth, *A History of Pentateuchal Traditions*, p. 31, and Coats, *Rebellion in the Wilderness*, p. 86, assigns verse 5 to the Yahwist.

[108]Coats, *Rebellion in the Wilderness*, p. 87, and Noth, *Exodus*, p. 136, attribute the two verses to a Deuteronomistic source.

[109]Childs, *Exodus*, p. 291.

[110]Testimony (עֵדוּת, עֵדֻת) is used predominately by the Priestly Writer (cf. Josh. 4:16 [JE]) during and after the Sinai event. Exodus 16:34 is the only occurrence prior to Sinai. Childs, *Exodus*, p. 291, states that its occurrence is an anachronism. *BDB*, p. 730, describes the "testimony" as the Ten Words on the Tables, or the ark containing the tables, or the tabernacle containing the ark.

[111]Childs, *Exodus*, p. 292.

[112]Von Rad, *Old Testament Theology*, vol. 1, p. 282.

[113]Noth, *A History of Pentateuchal Traditions*, pp. 18–36.

[114]Coats, *Rebellion in the Wilderness*, p. 56.

[115]Von Rad, *Old Testament Theology*, p. 12,

[116]U. Cassuto, *A Commentary on the Book of Exodus*, pp. 187–188; G. Henton Davies, *Exodus: Introduction and Commentary* (London: SCM Press, 1967), pp. 137–141.

[117]Benjamin W. Bacon, *The Triple Tradition of the Exodus* (Hartford: The Student Publishing Company, 1894), p. 67, seems to imply that the arrival and the establishment of the covenant at Mount Horeb control the shaping of Exodus 15:22–17:7. In fact, the exodus from Egypt and the arrival at Sinai fall under one block of material, constituting the first feature called the exodus, Exodus 13:17–19:25. Sinai is the second feature for Bacon.

[118]Davies, *Exodus*, p. 143.

[119]Coats, *Rebellion in the Wilderness*, p. 63, proposes that the "testing" of Yahweh at Massah and Meribah could have been nothing more than efforts to discover alternative courses of action to take in order to relieve the current need for water.

[120]Childs, *Exodus*, p. 308.

[121]This theme is further developed in Numbers 14:22, a key Yahwistic text, that summarizes the development of the relationship through the community's visible witness of Yahweh's "glory" and "signs" performed in the wilderness and through obedience of Yahweh's "voice" (See Numbers 13–14 below). Obedience is the product of witnessing Yahweh's glory and signs performed, thus building a solid relationship.

[122]Refer to Noth, *Exodus*, pp. 138–140, and Coats, *Rebellion in the Wilderness*, pp. 53–71, for discussion on the form critical and the traditio- historical significance.

[123]Zimmerli, *Man and His Hope in the Old Testament*, p. 60.

[124]Cassuto, *A Commentary on the Book of Exodus*, p. 187.

[125]Ralph W. Klein, *Israel in Exile: A Theological Interpretation* (Philadelphia: Fortress Press, 1979), p. 149.

[126]Hans Walter Wolff, "The Hermeneutics of the Old Testament," trans. Keith Crim, in *Essays on Old Testament Hermeneutics*, ed. Claus Westermann (Richmond: John Knox Press, 1964), 160–199.

[127]Cf. Childs, *Exodus*, pp. 326–329.

[128]Davies, *Exodus*, p. 143.

[129]Gray, *Numbers*, p. 97, assigns to the craving narrative 11:4–10, 13, 18–24a, 31–34, and to the seventy elders story 11:16, 17a, 24b–30.

[130]Ibid., p. 98.

[131]Milgrom, *Numbers*, p. 83, 379. In Exodus 12:38 the reference "mixed multitude" (עֵרֶב רַב) is possibly the same people as those he calls "riffraff" (הָאסַפְסֻף) in Numbers 11:4.

[132]John Sturdy, *Numbers* (Cambridge: Cambridge University Press, 1976), p. 80.

[133]David Jobling, *The Sense of Biblical Narrative: Structural Analysis in the Hebrew Bible*, vol. 1 (Sheffield: JSOT Press, 1986), p. 34; Coats, *Rebellion in the Wilderness*, p. 111.

[134]Hans Walter Wolff, "The Kerygma of the Yahwist," in *The Vitality of Old Testament Traditions*, 2nd. ed., trans. Wilbur A. Benware, ed. Walter Brueggemann and Hans Walter Wolff (Atlanta: John Knox Press, 1982), 41–66.

[135]Cf. John H. Sailhamer, *The Pentateuch as Narrative* (Grand Rapids: Zondervan Publishing House, 1992), pp. 385-386, who summarizes the problem in terms of the challenge to Moses' authority as leader by showing the failure of Moses' office as mediator for the people in Numbers 11.

[136]Noth, *A History of Pentateuchal Traditions*, p. 36, suggests that only J and P are present, with no Elohist elements in the narrative. The Elohist is not found in the book of Numbers, according to Noth, until Numbers 20:14. Coats, *Rebellion in the Wilderness*, assigns the following sources to Numbers 13–14: the Priestly Writer, 13:1–3a, (3b–16a [16b]), (17a), 21, 25–26, 32, 33aα (33aβ), 33b; 14:1a, 2–3, 5–10, 26–38. The Yahwist, 13:17b–20, 22a (22b), 23–24, 27–28 (29) 30–31; 14:1b, 4, 11a (11B–23a) 23b–24 (25a) 25b, 39–45.

[137]*GKC*, p. 396, explains that the repetition of words such as אִישׁ אֶחָד אִישׁ אֶחָד לְמַטֵּה אֲבֹתָיו (13:2) is used as distributive to mean "one each", i.e., "one each from the tribe of his father" or the whole of Israel represented. Also in 14:34 יוֹם אַרְבָּעִים יוֹם "forty days" or "for each day for one year." Both passages are from the Priestly Writer.

[138]Gray, *Numbers*, p. 141, states that the etiology is probably from the Elohist. The noun אוֹדָה "cause," used in the plural (always with עַל, for example, עַל אֹדוֹת "because of") is frequently from the Elohist (Gen. 21:11; 26:32 [J or E (?)]; Exod. 18:8; Num. 12:1 [J]). The causal phrase is used also to refer to the exodus (Exod. 18:8). Like the Valley of Eschol which receives its name and meaning through the spy narrative, the use of the term in Exodus 18:8, likewise, implies that Israel's existence and significance, as proclaimed by Jethro, is an act of Yahweh accomplished through the exodus.

[139]See Gray, *Numbers*, pp. 137–139, for a discussion on the Negeb.

[140]The popular phrase אֶרֶץ זָבַת חָלָב וּדְבָשׁ, used here by the Yahwist, appears to be shared by other literary traditions (See Num. 14:8 [P]).

[141]Waltke and O'Connor, *An Introduction to Hebrew Syntax*, p. 672, explain that the particle of negation אֶפֶס or אֶפֶס כִּי is used to restrict the immediately preceding material by clarifying the intention of the speaker. Thus in Numbers 13:28 the particle restricts the positive elements in v. 27. Therefore, the account in Numbers 13:28 reflects the unenthusiastic report, rather than a rebellion at this juncture in the narrative.

[142]The particle of interjection הָס is seldom used in the Hebrew Bible (8 times). Waltke and O'Connor, *An Introduction to Biblical Hebrew Syntax*, p. 683, suggest that הָס is a polite exclamation, more like promptings than cries of demand. The particle has come to be used in some instances as a verb which occurs here in the Hiphil imperfect.

[143]See Noth, *A History of Pentateuchal Traditions*, pp. 51–54, for a discussion of the theme "Guidance into the Arable Land."

[144]Martin Noth, *Numbers: A Commentary*, trans. James D. Martin (Philadelphia: Westminster Press, 1968), p. 107; Coats, *Rebellion in the Wilderness*, p. 138.

[145]Coats, *Rebellion in the Wilderness*, p. 142.

[146]*GKC*, p. 313, explain the conditional mode of a sentence when לוּ is used with a perfect (לוּ־מַתְנוּ v. 2). The conditional mode expresses actions or facts that are possible but not necessarily factual. The point suggests that neither in Egypt nor in the wilderness was death a certain threat. Yet, in the present narrative the land posed the greater threat for the people.

[147]Gray, *Numbers*, p. 152.

[148]George W. Coats, "Conquest Traditions in the Wilderness Theme," *Journal of Biblical Literature*, 95 (1976), 177–190.

[149]Coats, *Rebellion in the Wilderness*, p. 139.

[150]Noth, *Numbers*, p. 108, identifies Deuteronomistic concepts in 14:11–23.

[151]Olson, *The Death of the Old and the Birth of the New*, p. 138, identifies an important link between the judgment narratives and the structure of the book of Numbers. The link is made by the priestly account of the judgment. Numbers 14:28–30 is linked to the census in Numbers 1 through the reference by age of those responsible for their actions. The judgment in Numbers 14 is also linked to the census in Numbers 26 in which the judgment against the first generation is proclaimed to be fulfilled (Num. 26:63–65).

[152]Noth, *Numbers*, p. 108, attributes Numbers 16:11b–23a to later Deuteronomistic additions. Gray, *Numbers*, p. 155, retains the Yahwist as the principle literary source.

[153]Richard Elliott Friedman, "Sacred History and Theology: The Redaction of Torah," in *The Creation of Sacred Literature*, ed. R. E. Friedmann (Berkeley: University of California Press, 1981), pp. 25–34.

[154]Ernest W. Nicholson, *God and His People: Covenant and Theology in the Old Testament* (Oxford: Clarendon Press, 1986), p. 142.

[155]Wolff, "The Kerygma of the Yahwist," p. 61.

[156]Sean E. McEvenue, *The Narrative Style of the Priestly Writer* (Rome: Biblical Institute Press, 1971), p. 94, interprets the punishment as cancellation of the promises to the fathers. Olson, *The Death of the Old And the Birth of the New*, p. 140, on the other hand, points to the census in Numbers 26 as the fulfillment of the judgment in

Numbers 14, thus indicating that the census is a tangible sign that the promises of Abraham are extended to a new generation.

[157]Coats, *Rebellion in the Wilderness*, p. 148.

[158]The *Revised Standard Version* of *The New Oxford Annotated Bible*, ed. Herbert G. May and Bruce M. Metzger (New York: Oxford University Press, 1973), p. 182, places emphasis in verse 22a on the conditional particle אִם (see v. 23a אִם־יִרְאוּ אֶת־הָאָרֶץ), "none of the men who . . ." The literal translation falls more on the conditional particle אִם being used as a negative particle in its actual location. The text begins with another conditional particle כִּי that follows the beginning of the oath (כִּי כָל־הָאֲנָשִׁים), "*Surely* all the men who have seen my glory and my signs which I did in Egypt and in the wilderness and yet put me to the test now ten times and not listened to my voice *shall not* see the land which I swore to your fathers, but all of those who despise me shall not see it." See also Manfred R. Lehmann, "Biblical Oaths," *Zeitschrift für die alttestamentliche Wissenschaft*, 81 (1969), 74–92, for a full discussion of the use of conditional or hypothetical particles such as אִם in relation to oaths.

[159]The murmuring begins in a conditional mode by the speculation that the people may have died in Egypt or in the wilderness. The conditional particle לוּ in 14:2b(P) indicates that the potential death in Egypt is not a certain reality, no more than death in the wilderness. The entire judgment narratives of both the Yahwist and the Priestly Writer are influenced by the frequent occurrence of the conditional particle אִם, לוּ, כִּי (13:18–20; 14:2, 5–10, 8, 23, 30, 35). See Waltke and O'Connor, *An Introduction to Biblical Hebrew Syntax*, p. 678–670, for discussion on biblical oaths. The use of these particles creates a sense of uncertainty in regard to both the potential cause of actions and the response to those actions. They can also assume an interrogative role within the notion of uncertainty (Num. 13:18–20). Numbers 14:8–9 (P) establishes the clearest conditional statement which is directly related to the judgment texts.

[160]The use of the term נָאַץ implies the notion of despite, an act of willful disobedience, open disrespect, and dishonor. Ernest Klein, *A Comprehensive Etymological Dictionary of the Hebrew Language for Readers of English* (New York: MacMillan Publishing Company, 1987), p. 401, has the Piel stem of נִאֵץ, "he condemned, spurned, blasphemed." The thought is one of condemnation. In the Qal stem the sense of despite is expressed. Ludwig Koehler and Walter Baumgartner, *Lexicon in Veteris Testamenti Libros* (Leiden: E. J. Brill, 1958), p. 585, includes the idea of treating without respect.

[161]McEvenue, *The Narrative Style of the Priestly Writer*, p. 117, suggests that in the present shape of the spy narratives the Yahwist account indicates that the mission was initiated as a fact-finding mission to search for further ways of providing food for the community.

[162]Anthony F. Campbell and Mark A. O'Brien, *Sources of the Pentateuch: Texts, Introductions, Annotations* (Minneapolis: Fortress Press, 1993), p. 154, include 14:11–25 as part of the Yahwist strand while acknowledging Noth's conclusions that 14:11a and 14:23b constitute a break with the texts in between (14:11b–23b), a block of text Noth believes to be a later insertion into the Yahwist material. However, the relationship of the people's despite for Yahweh to the people's disbelief in the miraculous acts of Yahweh, and the judgment, are so smoothly narrated that such a distinction disrupts the final shape of the text. The object of the people's despite is Yahweh, revealed by, and understood as, their disbelief in the acts as the signs and glory of Yahweh.

[163]For a discussion on the Caleb/Hebron traditions see R. F. Johnson, "Caleb," *The Interpreter's Dictionary of the Bible*, vol. 1, ed. George A. Buttrick (Nashville: Abingdon Press, 1962), pp. 482–483; Martin Noth, *A History of Pentateuchal Traditions*, pp. 130–136.

[164]McEvenue, *The Narrative Style of the Priestly Writer*, p. 121.

[165]Coats, *Rebellion in the Wilderness*, p. 146, states that 14:11 suggests an overt rejection of Yahweh.

[166]James L. Mays, *Amos: A Commentary* (Philadelphia: Westminster Press, 1969), p. 111, notes that the length of time spent in the wilderness, forty years, began in Deuteronomic circles and became a later feature when references were made to that period (See Deuteronomy 2:7; 8:2, 4; 29:5; Josh. 5:6; Exod. 16:35; Num. 14:33; 32:13; Ps. 95:10; Neh. 9:21).

[167]Ibid., p. 161. Coats assigns Numbers 16–17 (Hebrew 16:1–17:17) as follows: the Yahwist; 16:1b–2a, 12–15, 24bβ–26 (after "the dwelling of Korah"), 27aβb–31. The Priestly Writer (core material); 16:1a, 2aβb–7a, 18–24ab (including "the dwelling of Korah"), 27a, and 32–35. The priestly secondary expansions: 17:7b, 8–11, 16–17. Liver, "Korah, Dathan and Abiram," pp. 189–217, argues that the separation of the story into documents does not stand up to close examination, though the story is not a unity. Other traditions provided distinctive features, some independent of the Pentateuchal narrative.

[168]Von Rad, *The Problem of the Hexateuch*, p. 76, has a similar observation by stating that the Yahwist portrays God's activity in an "almost secular manner."

[169]The priestly emphasis is illustrated through the use of the term לְהַקְרִיב, (Hiphil Inf. Cst.) "bring near," specifically in 16:9–10, which indicates that the problem associated with the rebellion involves priestly functions in the tabernacle. See *BDB*, p. 899, where the term is defined and used, for example, in the selection of Aaron and his sons for service in the tabernacle (Exod. 29:4, 8). The term is also used in relation to dedication, sacrifice, and other cultic functions.

[170]Milgrom, *Numbers*, p. 417.

[171]Ibid., p. 130. See Coats, *Rebellion in the Wilderness*, p. 168f., for a discussion of the identity of Korah.

[172]*BDB*, p. 672, נָשָׂא in the Hithpael can be translated "exalt oneself" See also *BDB*, p. 239, where a similar use of the Hithpael with הָלַל, "be boastful," "praise" (Piel), is rendered as a self-confident boasting, "make one's boast." The Hithpael stem indicates self-serving intention.

[173]Coats, *Rebellion in the Wilderness*, p. 170.

[174]Murray L. Newman, *The People of the Covenant* (Nashville: Abingdon Press, 1962), pp. 72–101.

[175]Trent C. Butler, "An Anti-Moses Tradition," *Journal for the Study of the Old Testament*, 12 (1979), 9–15, identifies five narratives that reveal a negative view of Moses in Israelite traditions (Exod. 2:11–25; 4:24–26; 18; Num. 16; 25).

[176]Milgrom, *Numbers*, p. 133. Coats, *Rebellion in the Wilderness*, p. 166. See also J. G. Vink, "The Date and Origin of the Priestly Code in the Old Testament," in *Oudtestamentische Studiën*, vol. 15, ed. P. A. H. De Boer (Leiden: E. J. Brill, 1969), p. 120, who interprets לֹא נַעֲלֶה, "we will not come up," as the people's refusal to enter the land. The connection between Numbers 16 and Numbers 13–14 is made by interpreting the revolt in Numbers 16 in terms of entrance into the land. Vink's

point appears to be contradictory to the content of the complaint which includes the expressed disappointment of not coming into a habitable land.

[177]Milgrom, *Numbers*, p. 133.

[178]Gray, *Numbers*, p. 426. Fohrer, *Introduction*, p. 148. Eissfeldt, *The Old Testament: An Introduction*, pp. 200–201. Noth, *Numbers*, p. 238, states the narrative is a late work and was integrated with the Deuteronomistic historical work.

[179]Noth, *Numbers*, p. 127, assigns vv. 25–34 to the conclusion of the Dathan and Abiram narrative. 16:35 is therefore the conclusion to the Korah story. Verse 32b appears to be a priestly intrusion which is linked with verse 35. Coats, *Rebellion in the Wilderness*, p. 162, on the other hand, assigns 16:32–35 to the core tradition of the Korah rebellion. Coats suggests a distinction can be made between the Yahwist and the Priestly Writer through the use of הָאֲדָמָה, common to the Yahwist (v. 30a), and הָאָרֶץ, from the Priestly Writer (v. 32a). Therefore, verse 32, which contains הָאָרֶץ, must be from the Priestly Writer. However, the similarity in the language of 16:30 and 16:32a indicates a Yahwist influence (Cf. the anthropomorphic language of the Yahwist in וּפָצְתָה הָאֲדָמָה אֶת־פִּיהָ וּבָלְעָה אֹתָם [v. 30a], and וַתִּפְתַּח הָאָרֶץ אֶת־פִּיהָ וַתִּבְלַע אֹתָם [v. 32a]).

[180]Noth, *Exodus*, states that Exod. 3:10–12 are from the Elohist since the fundamental difference between J and E is that the Elohist has Yahweh instructing Moses to bring the people out of Egypt whereas the Yahwist has Yahweh personally bringing them out (Exod. 3:8, 17). In Numbers 16 the Elohist emphasis is present. The distinction, though perhaps evident, is not important for the narrative's present purpose. What is important is that the exodus and the mountain experience at Sinai are to be understood as signs revealing that Yahweh sent Moses.

[181]Noth, *Numbers*, p. 133, states that Numbers 17:12–13 provides a transition between the Korah rebellion narratives and the ordinances that follow. The two verses provide a summary statement reflecting the problem of encroachment on the realm of the "holy" (16:19ff.; 16:41ff.). The danger of increased familiarity with the sanctuary was considered "potential iniquity" (18:1).

[182]Gray, *Numbers*, p. 218. הַאִם is a strengthened interrogative, "Shall we ever finish dying?"

[183]Liver, "Korah, Dathan and Abiram," p. 191.

[184]Ibid., p. 193.

[185]Thomas W. Mann, "Holiness and Death in the Redaction of Numbers 16:1–20:13," in *Love & Death in the Ancient Near East: Essays in Honor of Marvin H. Pope*, ed. John H. Marks and Robert M. Good (Guilford, Conn.: Four Quarters Publishing Company, 1987), pp. 181–190, attributes the form of Numbers 16:1–20:13 to the internal themes of holiness and death. The narrative unit is understood as a complement to Numbers 11–14; Gray, *Numbers*, p. 256. Milgrom, *Numbers*, p. 157, 438–447, discusses the nature and structure of Numbers 19, a chapter considered by many to be unrelated to the wilderness narratives.

[186]Coats, *Rebellion in the Wilderness*, p. 71.

[187]Klein, *Israel in Exile*, p. 134.

[188]George W. Coats, *Moses: Heroic Man, Man of God* (Sheffield: JSOT Press, 1988), pp. 145–153.

[189]Gray, *Numbers*, p. 261.

[190]Mann, "Holiness and Death in the Redaction of Num. 16:1–20:13," pp. 181–190, points out that Numbers 17:12–13 [Heb. 16:27–28] and 20:3 are redactional touches that point to a continuous reading of the two narratives. He overlooks the significance of 20:29 in that reading.

[191]Noth, *A History of Pentateuchal Traditions*, p. 121. See Campbell and O'Brien, *Sources of the Pentateuch*, p. 156.

[192]Noth, *A History of Pentateuchal Traditions*, p. 122; *Numbers*, pp. 156–157.

[193]Coats, *Rebellion in the Wilderness*, p. 117.

[194]John Sturdy, *Numbers* (Cambridge: Cambridge University Press, 1976), p. 147.

[195]Karen Randolph Joines, "The Bronze Serpent in the Israelite Cult," *Journal of Biblical Literature*, vol. 87 (1968), 245–256.

[196]Sturdy, *Numbers*, p. 148. See also Jesús Asurmendi, "En Torno a la Serpiente de Bronce," *Estudios Biblicos*, vol. 46 (1988), 283–294.

[197]Sailhamer, *The Pentateuch as Narrative*, pp. 402–403.

[198]Odil Hannes Steck, "Theological Streams of Tradition," in *Tradition and Theology in the Old Testament*, ed. Douglas A. Knight (Philadelphia: Fortress Press, 1977), pp. 183–214, suggests that traditions have distinct features that enable them to preserve their own identity while maintaining control over new additions to the tradition. Traditions maintain particular content and goals. However, in the Exodus narratives the wilderness traditions have not developed along lines of independence like those in the book of Numbers.

[199]Paul D. Hanson, *The People Called: The Growth of Community in the Bible* (San Francisco: Harper & Row, Publishers, 1986), p. 525.

[200]Blenkinsopp, *The Pentateuch*, p. 135. Cf. Sailhamer, *The Pentateuch as Narrative*, pp. 62-66, who views the focus of the Pentateuch as a biography of Moses over that of interest in the nation of Israel, agreeing for the most part with Rolf Knierim, "The Composition of the Pentateuch," *SBL 1985 Seminar Papers* (Atlanta: Scholars Press, 1987), pp. 393-415.

[201]Ibid., p. 160.

[202]Noth, *A History of Pentateuchal Traditions*, pp. 116–117. Newman, *The People of the Covenant*, p. 75.

[203]Hanson, *The People Called*, p. 24. See J. G. Vink, "The Date and Origin of the Priestly Code in the Old Testament," p. 142, who suggests a parallel meaning as a military term, a military colony.

[204]F. Charles Fensham, "Covenant, Promise and Expectation in the Bible," *Theologische Zeitschrift*, 23 (1967), 305–322.

[205]Milgrom, *Numbers*, p. 377, implies that the quails narrative provides the setting for both punishment of the people and Moses himself. Moses' punishment is the lessening of his spiritual powers because he failed to intercede for the people, and trust that God would provide. Coats, *Moses*, p. 120, suggests the contrary, thus attributing to Moses a heroic stature.

[206]Robert H. Pfeiffer, *Introduction to the Old Testament* (New York: Harper & Brothers Publishers, 1941), pp. 250–251, discusses the priestly use of the various narratives by listing narratives with legislative purposes in the Priestly Document. The legislation is presented in two forms, narrative and juristic (in the form of

commandments). According to the priestly legislative prerogatives some of the narratives contain legal precedents. Examples are Exodus 16, illustrating observance of the Sabbath; Numbers 13–14, the priestly concern is with the sentencing of those who murmured against the Lord; Numbers 16–17, the punishment of those who murmured against the ecclesiastical system; Numbers 20:1–13, sentencing of Moses and Aaron for their actions at Meribah; and Numbers 20:22–29, the death of Aaron in compliance with the sentencing in Numbers 20:1–13.

[207]Ronald E. Clements, *God and Temple* (Oxford: Basil Blackwell, 1965), p. 112.

[208]James A. Sanders, *Torah and Canon* (Philadelphia: Fortress Press, 1972), p. 51.

[209]Von Rad, *The Problem of the Hexateuch*, p. 4.

[210]Joseph Blenkinsopp, *A Sketchbook of Biblical Theology* (London: Burns & Oats, 1968), p. 64, adds that the Torah as a body of customary rules was recognized by the community as binding. See also Joseph Schreiner, "The Development of the Israelite 'Credo'," in *The Dynamism of Biblical Tradition*, ed. Pierre Benoit and Roland E. Murphy (New York: Paulist Press, 1967), p. 34, who likewise suggests that the Torah is binding and therefore its confessional stance is law. The implication from these points is that confession may be a requirement more than a response of the faithful.

[211]Joseph Blenkinsopp, *Wisdom and Law in the Old Testament* (Oxford: Oxford University Press, 1983), p. 105.

[212]Sue Boorer, "The Kerygmatic Intentions of the Priestly Document," *Austin Biblical Review* 25 (1977), 12–20.

[213]Hanson, *The People Called*, p. 18.

[214]Benjamin W. Bacon, *The Triple Tradition of the Exodus* (Hartford: The Student Publishing Company, 1894), p. 94, identifies the Yahwist as the source for the confession in Exodus 18:8-11. Since a shift has occurred from the divine name אֱלֹהִים [E] to יְהוָה, the Yahwist is assumed to have produced the confession.

[215]Nahum Sarna, *The JPS Torah Commentary: Exodus* (Philadelphia: The Jewish Publication Society, 1991), p. 99, suggests that Exodus 18 is most often associated with the ceremonial (Exod. 18:12), implying a treaty consummated between the Midianites and Israel.

[216]Davies, *Exodus*, p. 148.

[217]Gray, *Numbers*, p. 197.

[218]Clements, *God and Temple*, p. 116.

[219]Olson, *The Death of the Old and the Birth of the New*, p. 160.

[220]Walter Brueggemann, *The Creative Word: Canon as a Model for Biblical Education* (Philadelphia: Fortress Press, 1982), p. 4.

[221]Campbell and O'Brien, *Sources of the Pentateuch*, pp. 21–22.

Chapter Three

The Wilderness Traditions in Deuteronomy

The book of Deuteronomy is set in the framework of a retelling of certain Israelite traditions through the voice of Moses. The events in the retelling primarily reflect the experiences of the community since its departure from Sinai. As popular consensus suggests, the book in its final literary shape functions as Moses' last will and testament.[1] Since the most distinctive feature of the book is its urgent preaching style, Deuteronomy is considered more a book of instruction than a law book in the strictest sense. Deuteronomy is concerned with how the law is received, acted upon, and understood.[2] The sermons or teaching discourses, given in an atmosphere of threat, are presented as an appeal to love the only true God.[3]

Scholars have identified chapters 1–11 to be the introductory discourse to the Deuteronomic work, with distinct divisions in the material (1:1–4:40; 4:41–43; 4:44–49; 5:1–11:32).[4] Noth further suggests that chapters 1–3, and possibly 4, constitute an introduction to the Deuteronomistic history while chapters 5–11 form the original introduction to the book.[5] The following structure of the book of Deuteronomy will assist in the analysis of the wilderness traditions:[6]

1:1–4:40 (1:41–43), First Introduction
4:44–11:32, Second Introduction (to chapters 12–26)
12:1–26:19, Collection of Laws
27:1–34:12, Concluding Section

The book contains three major categories of materials: the historical (chapters 1–4), legislative (chapters 12–26, 28) and the parenetic (chapters 5–11). The parenetic is the more significant, for in this type of material are found the fundamental teachings of the religious and moral principles. Furthermore, the historical material also serves a parenetic function.[7] The historical review in Deuteronomy 1:1–4:40 stresses the providence of God revealed in the events of the exodus, the wilderness wandering, and an account of Israel passing through their neighbors' lands on their way to Palestine. Chapters 5–11 constitute a hortatory introduction to the laws of chapters 12–26, which, among other important concerns, emphasizes the first commandment.[8] Chapters 27–34 is the closing section of Deuteronomy, and chapters 28–30 contain a concluding speech by Moses, which may be a continuation of the double introductory speech (1:1–4:40, 4:44–11:32).[9]

Table 5

THE WILDERNESS TRADITIONS IN DEUTERONOMY 1:1–11:32

1. 1:1–3:17	Israel's wanderings from Horeb to the Jordan		
		1:9–18	Exod. 18, Num. 11, Moses' leadership
		1:20–46	Num. 13–14, Spy narrative
		1:37	Num. 20 (?), punishment of Moses
		2:2–7	Num. 20.14–21, Edom passage
3:18–29	The prospect of the land		
		3:23–28	Num. 20, 27, account of Moses' death
4:1–43	Idolatry warnings		
		4:21	Num. 20 (?), Moses' punishment
2. 4:44–49	Introduction of the law		
5:1–21	The Ten Commandments		
5:22–6:25	The principal commandments		
		6:16	Exod. 17, Num. 20, Massah
7:1–8:20	Homilies concerning the law		
		8:1–6	Forty years in the wilderness
		8:11–20	Exod. 16, Manna; Num. 20, Meribah
9:1–29	Lessons from the past		
		9:1–7	Num. 13–14, Anak
		9:8–21	Exod. 32, The Golden Calf
		9:22–29	Num. 13–14, Spy narrative
10:1–22	The majesty of God		
11:1–32	Israel's response commanded		
		11:1–7	Num. 16, Dathan and Abiram rebellion

According to von Rad, the structure of the book reflects a liturgical movement in the form of a cultic ceremony of covenant-making or covenant renewal.[10] The covenant renewal form also appears in the Sinai material of Exodus 19–24. Von Rad identifies the structure to include four basic movements: historical and parenetic introduction (chapters 1–11); the presentation of the law (12–26); the sealing of the covenant (26:16–19); and the blessings and curses (chapters 27ff.).[11]

The law code in Deuteronomy 12:1–26:15 represents a more uniform and consistent literary style than do the introduction and the conclusion.[12] Both chapters 1–11 and 27–34 contain a complex mixture of traditions and literary techniques, thus displaying the consistent appropriation of the stories derived from the wilderness traditions of Exodus and Numbers.[13] Four major sections are marked by what Clements identifies as headings: 1) 1:1 "Words" of Moses, 2) 4:44–49 "law" Moses set forth, 3) 29:1 "Words" of the covenant, and 4) 33:1 "Blessing" of Moses.[14] The four sections occur primarily in the two divisions of the Introduction (1:1–11:32) and the Epilogue (26:16–34:12). The first division is outlined in Table 5 above. References to the wilderness traditions in the law code (12:1–26:15) are very limited (for exceptions, see 24:9 [Miriam's leprosy], 25:17–19 [Amalek opposition]); however the role of the traditions is more significant in the epilogue. Table 6 outlines the wilderness traditions in this last major division of the book of Deuteronomy.

Table 6

THE WILDERNESS TRADITIONS IN DEUTERONOMY 26:16–34:12

1. 26:16–27:10	Law as the way to holiness		
27:11–26	The twelve curses		
28:1–68	The two ways––blessing and curse		
2. 29:1–29	The covenant in Moab		
		29:1–9	Yahweh's care in the wilderness
30:1–20	Perspectives on the law		
3. 31:1–29	Provisions of the law		
4. 31:30–32:52	The Song of Moses		
		32:1–27	Care in the wilderness
		32:48–52	Num. 20, Deut. 3:23–36, Moses' death
5. 33:1–29	The Blessing of Moses		
		33:8–11	Exod. 17, Num. 20, Massah and Meribah
34:1–12	The death of Moses		

Application of the wilderness traditions by the writer of Deuteronomy occurs primarily in chapters 1–11, with less frequent occurrences in chapters 29–33. Chapters 1–2, 8, and 9 evidence the most extensive use of the traditions. The Spy narrative and the golden calf episodes are appropriated extensively in Deuteronomy. In chapter 4, the golden calf narrative retains its usual independence from the wilderness period, and, according to the scope and content of the wilderness traditions in Exodus and Numbers, they are not mentioned in chapter 4. On the other hand, as the following analysis will suggest, the golden calf event is considered by the writer of Deuteronomy as part of the wilderness traditions (cf. Deut. 9). In the majority of other passages, the wilderness traditions appear as brief illustrations.[15]

Literary Analysis of the Wilderness Traditions

The historical prologue (1:9–2:16) and the introduction to the law corpus (chapters 8–9) are firmly grounded in the traditions that reflect the period of the wilderness. Analysis of the wilderness traditions in the book of Deuteronomy will be organized as follows: 1:9–46; 6:1–25; 8:1–20; 9:1–29; 11:1–9. The major texts in which the traditions are appropriated in the epilogue (27:1–34:12) are Deuteronomy 29:1–9, the Song of Moses (chapter 32), and 33:8–11.

Deuteronomy 1:9–46

According to Deuteronomy 1:6, the setting for Moses' discourse in Deuteronomy is at Mount Horeb. The traditions of 1:9–18 reflect a time before the community left Horeb to enter the wilderness (1:19), perhaps the situation revealed in Exodus 18.[16] Following the introduction to the historical prologue in 1:1–5, Moses continues his address by recalling his own situation as their leader (1:9–18). The discourse begins by describing Moses' exceptional will and ability in leading the people, as though Moses is co-equal as the savior of the people. The claim by Moses "I am not able alone to bear you" (1:9) may refer to the traditions of Moses' leadership of the community in Exod. 18:14–27 and Numbers 11, though certain elements are missing in the Deuteronomic account, such as the commissioning of the seventy elders to assist Moses (Num. 11:24–25).[17] As in the two wilderness narratives of Exodus 18 and Numbers 11, Deuteronomy 1:9–46 is primarily Moses-centered.

The covenant tradition from Abraham to Moses is the primary concern in these initial statements (1:9–10), stressing that God is at work in history fulfilling the promises.[18] The recitation of the historical fact of Israel's growth is a confession of God's abilities as a faithful God. The blessing pronounced by Moses in 1:11 not only supports the confession that God is behind the blessing, but the blessing also creates a positive view of Moses that tones down the negative implications of Moses' initial complaint in verse 9, thus separating him from the blame for the people's fate in the wilderness.[19] The covenant promises, then, stand at the heart of the motive for choosing the leaders. The fact that Israel has become as "the stars of the heaven" denotes the fulfillment of the promises, at least in part.

Significant to the present account is the cooperative nature of the people in this organizational effort. The community is responsible for the choice of the leaders, which is an element absent in Exodus 18 and Numbers 11, though Moses remains the primary catalyst in the structuring process. Weinfeld believes that national pride, which prevails in Deuteronomy as a whole, is fully expressed here. The Deuteronomist would not allow a foreigner to contribute in such a way as Jethro in Exodus 18.[20]

Within the implications of the question, "How can I bear alone the weight and burden of you and your strife?" (1:12) lies the common characteristics of the murmuring or rebellion motif.[21] The evidence of the difficulties and conflict associated with the wilderness traditions is found in the three words: טֹרַח, "weight," מַשָּׂא, "burden," and רִיב, "strife." The structure of 1:9–18, however, reveals a pattern that is basically positive in the wilderness traditions.[22] Moses' statement in Deuteronomy 1:9, though hinting in a negative way to the difficulties surrounding his task as the leader, actually relates to the affirmation in verses 10–11, which is a positive kerygmatic statement regarding Yahweh's fidelity to the promises and the people. On the other hand, a negative note is struck in verse 12 when the emphatic question is voiced by Moses. Taken in contrast to the confessional in 1:10–11, Moses' question gives the picture of a community in stress and conflict, thus laying ground for the fuller development of the rebellious actions of the community in the texts that follow (cf. 1:26).

The third division in the historical prologue (1:19–46) recalls the journey from Horeb. Deuteronomy 1:20–46, the spy episode (cf. Num. 13–14), represents the most extensive use of the wilderness traditions in the book of Deuteronomy. From a traditio-historical standpoint, Noth identifies three functions of Deuteronomy 1:19–46:

1) The narrative anticipates the theme of occupation which the Deuteronomistic historian proposes to treat later in detail.
2) The recollection helps to explain why the wanderings in the wilderness lasted forty years, hence justifying the Deuteronomistic historian's chronology.
3) The narrative provides an explanation for Caleb's special role in the conquest (Josh. 14:6–14).[23]

But in the literary structure, the narrative functions to reveal "the proof of God's right to Israel's worship, which preceded any human act," "the inexplicable conduct of the people," and "the punishment reaction of God."[24]

In Deuteronomy 1:19–46, and the historical prologue as a whole, the land theme is central. In the spy episode of Numbers 13, the order to form a scouting expedition comes from Yahweh, but in the retelling here, the people themselves initiate the spy mission (v. 22). Moses' response to the community's request (וַיִּיטַב בְּעֵינַי, v. 23) implies that Moses intended good but failed because he listened to the people instead of God. The last word or command from God, prior to the community's arrival at Kadesh-barnea, had been to "go in (בֹּאוּ) and take possession of the land" (1:8a), indicating immediate action to obey the command and fulfill the promise made to the patriarchs. The actual mission does not occur until the people arrive at Kadesh-barnea. In Deuteronomy 9:23, where the spy narrative is mentioned briefly, the expedition also originates from Kadesh-barnea (1:19). The command by Yahweh to "go up (עֲלוּ) and take possession of the land" (9:23), using the same language as 1:8 (וּרְשׁוּ "and take possession of"), is only met with rebellion and disbelief, with no mention of the spy expedition as a motive for rebellion. The common elements found in the simplest recollection, such as chapter 9, include: the command by Yahweh to enter the land, the place of departure is from Kadesh-barnea, and the community's response by rebellion and disbelief.

The scouting expedition, as in Numbers 13, traverses the Valley of Eshcol, where a sampling of the fruit of the land is gathered. The fruit is an outward sign, while the report of the spies affirms the goodness of the land and the fact that the land is a gift.[25] The proclamation, "It is a good land which the LORD our God gives us," is a general affirmation given without reservation and not attributed to anyone in particular. The great contrast between the good report (v. 28) and the negative response by the community indicates the unusual reaction of ingratitude. Since there are no grounds for the skepticism, the people's response is to be interpreted as a lack of faith and trust in God.[26] The recollection of the spy narrative is therefore divided to show the contrast between the positive aspects of the goodness of the land (1:19–25) and the negative response by the people (1:26–33).[27]

The complaint, which reflects the murmuring motif in verse 26, is that God has taken the community into the wilderness so as to kill them. The threat which caused the complaint is created by the presence of the Amorites. The excuse is compounded when the people claim that the inhabitants are too great, the cities are fortified, and the Anakim are in the land.[28] Moses' intervention specifically reminds the people that God will fight for them, just as God had done in Egypt and during their stay in the wilderness (1:30–31). Like the Yahwist, the two kerygmatic elements, deliverance and guidance, are combined to encourage the recollection of the community's relationship to their God in times past.

The kerygma of Deuteronomy 1:20–46 is revealed in the affirmations of verses 31 and 33. Verse 31 proclaims the gracious leadership of God, which allowed Israel to arrive successfully at the borders of the promised land. The affirmations of verse 31, Yahwistic in content, are repeated in verse 33. The language reflects, in part, what Coats identifies as an exposition of the wilderness traditions. The theme of the leadership of Yahweh, for example, is symbolized by the pillar of cloud and the pillar of fire.[29]

Additional language of affirmation regarding the guidance theme can be identified in association with these symbolic elements. Coats identifies two important terms to depict the leadership as a whole, לַנְחֹתָם and הַדֶּרֶךְ (Exod. 13:21).[30] A comparison between Exodus 13:21 and the texts of Numbers 14:14 and Deuteronomy 1:30–33 will clarify the important role of the guidance or leadership theme.

Exodus 13:21

וַיהוָה הֹלֵךְ לִפְנֵיהֶם יוֹמָם בְּעַמּוּד	And the LORD went before them by day in a pillar
עָנָן לַנְחֹתָם הַדֶּרֶךְ וְלַיְלָה בְּעַמּוּד	of cloud to lead them along the way and by night in a pillar
אֵשׁ לְהָאִיר לָהֶם לָלֶכֶת יוֹמָם	of fire to light for them to go
וָלָיְלָה׃	by day and by night.

Numbers 14:14

. . . וַעֲנָנְךָ עֹמֵד עֲלֵהֶם וּבְעַמֻּד	and your cloud stands over them and in a pillar
עָנָן אַתָּה הֹלֵךְ לִפְנֵיהֶם יוֹמָם	of cloud you go before them by day
וּבְעַמּוּד אֵשׁ לָיְלָה׃	and in a pillar of fire by night

Deuteronomy 1:30

יְהוָה אֱלֹהֵיכֶם הַהֹלֵךְ לִפְנֵיכֶם . . .	The LORD your God who goes before you

Deuteronomy 1:31

בְּכָל־הַדֶּרֶךְ אֲשֶׁר הֲלַכְתֶּם . . .	in all the way that you went

Deuteronomy 1:33

. . . הַהֹלֵךְ לִפְנֵיכֶם בַּדֶּרֶךְ	who went before you in the way
. . . בָּאֵשׁ לַיְלָה . . .	by fire at night
בַּדֶּרֶךְ אֲשֶׁר תֵּלְכוּ־בָהּ	by what way which you should go
וּבֶעָנָן יוֹמָם	and in a cloud by day

Putting aside the differences between the singular and plural pronominal references, the similarities among the passages establish a central theme of God's leadership and care for Israel during the exodus and the wilderness period. The repeated emphasis upon Yahweh going before the people (הֹלֵךְ לִפְנֵיהֶם) is well-established in the exodus and wilderness traditions. Yahweh has been their guide, directing their way (דֶּרֶךְ), while Yahweh's presence is symbolized by the fire and cloud pillars. In Deuteronomy, the traditional elements of Yahweh's leading, guiding, and presence have become integrated within the entrance into the land motif.

A similarity exists between one of the terms Coats identifies in the leadership motif, לַנְחֹתָם "to lead" (Exod. 13:21), and לַחֲנֹתְכֶם "to pitch your tents" (Deut. 1:33).[31] Both Exodus 13:21 and Deuteronomy 1:33 stress the guidance theme and emphasize the fact that Yahweh "goes before" the people, in search of a way through the wilderness or through the land. The presence of תּוּר in Deuteronomy 1:33 further connects the narrative to Numbers 13–14.[32]

Deuteronomy 1:22 illustrates the central role of the care and guidance theme in Deuteronomy by contrasting the concerns and actions of the people with the kerygmatic affirmations in 1:33.

Deuteronomy 1:22

וַתִּקְרְבוּן אֵלַי כֻּלְּכֶם	Then all of you came near to me
וַתֹּאמְרוּ נִשְׁלְחָה אֲנָשִׁים	and said "Let us send men
לְפָנֵינוּ וְיַחְפְּרוּ־לָנוּ	before us and they can explore
אֶת־הָאָרֶץ וְיָשִׁבוּ אֹתָנוּ	the land for us and bring us
דָּבָר אֶת־הַדֶּרֶךְ אֲשֶׁר	word of the way by which
נַעֲלֶה־בָּהּ וְאֵת הֶעָרִים	we may go up to it and the cities
אֲשֶׁר נָבֹא אֲלֵיהֶן׃	into which we may come"

In Deuteronomy 1:22 the people approach Moses and suggest the formation of a spy expedition to search out the land for them (וְיַחְפְּרוּ־לָנוּ). The task of the men is to go before the community (נִשְׁלְחָה אֲנָשִׁים לְפָנֵינוּ) with the purpose of searching out the best way (דֶּרֶךְ) to enter the land successfully. The response in 1:33, which has Yahweh as the one who performs the scouting task, is given in consideration of the community's initiatives in verse 22. The corresponding themes in verses 22 and 33 imply that the spy mission itself was in error. Deuteronomy 1:33 implies that Yahweh is the scout who customarily goes before the people to scout out the terrain (תּוּר); and the affirmation suggests that Yahweh had already accomplished the task of spying out the land (1:8, 21). Further, in Deuteronomy 1:42, where an effort is made to correct the mistake, the stress is placed on the proper entrance into the land. Failure results because God is not in their midst (Num. 14:14, 42), and success is only possible when Yahweh goes before them.

To conclude the discussion of Deuteronomy 1:19–46, a few points are necessary regarding the interpretation of the Deuteronomist's use of the spy tradition. First, seen in its kerygmatic purpose, the spy mission itself is an act of rebellion against God and a demonstration of unfaithfulness on the part of the people. Unlike the same tradition in Numbers 13–14, where God commands the mission, here the whole endeavor is initiated by the people; and, understood as an act of rebellion in itself, the spy expedition is viewed by the Deuteronomist as an insult to the very nature of God's relationship to the community. The command had been given already to enter and to take possession of the promised land (1:8). God's anger (קָצַף) is expressed as a wrathful rage against the people (1:34) and against Moses as well (אָנַף, v. 37). In the final shape of the historical prologue, that anger appears to have as its antecedent the actions of the people in carrying out the spy expedition and the subsequent murmuring of the people (1:27–28).

Second, although Moses does not suffer the curse of death that the "men of war" were doomed to experience (Deut. 2:15), he is nevertheless not permitted to enter the land. The fact that Moses accepted the request as "pleasing" (וַיִּיטַב) indicates that he was mistaken in his assessment of the situation.[33] In Deuteronomy 1:37, the traditional view of Moses' fate is interpreted in relation to his role as the community's leader. Moses' death is explained as strikingly vicarious.[34] Coats does not follow this interpretation completely, but his views help to clarify Moses' place in the spy episode. He concludes that in Deuteronomy 1:37 בִּגְלַלְכֶם ("on your account") can be interpreted to mean that Moses cannot enter the land *because* of the people.[35] The preposition (בִּגְלַלְכֶם), when used elsewhere (for example, Gen. 39:5), indicates the notion of agency. Thus, Moses must remain outside the land for the sake of the people. The most significant point in Coats' discussion appears in the brief statement, "But the real point in this tradition lies in the identification of Moses with his people."[36] By identifying with the people, Moses remains outside the land due to the fact that he participated in the plotting and improvising of the mission. In other Pentateuchal traditions, Moses is identified with the people usually through his acts of intercession. Craigie suggests that Moses' identification with the people meant that in his leadership position he accepted the result of their failures alongside them.[37] Moses himself confessed that at the time "it seemed good (was pleasing) to me" (1:23). This statement by Moses in 1:23 is definitely an identifying remark, not necessarily an attempt to exonerate Moses of the sin, as Mayes would suggest.

Decisions to act in the narrative involve the people's initial effort (1:22) and Moses' favorable response (1:23). Nevertheless, the goodness of the land and the sovereignty of God are still proclaimed (1:25 "the land is good," and 1:29–30 "Do not fear . . . Yahweh your God goes before you."). As in the Numbers 20:10–11 account of Moses' transgression, where he is judged for acting presumptuously by striking the rock, here presumption seems to have caused the judgment as well. The tendencies of the community to function alone and ignore Yahweh are juxtaposed to the confession of God's sovereignty and faithfulness to them. Moses' words of encouragement (1:29) emphasize that fear can overcome the people if they do not seek the leadership of Yahweh and act in accordance with divine mandates that establish the structure of life for the community (1:30). The community and its leadership provide the antithesis to proper community life centered upon faith and trust in the God, who cares and leads them into their future. The kerygma, revealed through the appropriation of the spy tradition, is one that affirms the sovereignty of God, while appealing to the community's renewed trust in God.

DEUTERONOMY 6

One reference to the wilderness traditions occurs in Deuteronomy 6:16 where the list of instructions, which are given in apodictic style, includes the warning against putting Yahweh to the test (נִסָּה). The interpretation of the nature of this testing is rather ambiguous, and the implications of the verse must be viewed in relation to the entire passage. The writer utilized the wilderness traditions, represented by the Massah event, to stress proper living as a community of God. Mayes interprets the "testing" as a challenge that proves the faithfulness of God to the covenant.[38] In this respect, the reliability of Yahweh is brought under suspect. Von Rad adds that when the community's faith, and its worship of Yahweh, depend on putting God to the test, the people fail to appreciate God and, therefore, the testing is a defiance of God.[39] Driver is perhaps more concrete by interpreting the testing in Deuteronomy 6:16 as the community's challenging the belief in God's presence and doubting God's word.[40] In this view, the interpretation relies heavily on the narrative in Exodus 17:1–7.

The reference to Massah occurs in the middle section (6:10–18) of a basic three-part sermon. In 6:4–9 the commandments of God are venerated as the highest goals in life and faith, and 6:20–25 lists the miraculous acts of God toward Israel, which include the law as one of the miraculous provisions. Like other acts of mercy, the laws are also given for the good of the people, so that life will go well for them in the land (6:24). For instructional purposes, a series of warnings are strategically inserted between the great confessionals in 6:4–9 and 6:20–25. In 6:12 a warning is given against prosperity and forgetfulness, which can lead to presumptuous living. Deuteronomy 6:14 is a warning against the worship of other gods. The two warnings in 6:12 and 6:14 are concerned with departing from God because of or in pursuit of other things. The force of the anger of God is expressly related to these two problems.

Three commands follow that relate to proper living in the land: "you shall not test" (6:16), "you shall keep (emphatic) the law" (6:6:17), and "you shall act accordingly" (6:18). Obedience to these three commands is required if the people are to go in and successfully take the land. Of the three, the command not to test Yahweh is the most ambiguous. A close reading and interpretation will depend on the knowledge of Exodus 17:1–7, though caution must be taken in assuming Exodus 17 is the source for the statement.

In Exodus 17:1–7 the underlying problem is the community's disbelief in the presence of God in the wilderness. The difficulties experienced in the wilderness by the community create disbelief in God and skepticism toward the leadership. In Deuteronomy 6:16 the testing, therefore, can be understood to be a restatement or a furtherance of the notion of God's presence expressed in 6:15. In other words, in connection with 6:12–13, which stressed the demands for the community's loyalty to Yahweh, the people are commanded not to be presumptuous toward God's presence. Understood in relation to the emphasis on the presence of God, the command in 6:16, "you shall not put the Lord your God to the test," is an affirmation of God's presence and an appeal to the community's fidelity to God.

Since Deuteronomy as a whole elevates the status of the law, then fidelity to God finds its expression in obedience and loyalty to the laws of God.[41] The Deuteronomist implies that the wilderness period had as its main purpose the testimony to the important place of the law within the life of the community. But, as Childs concludes, the motive for observing the law is to remember and affirm Israel's past traditions.[42] If Deuteronomy 6:16 is to be considered along with 6:20, which is fully concerned with the transmission of tradition, then the provocation of the Massah incident can be prevented through observance of the law. Through the law, the presence of God is actualized and understood, and personal faith is renewed. The faithful obedience to God's laws confirms the reality of God's presence. For future generations far removed from the experiences of Israel's beginnings, the law is intended to provide continuity.

DEUTERONOMY 8

The wilderness traditions are perhaps integrated into the text of chapter 8 more than in any other texts in chapters 5–11. The whole chapter, then, is crucial for understanding the kerygma of the wilderness traditions in the book of Deuteronomy. Deuteronomy 8 stresses the nature of Yahweh's relationship to the community. Chapter 8 departs from the previous negative presentation of Israel in the wilderness (Deut. 1:19–46; 6:16) and represents a positive experience for the community. In fact, here, the text is entirely focused on the kerygmatic theme of the care and leadership of God in the wilderness traditions (see Deut. 2:7).

Christensen identifies Deuteronomy 7:12–8:20 to be centrally positioned according to the structure of chapters 4–11, with 8:1 as that center. This central section (7:12–8:20) emphasizes the necessity of obedience to God through observing and learning from the laws of God, in order that the blessings of God will be experienced in the land.[43] Covenant loyalty, both of Yahweh and the people, is pivotal in the message of chapters 4–11 as a whole. The necessity of loyalty to the covenant by the community is expressed pointedly in chapters 7–8, wherein the community is called to response by faith and obedience.[44]

The wilderness traditions in chapter 8 are utilized to teach the community that God is their true source of life. Miller summarizes the message of Deuteronomy to be:

> the word of a good life (5:16; 6:18; cf. 28:11) in a good land and the offer of that as a genuine option to later generations . . . In other words, Israel receives the possibility of a special kind of life—good, undefiled, life in community, life in the worship of Yahweh, life at its fullest and best . . . Ultimately, therefore, it is not possible to speak of the gift of the land apart from obedience to Yahweh and his law.[45]

The phrase "man lives by everything that proceeds out of the mouth of God" (8:3) is the heart of the kerygma of both the wilderness traditions in Deuteronomy and the book as a whole. Deuteronomy 8:3 suggests that life is more than the material, and God is more than a material provider. Implied within this exhortation lies the competitive nature between the traditions of God's presence and actions in the exodus and the wilderness and the transformation of those actions when the *Sitz im Leben* of the community changes in the urban world of Palestine. In other words, the land is a peculiar competitor to God's presence and place in the community. Life of prosperity in the land that becomes overly confident can produce similar actions by the people that mirror their behavior during the wilderness period. The warning expressed persistently in chapter 8 is for the people not to lose sight of the one who still miraculously provides for the people. The constant reminder of God's presence, as well as the gift of the land, is the law (8:11).

The wilderness period and life in the land are afforded an equal degree of importance in chapter 8, because both are seen as vital to Israel's survival. God is at work in both to bring about the fulfillment of the promises and confirm the covenant (8:18). The Deuteronomist interprets the wilderness period as a time that was more than a journey with its hardships and tragic outcome for the first generation. The wilderness period was an integral part of the progress toward the fulfillment of God's promises. Actually, for the Deuteronomist, the land, though a part of the promises of Abraham, is potentially more tragic than the wilderness. For example, the fear expressed in the wilderness, "Behold we perish" (Num. 17:12), can be understood as an implied warning against those who will forget Yahweh after they arrive in the land (8:19b–20).

McCarthy points out that Deuteronomy 1:31 is the only text, other than Hosea 11:1, that attributes Yahweh with a tender nature like that of a loving father to a son. In Deuteronomy, the period used to illustrate the father–son relationship is the wilderness. According to McCarthy, the relationship of Yahweh and Israel, pictured in the image of a father's love for the son, is identical to the Deuteronomic conception of the covenant relationship between Yahweh and Israel.[46] In Israel's relationship to Yahweh, certain demands are placed upon them as the subject–party to the covenant, and such a relationship is characterized as a father's discipline of the son (8:2–5).

Mauser identifies two important verbs in 8:2, נִסָּה "test" and עִנָּה "humble," that convey the impression that God was dealing rather severely with the community during the wilderness period.[47] The manna, which is miraculously given in the wilderness, is used to illustrate the community's dependence on God for the whole of Israel's existence (8:3). In the process of the testing, disciplining, and humbling, Israel should come to understand herself and her election. Understood in its instructional function, as Mauser perceives it to be, Deuteronomy 8:2 illustrates the theme of knowledge. One phrase in 8:2, however, is potentially ambiguous, לָדַעַת אֶת־אֲשֶׁר בִּלְבָבְךָ, "to know what is in your heart." The subject of the infinitive construct לָדַעַת, "to know," could be Israel.[48] According to this interpretation, the testing of the people was done not so that Yahweh would come to know the character of the people, but that the community would grow to understand itself. The point seems convincing since 8:2–5 is entirely concerned with increasing the wisdom of the community, though Mauser does not expand upon the point and its relation to 8:3. In Deuteronomy 8:3 the purpose for the disciplinary action in the wilderness is that the community will come to know that they depend on God for all areas in life. Consequently, 8:2–5 constitutes an instructional prologue grounded in Yahweh's disciplinary intentions for the community during the wilderness period.

The affirmation of the care and leadership of Yahweh during the wilderness period is illustrated in Deuteronomy 2:7, לֹא חָסַרְתָּ דָּבָר "you have lacked nothing." Also, in 8:9 the phrase occurs again in a slightly different manner, לֹא־תֶחְסַר כֹּל "you will not lack anything." With the two phrases the dichotomy of the wilderness traditions and the land theme is overcome. Deuteronomy 2:7 refers to the ability of Yahweh to provide for the people in a landless situation, specifically during the wilderness period. The ability of the land to provide for the people is stressed in 8:9. In both instances, Yahweh is the one who provides, for the land is a gift from God equally miraculous and given for the good of Israel.

For the Deuteronomist, the wilderness is viewed as a time when the people were taught to understand life in a divinely spiritual/physical way (8:3). The contrast is between earthly provisions, illustrated by the manna in Exodus 16, and divine instruction and laws originating from God. Law and provision being brought together in 8:3, as Von Rad proposes, the manna is now entirely spiritualized; whereas, the Priestly Writer, in Exodus 16, has the incident of the manna serving a physical role.[49] As stated above, 8:4–5 recalls the care of God, which previously sustained the community in the wilderness, while 8:9–10 shifts in focus to the land, which will eventually provide the community with its material needs. The cautious pleadings of the text indicate that forgetfulness and rebellion are dangers both in the wilderness and, potentially, in the land (8:17). The law is therefore elevated in its degree of importance so as to guard against religious apathy, to provide stability for the community, and to preserve their religious heritage. The link between the historical prologue (chapters 1–4) and chapter 8 is possibly through the use of the expression פִּי־יְהוָה (v. 3; אֶת־פִּי־יְהוָה, 1:26, 43).[50] In Deuteronomy, community failure is caused from not listening to the commandments of Yahweh, regardless of whether it is during the trials of desert life, in holy war, or at peace in the land.

In Deuteronomy 8:11–20, "Lest you forget" is the key element, and the exodus and wilderness traditions are used as illustrations. The concern in this section is the fear of prosperity and the loss of continuity with traditions. In the wilderness traditions (Exodus through Numbers), the laws of God have been there, in part, from the beginning (Exod. 15:25), providing the same function as in the land. Christensen states that the essence of forgetfulness is not observing the laws of God.[51] However, the function of the commandments and laws of God in chapter 8 is related to the prevention of forgetfulness. Deuteronomy 8:11 illustrates this point.

הִשָּׁמֶר לְךָ פֶּן־תִּשְׁכַּח	Take heed lest you forget the
אֶת־יְהוָה אֱלֹהֶיךָ לְבִלְתִּי שְׁמֹר	LORD your God by not keeping
מִצְוֺתָיו וּמִשְׁפָּטָיו	his commandments and his ordinances
יְחֻקֹּתָיי . . .	and his statues . . .

The object of the statement is the commandments, laws, and statutes of God. Likewise, the second reason for forgetfulness is the prosperous life in the land,

פֶּן־תֹּאכַל . . .	lest, when you have eaten (8:12a)
וּבְקָרְךָ . . .	and when your herds . . . (8:13a)
וְכֹל אֲשֶׁר־לְךָ יִרְבֶּה . . .	and all that you have is multiplied (8:13b)
וְרָם לְבָבֶךָ וְשָׁכַחְתָּ	and your heart be lifted up and you
אֶת־יְהוָה אֱלֹהֶיךָ . . .	forget the LORD your God (8:14)

The contingent statement is 8:11, which stresses the role of the law in providing the stabilizing element for prosperous living in the land. The prosperity of the land can therefore become a curse instead of a blessing, if the new setting in the land causes Israel to depart from God. The law, in essence, prevents forgetfulness and Israel's departure from her religious mooring with the past traditions of the fathers.

The Deuteronomist interprets the traditions of Israel for a later generation, which had not itself participated in the redemption from Egypt and the Sinai covenant. Understood in this manner, the wilderness traditions are appropriated to teach the people that rebellion and disobedience have their consequences. In order to arrive at a continuity with Israel's traditions, the community must come to appreciate the traditions. The community can then recognize its vulnerability as a people who share in the same temptations of rebellion and apostasy. In essence, the Deuteronomist lays out the prerequisites for the nation so that Israel can maintain, or once again find, its place as the people of God. Within this purposeful use of Israel's ancient traditions, one would expect to find a fresh presentation of the old traditions that can address new situations for a new generation.[52]

The parenetic style of the writer intends to evoke a response, and, in order to accomplish this task, the Deuteronomist seeks to find a common ground on which Israel can once again relate to its past.[53] However, the key to continuity is in keeping the present rooted in the past. The Deuteronomist endeavors to avoid departing from the past by calling upon the memory, and recollection of the past is the task of the law. The continuity with past traditions is achieved when the new generation understands and affirms that God is still active in the life of Israel and is bringing about the fulfillment of the covenant promises.[54]

Israel is therefore commanded to observe and obey the commandments of God for an important constitutive reason. By remembering the past, Israel can regain a sense of "belonging," and the God of Israel's history becomes the God of the people. At the heart of this notion is the call to fidelity to the God of the fathers.[55] Childs writes, "Israel is commanded to be obedient to the commandments *in order to* remember the redemptive history."[56] After the Deuteronomist states the origins of Israel's dependence on Yahweh, firmly established in the wilderness period (8:2–5), the goodness of the land is expounded (8:6–10). The following instructional point in 8:11 is a firm and cautious reminder not to forget Yahweh who has accomplished these things. The law provides the means whereby Israel can prevent her tendencies toward forgetting her past, and in essence regain her sense of identity as the elect of God.

DEUTERONOMY 9–10

Craigie states that with the call to remember in 9:7 the basic themes of Deuteronomy 8 once again appear.[57] The mood in Deuteronomy 9 is yet changed due to the recollection of the people's stubbornness in the wilderness, a trait not emphasized in chapter 8. Israel is epitomized as a "stubborn people" (9:6), which is given in contrast to the potential claims of the people that God gave them the land because of their righteousness. The statement introduces the sin motif that now controls the sermon of Moses. With the introduction of the sin motif, the positive view of the wilderness period, commonly characterized by Yahweh's divine leadership and care for the people, now shifts to a negative view reflecting the people's actions. The eulogy of the first generation in 9:6–7 provides the introduction to the Horeb illustration (9:8–29). The reference to events from the wilderness period in 9:22–24 is a later addition inserted into the Horeb narrative.[58] In the final shape of chapter 9, all of the events are retold as though they fall within the same time frame.

For chapter 9, the rebellions of Israel in the wilderness include the golden calf incident. The chain of conjunctions indicate the progression of the sermon:

v. 8 וּבְחֹרֵב . . .
v. 22 וּבְתַבְעֵרָה וּבְמַסָּה
וּבְקִבְרֹת הַתַּאֲוָה . . .
v. 23 וּבִשְׁלֹחַ יְהוָה

The conjunction in 9:8a (וּחֹרֵב) can be translated to mean "in particular," which would imply that what follows are examples of the rebellious nature of the people that provoked Yahweh to wrath in the wilderness (9:7b), thus placing the golden calf event alongside other wilderness incidents (9:22–24).[59] No distinction is made for which events occurred in the wilderness following the exodus. Therefore, the kerygma of the wilderness traditions in the sermon should be understood accordingly.

Von Rad states that Deuteronomy 9:7–29 is basically the same in form to that of the historical prologue in chapters 1–3.[60] Like the historical prologue in chapters 1–3, 9:6–29 recounts the events that created a disdainful image of the people. An unusual combination of events and actions are contained in these accounts of Israel's rebellion in the wilderness. The sermon makes a contrast between the potential claims on the part of the people to be a nation deserving their fortunes in the land and their persistent disloyalty to God. The presentation of the negative nature of the people is expressed by עַם־קְשֵׁה־עֹרֶף (v. 6, 13) and מַמְרִים (v. 7, 24). Driver explains that the use of this appellation connotes that "Israel has never yielded itself readily to God's will."[61] The purpose in using the golden calf narrative, for example, is to show that from the beginning of the covenant relationship Israel has been rebellious against her God.[62] The fact is that from the beginning they have been a עַם־קְשֵׁה־עֹרֶף and a מַמְרִים people, implying that the gift of the land is completely through the grace of God, in fulfillment of the promises to the fathers (9:5). Deuteronomy 10:16 is a final exhortation, within the concluding section of the sermon, that implies a similar rebellious tendency within the new generation, "Circumcise the foreskins of your heart, and be no longer stubborn (וְעָרְפְּכֶם לֹא תַקְשׁוּ עוֹד)."

The intercessory prayer of Moses in 9:25–29 holds a peculiar, but crucial, place in the traditions of Israel's rebellions in the wilderness. The prayer is a continuation of the scene in verse 18, whose conclusion in verse 29 leaves the requests of Moses unresolved, though von Rad suggests that 10:10–11 concludes the prayer by affirming the fulfillment of the promises.[63] In the traditions of the golden calf in Exodus 32, the prayer varies in its content (32:11–13, cf. עַם־קְשֵׁה־עֹרֶף 32:9), as does the prayer from the spy tradition (Num. 14:13–16).[64] By the intercessory prayer of Moses being split at verse 18, all of the wilderness rebellions are included in the prayer. The unusual inclusive nature of the prayer points to the central kerygma of the chapter. Chapter 8 deals with the issue of the people's loyalty to God, which could be maintained through obedience to the laws of God. In chapter 9, the confession of Yahweh's loyalty to the covenant, in spite of the people's rebellious nature, is the motive for shaping the traditions of the wilderness period into their present form. Where the wilderness traditions hold a prominent place in chapters 8 and 9, the theme of God's loyalty to the covenant is prominent (8:18; 9:27). Moses' prayer of intercession concentrates on the importance of the fulfillment of the covenant. Christensen points out that the use of the various events from the wilderness period is to "emphasize the fact that the gift of the land could never be considered a reward for the righteousness of the people."[65] The covenant promises are really the motivating force of God's goodness toward Israel, not the goodness of the people.

The prayer of Moses gives emphasis to the fact that the golden calf incident, along with other wilderness rebellions, is not grounds for the nullifying of God's promises.[66] In Balentine's analysis of prayer in the wilderness traditions of Numbers, he concludes that where the Deuteronomistic texts deal with Moses' practice of intercession, the prayer of Moses "functions to introduce into the narrative questions about divine intentions, particularly the justice of divine intentions, and thereby to persuade God to alter or modify these intentions."[67] The rebellions of Israel work as an antithesis to the covenant, and through the joint function of the rebellions of Israel (עַם־קְשֵׁה־עֹרֶף and מַמְרִים) and the prayer of Moses, the persistent fidelity of Yahweh to those promises is proclaimed. In essence, Israel's God is greater than all the failures of the people.

Deuteronomy 11:1–7

In Deuteronomy 11:1–7 two events of the exodus and wilderness traditions are mentioned: the exodus with particular emphasis on the Reed Sea (11:3–4) and the Dathan and Abiram rebellion of Numbers 16 (11:5–6).[68] Traditionally, Israel's wilderness experience is interpreted as a time of purposeful discipline and education. In this regard, the generation who has not experienced such discipline firsthand (cf. Num. 26:63–65) is exhorted to learn from the period through the recollecting or contemporizing of the experiences of the first generation (11:2).[69] The translation of וִידַעְתֶּם (11:2a) could be in the future mode, "And you shall know," but considering the instructional purpose of the repeated illustrations, the opening verb וִידַעְתֶּם is perhaps best translated "And you know," which affirms the fact of the community's experiences in the past. Additional evidence to this affirmation of knowledge is given by way of contrast between what the community knows and what their children do *not* know. The long affirmation in 11:2–6 is given in an indirect manner. The actions of God in the life of Israel are presented as what the children do *not* know. A translation of 11:2 will clarify this interpretation:

וִידַעְתֶּם הַיּוֹם כִּי לֹא	And you know today, for not
אֶת־בְּנֵיכֶם אֲשֶׁר לֹא־יָדְעוּ	your children, who do not know
וַאֲשֶׁר לֹא־רָאוּ אֶת־מוּסַר	and who have not seen the discipline
יְהוָה אֱלֹהֵיכֶם אֶת־גָּדְלוֹ	of Yahweh your God his greatness,
אֶת־יָדוֹ הַחֲזָקָה	his mighty hand,
וּזְרֹעוֹ הַנְּטוּיָה׃	and his outstretched arm,

The acts of Yahweh are indicated through the repeated phrase אֲשֶׁר עָשָׂה (v. 3, 4, 5, 6). The final clause in this long sentence occurs in verse 7, indicated by the conjunction כִּי (see 11:2, 10). With 11:7 the indirect affirmation is returned to the subject of 11:2a by confirming their knowledge of what God has done, "for your eyes have seen" (v. 7a). The wilderness traditions are utilized to affirm the greatness of God's actions, which are understood as disciplinary (11:2b, 5) and demonstrative of divine judgment for rebellion (11:2b, 6).

Two interesting parallels are drawn between the exodus and the wilderness traditions, which are set up by 11:2b. The first parallel is between what occurred both in Egypt (verse. 3) and in the wilderness (verse 5). The second parallel is between what happened both to the army of Egypt (verse 4) and the rebels, Dathan and Abiram (verse 6). The former parallel appears to illustrate the discipline of Yahweh, while the latter definitely reveals the miraculous power of God. In verse 2 a specific reference is made to the signs and wonders that are witnessed by the community. The common elements in the latter parallel of events are the miraculous actions of God, illustrated by the sea overflowing the Egyptians (11:4), and the earth swallowing up the wicked (11:6). The two-fold purpose of Yahweh's actions is therefore affirmed as disciplinary and revelatory of the sovereign power of God. Verse 7, then, concludes the short kerygmatic statement in 11:2–6 by reminding the community that they have seen and experienced these events. Deuteronomy 11:8–9 continues the previous instructional motive by making an appeal to keep the commandments. The acts of God in 11:1–9 are the historical witness that provides the reason for the requirement to keep the law.

DEUTERONOMY 29:1–9

Deuteronomy 29:1–32:52 contains the account of a covenant established on the plains of Moab, which is a different covenant from that of Horeb (28:69). This covenant stands apart from the rest of Deuteronomy, since the book of Deuteronomy is considered basically to be a book of the covenant at Horeb.[70] The saving acts of Yahweh are recited in 29:1–9, and the motif of the care of Yahweh in the wilderness is indicated by the statement in 29:5–6, which suggests that the people lacked nothing during the wilderness period. With this statement a new interpretation is introduced into the account of the wilderness experience. In the wilderness the people were adequately clothed and did not eat bread nor drink wine (29:6).

The purpose underlying the wilderness experience is for the community to attain the knowledge that Yahweh is the God of the people. Knowledge is perhaps related to the similar concerns expressed in Deuteronomy 8:3, where the wilderness experience is understood as the occasion for the instruction of the community regarding its relationship to God. In 29:1–9 the means for obtaining this knowledge (8:6) and blessing (8:9), actualized by living wisely (תַּשְׂכִּילוּ) in the land, is now through the experience of the wilderness and obedience to the "words of the covenant" (29:9). The writer's interpretation of the wilderness period in 29:5–6, which is a time in which Israel owes her survival to her God, is consistent with the kerygma of the wilderness traditions in Deuteronomy as a whole.

Deuteronomy 32

Deuteronomy 31–34 constitute the second part of a framework around the law (4:44–26:19, 28:1–69), with the historical prologue (Deut. 1:1–4:43) as the first portion.[71] Deuteronomy 31:16–30 is the introduction to the Song of Moses in 32:1–43, while 32:44–52 contains the closing statements of Moses. Though the psalm may appear to be an independent work within the Deuteronomy text, as von Rad believes, Clements proposes that the Song of Moses concludes the covenant texts which began in 29:1. The two headings in 29:1 and 33:1 distinguish the material contained therein.[72] Labuschagne adds that the most striking feature of the song is its relationship to the context of the covenant at Moab in which the song was placed in this larger framework to appeal to Israel as a witness.[73] In this regard, the kerygma of the Song of Moses is to be understood in connection to the covenant at Moab.

The pattern of the covenant lawsuit is identified with the official summons in verse 1, the indictment in verses 15–18, and the verdict in verses 19–29.[74] The elements in the covenant lawsuit vary according to the context calling for its use in biblical traditions. In the Deuteronomic tradition, the celebration of covenant renewal, in the course of time, embodied elements of the lawsuit."[75] Deuteronomy 32:6b–14 is the historical prologue to the covenant lawsuit, in which reference is made to the exodus, the wilderness wandering, and the entrance into the land.[76] The kerygma is revealed in the recitation of the mighty acts of God in verses 7–14.[77] The kerygma states that Yahweh's inheritance is Israel (v. 9), Yahweh "found" Israel (v. 10), Yahweh cared for them (v. 10), and Yahweh alone provided the care (v. 12).

In 32:10 the interpretation of Israel's origin is a highly debated issue among scholars. Since there is no explicit mention of Egypt in verse 10, the interpretation of the "desert land" (בְּאֶרֶץ מִדְבָּר) remains ambiguous. Reference to the exodus could be given figuratively in Deuteronomy 32:10, since בְּאֶרֶץ מִדְבָּר could refer to Egypt; and for the Israelites, Egypt could have represented a desert experience.[78] Hosea 9:10, on the other hand, has the Israelite community's origin in the wilderness and not Egypt, and Deuteronomy 32:10 seems to suggest the same interpretation. In the book of Hosea, Israel is compared metaphorically with the first fruit of a fig tree, implying that when they first appeared God "saw" and "found" them. The imagery accompanying Deuteronomy 32:10a stresses the care of Yahweh (Deut. 32:10b–11) and appears to be related more to Israel's wilderness experience revealed in the traditions of the books of Exodus and Numbers and other passages in the book of Deuteronomy. However, if 32:10 reflects a tradition of Israel's origin in the wilderness, then the exodus is not mentioned in Deuteronomy 32:1–29, which is itself a phenomenon in confessional texts.

Von Rad proposes that 32:8–9 responds to the question of Israel's origins and relationship to God and is, therefore, an etiological statement expressing a Deuteronomistic view of Israel's history.[79] The kerygma in Deuteronomy 32:10 answers the question of Israel's origin and relationship to God through both affirmation and appeal. The relationship between Israel and God is unlike the other nations' relationship to their own gods. Yahweh chooses Israel directly as God's inheritance, and this is accomplished by a decision of God. Accordingly, the notion of election is not rooted in any earthly enterprise (a strong Deuteronomistic idea) but only through divine mercy and purpose. To be sure, the emphasis is not on the origin of Israel alone, but on the subtle distinction between life in the desolate places of the desert through which Israel was led and the life of prosperity in the land.

Israel's origin in the wilderness can therefore be understood to reflect the enormous contradistinction between the prosperity in the land and the near nothingness in the wilderness (תֹּהוּ 32:10). The writer starts not with the exodus but the desert to describe better the "homeless" condition of Israel.[80] The waste (תֹּהוּ) land is a barren desolate place, and it is here that Yahweh protected Israel from the wilds of chaos. In Deuteronomy 32:10 "encircle" (יְסֹבְבֶנְהוּ) means to encompass in order to protect, possibly a play on the imagery of military practices (Josh. 6). Other imagery of the care motif includes בִּין "care," which in a fuller definition means to perceive with the eyes and understand or have insight.[81] The figurative reference to Israel as the "pupil of his eye" reveals the most intimate of relationships between Yahweh and Israel. In 32:11 the metaphoric parallelism provides the depth of the care motif; God cared for and kept Israel in the wilderness, like the great bird that carries and bears its young on its wings.

Following the initial affirmation of the election of Israel and the parceling out of the lands of the world (32:8–9), Deuteronomy 32:13–14 then stresses the goodness of the land.[82] The language of the poem at this point anticipates the period of the occupation through the skillful blending of the images of the wilderness traditions with the language and imagery of the land. In 32:13 the unusual poetic term סֶלַע, "cliff," is used in conjunction with דְבַשׁ, "honey," while צוּר, "rock" (Exod. 17:6), is used in conjunction with שֶׁמֶן, "oil." The only other appearance of סֶלַע in the Pentateuch is in the water miracle story of Numbers 20 (20:8, 10, 11; cf. Neh. 9:25; Ps. 78:16). In the Pentateuch, חַלָּמִישׁ, "flint," only occurs in Deuteronomy 8:15 and 32:13. Deuteronomy 8:8 refers to honey and oil (olive) as products of the land of Canaan. The balance of the images in 32:13–14 reflects traditions of the land.

The recitation in Deuteronomy 32:7–14 is completely focused on the acts of Yahweh. In the wilderness, it was Yahweh alone who led the people. The actions of Yahweh are expounded through the causative Hiphil in which Israel is then able to live in the good land, obtain nourishment from the rock, and enjoy the products of the field and flock. The kerygma of 32:7–14 is that Yahweh has caused all that has happened in the world and has directed the course of life for Israel.

Deuteronomy 32:7–9 appears to recognize the existence of other gods in connection with each of the other nations.[83] The affirmative aspect of the kerygma, however, quickly subsumes the implication under the motif of God's sovereignty; a motif which runs throughout the song. Yahweh is proclaimed to be the only true God (32:39), and the gods of the nations are referred to as "no gods" and the foreign nations as "no people" (32:21). Albright's translation of 32:21 is sufficient to point out the idea:[84]

> They set up a no-god as my rival,
> They made me angry by their follies;
> So I will set up a no-people as their rival,
> I will make them angry with a foolish nation.

The sin of the people is idolatry. The kerygma of the passage is concerned with proper appreciation of the identity of both Yahweh and Israel. Since the "no gods" cause God to act because of God's jealous nature, the people who are jealous for their own identity as Israelites will likewise be angered because of what the nations will do to them. The jealous anger of God is caused by the idolatry of the people of God; and the jealous anger of the people is caused by the overbearance of the nations. Within this parallelism lies the prophetic appeal against presumptuous living. God gains the attention of the people through the one thing they love the most: their national identity, not necessarily their love for God. Deuteronomy 32:1–7 has as its main theme Israel's denial of God.

In the soliloquy (32:25–35), God recognizes that regardless of Israel's sinfulness she cannot be destroyed, even though she deserves utter destruction (cf. chapter 9). The mercy given by the restraint of God's anger is not for the sake of Israel but for Yahweh's honor, a motif common to divine reaction to the rebellious nature of the generation of the wilderness period. Yahweh's honor would be misconstrued, and the enemy would fail to recognize God's purposes if they were allowed to completely destroy Israel. Their claim to victory would imply that God had failed to protect his people, instead of proving that God had acted to punish them.[85] The adversaries would dishonor God by taking credit for their victory over God's people since they fail to recognize the truth that God allowed or permitted their victory.[86]

In Deuteronomy 32:27, the verb נִכֵּר (Piel) means to disguise or to misconstrue the facts, as in Jeremiah 19:4 where the same word is used to describe the intentional act of turning the temple into a place where incense is burnt to other gods. In any event, God is presented in a peculiar dilemma. Both Israel (cf. Deut. 8) and the nations (32:27) claim credit for events and circumstances that should be understood as originating from God. The law once again provides the stability and testifies to God's presence and purpose (8:11), while history, transmitted through Israel's traditions, reveals the same (32:7). The motif of the sovereignty of God permeates the song and is its ultimate resolve for the community.

The message in 32:28–29 is clear: wisdom comes from the counsel of God. The subject of these verses is ambiguous, though Israel is presumed to be the subject.[87] On the other hand, according to verse 30, which has the adversaries as the subject, the subject appears to have been the enemies of Israel and God. Considering that the text in 32:26–34 refers to the final outcome for Israel and the adversaries, the ambiguity is resolved by looking forward to 32:40–41. The oath in 32:40–41 affirms the integrity and sovereignty of God in the face of idolatry and presumptuous actions. The enemies of God are the adversaries who hate God and those who choose to attribute events and circumstances to the powers at hand instead of God. The actions of disobedience and disrespect can originate from within God's own people as well as from without among the adversaries. The identification of the subject of these transgressions is therefore difficult because of the text's instructional purpose, which makes its message timeless and faceless in subject.

The wilderness period provides the setting from which the entire song evolves. Verses 13–15 either reveal a transition from the wilderness context or speak of the wilderness in euphoric style, but, because of the timeless quality of the poem, either view is uncertain. Certainly, the text of verses 13–15 suggests a change within the community that caused Israel to forget and leave their God in pursuit of other gods. According to the wilderness traditions of the Tetrateuch, the apostasy occurred at Sinai and after Israel left the wilderness (Num. 25).

In conclusion, there appears to be no progression of periods in the psalm. The apostasy, judgment and deliverance are timeless.[88] The kerygma of the wilderness traditions in Deuteronomy 32 is revealed in the confessions of the entire song. The beginnings for Israel are rooted in the wilderness period, and the exodus event has been excluded from its normal place within Israel's confession. Israel's beginnings are characterized by God's parental care and leadership, yet, Yahweh punishes the transgressor who commits idolatry to avenge the honor of God thus affirming the sovereignty of God. The song also proclaims the destruction of Israel's enemies and the glorification of Israel as the people of God.

DEUTERONOMY 33:8–11

In Deuteronomy 33:1–5, the beginnings of the relationship between the community and Yahweh are linked to the giving of the law at Sinai through Moses (cf. Deut. 32:10). Sinai is the event where Yahweh becomes the Lord, or King, of the people (33:5). Among the most significant kerygmatic elements in the blessing are the rule of Yahweh in the world and the fundamental relationship between the community and its God that is grounded in the Mosaic traditions and institutions.[89] The blessing of the various tribes is recorded in 33:6–25, with 33:26–29 containing the concluding praise of Yahweh.

The blessing of Moses in Deuteronomy 33 is linked to the wilderness traditions through the brief reference to the Massah–Meribah story (Deut. 33:8). The connection with the Massah–Meribah narrative is further indicated by the use of the two terms נִסָּה, "he tested" and רִיב, "to strive, contend." The Levites are not mentioned in the water miracle stories of the Tetrateuch. In the Deuteronomist's use of the traditions, Yahweh tests and contends with the Levites, which is more focused on a segment of the community than either the Exodus 17 or the Numbers 20 versions allow; unless the conduct or actions of Moses and Aaron are viewed as representative of the tribe of Levi. In Exodus 17:7, the etiological summary implies the testing and striving with Yahweh by the community, whereas the reverse is indicated in the Deuteronomy recollection.

Information about the actual early history and duties of the Levites is very limited. The Pentateuchal traditions, in particular the Deuteronomist, support the view that the priesthood is associated with the tribe of Levi (cf. Deut. 10:8f.; 18:1–8).[90] The Levites are granted the Urim and Thummim, which suggests a duty of the office as priest. Two duties are implied in the office: to guard the sacred traditions and to exercise an authority to teach the law to the people. The second duty involves the operation and overseeing of the cult.[91] The recollection or appropriation of the wilderness traditions is recited to provide support and validity to the Levite office and function. In the traditional view, the office of priest originates with Moses, who is himself a Levite. With the blessing of the Levites, thus stressing their role in the community, the Levitical line is established from Moses throughout Israelite history.[92] Aaron is the anointed priest, and his office is validated through the incidents at the rebellion of Korah (Num. 16) and the events that follow (Num. 17). The association of the Levites with the wilderness traditions in Deuteronomy 33:8–11 indicates that the origin of the Levitical role within the community and within the cult goes back to the period of the wilderness.

In Exodus 32:25–29, the Levites are elevated to the regular priesthood as a reward apparently for their faithfulness and obedience to Yahweh during the golden calf rebellion. Likewise, in Numbers 25:1–9 the Levites, portrayed through the persons of Moses and Phinehas, respond in faithful and obedient service in the incident at Shittim. In Deuteronomy 33:8, Levi and Moses may occur in parallel poetic fashion since Levi represents the continuation of that which began with Moses in the wilderness.[93] Cross interprets the "faithful one" (לְאִישׁ חֲסִידֶךָ) as referring to Moses. By occurring in parallel, both Moses and the tribe of Levi represent the priestly family who are judged as faithful from the beginning in the wilderness. The inclusion of a positive view of Moses' role is, without a doubt, due to the ambiguity created by the singular and plural references to the tribe of

Levi (cf. 32:8 and 32:9–10) which, along with archaic forms and change in metre, suggest a possible merging of literary traditions.[94] If the reference to the "faithful one" is Moses, then, in the Deuteronomy recollection, he is portrayed in a better light than in Numbers 20:2–13.

The function of the wilderness traditions is also different in the Deuteronomy account. The primary focus in Deuteronomy 33:8 is the role of the Levites within the life and structure of the Israelite community. The Levites are the administrators and teachers of the Mosaic law. They receive their authority, in part, due to their faithfulness in obeying the word of Yahweh and keeping the covenant in the wilderness, an accomplishment unmatched by the community as a whole in either accounts of the water traditions (Exod. 17:1–7, Num. 20:2–14). The use of the Massah-Meribah tradition in Deuteronomy 33 reflects yet another positive account of the wilderness traditions that appear to center around the water stories, while other stories in the wilderness traditions have developed into negative accounts that stress the failures of the first generation after leaving Egypt.[95] The kerygma of the wilderness traditions takes a definite shift in Deuteronomy 33, since the connection is made in 33:8–11 between the success of Yahweh's discipline in the wilderness and the reward for faithfulness; but, then, the blessing of Moses exhibits hopeful optimism. The Levites provide the example of faithfulness in much the same manner as Joshua and Caleb in the wilderness traditions of the Tetrateuch.

THE KERYGMA OF THE WILDERNESS TRADITIONS IN DEUTERONOMY

The historical prologue in chapters 1–3 maintains the chronological order of the wilderness traditions to some extent, but in the rest of Deuteronomy that concern is less evident. The complex nature of the traditions is due in part to the homiletical nature of Deuteronomy. The wilderness traditions are primarily used as illustrations, and in that function, the wilderness traditions exhibit an unusual shape and character. In chapter 9, for example, Horeb and certain wilderness events are joined because of the context of the sermon.

The explicit use of the wilderness traditions is usually recognizable. Apart from the historical prologue in chapters 1–3, the wilderness traditions usually appear in brief statements (Cf. 6:16). For the Deuteronomist, the wilderness period is the primary period for the origin of the community and the giving of the Law. The wilderness period provides the only setting for the history of the community, and as such, the relationship between Yahweh and the community evolves from the desert experience.

Through the use of the wilderness traditions, Moses speaks in a future sense to the people prior to entrance into the land. The approaching conquest of Canaan is important, but the dangers of the land are prominent in the thoughts of the Deuteronomist, and such alarm leaves the impression of foresight into the events that will come to pass. The book of Deuteronomy foresees the future destruction of Israel to be the result of her disobedience, and, as Noth suggests, the Deuteronomic historian saw the outcome as an accomplished reality.[96] The theme of the Deuteronomic history is the conduct and fate of the people in the land, which is reflected in the repeated parenetic exhortations of Deuteronomy chapters 5–11 and chapters 29–34.[97] The hazards to the community of faith are expressed as idolatry, forgetfulness, and excessive pride.[98] The wilderness traditions are used, through the parenetic effort, to encourage faith in God and obedience to the laws, in order to avoid the fate of the previous generations who are judged because of their sin and rebellion. In an effort to address the crises of faith in the community, three basic points are identified, in which the wilderness traditions have come to be incorporated into the message of the book of Deuteronomy: the sovereignty of God in the life of the community, the central role of the laws of God, and the promises of the fathers.

One of the most important contributions of the wilderness traditions to Deuteronomy is the role they take in affirming the fidelity and sovereignty of Yahweh. The wilderness traditions affirm the historical fact that God chose, delivered, and cared for the people before they became a prominent nation among the nations of the world. Israel therefore owes her existence, prosperity, and future to Yahweh. The contrary attitude of the community toward this notion is demonstrated through the appropriation of the wilderness traditions, for example, in the spy episode in 1:19–46. The distinction between the spy narrative in Numbers 13–14 and the historical prologue in Deuteronomy 1:19–46 is revealed through the speech and actions of the people. The community participates in the decision making process in the life of the people (also in 1:9–18), and, in essence, they have a greater sense of self-determination. The distinction is not without significance for the kerygmatic intention of the sermons in Deuteronomy. The conflict in the spy episode is between the forgetful, bold nature of the people and the divine purpose for them; a theme that continues in various forms throughout Deuteronomy 1–11 and 29–34.

At the center of the conflict lies the issue of God's sovereignty. The command to go in and take the land (1:8, 21) is met by rebellion and careless actions from the community (1:41–46). The proper actions of the people should be guided by trust and obedience. Deuteronomy 1:33, a crucial passage in the kerygma of the narrative, affirms the sovereignty of God while appealing to the community's trust in God. To be sure, in the introductory passages in the book of Deuteronomy, the motif of the conflict between individual initiative and the sovereignty of God is established. By addressing the important issue of the nature of community, the kerygma of the wilderness traditions affirms the structure of the community as a theocracy and appeals to that ideal.

Deuteronomy affirms that Yahweh is God *par excellence*, the sole creator and sustainer of the cosmos (see 32:8, 39). Though the universal rule of God is not primary for the Deuteronomist, the concern is however with the continuity of the historical rule of God over Israel and with Israel's national identity (32:21).[99] The identity of Israel as a people of God is defined by the terms of the covenant at Horeb. Israel is exhorted to guard against the potential threats that impede the relationship, and the wilderness traditions provide an invaluable frame of reference. In essence, Israel is to protect itself from these threats while Yahweh at the same time will be "guarding his exclusive claim upon Israel's loyalty."[100] A juxtaposition of motives is evident in the fidelity of Yahweh to the people and the people's fidelity to Yahweh.

The Deuteronomist makes an appeal to a fragmented community that is at risk in the world. The community has possibly lost, or is about to lose, its link with traditions that at one time had been able to sustain them. One of the reasons for this crisis of identity is the great expanse of time between the community's present context and the period of Israel's origins. Von Rad suggests that the book makes a plea for Israel to be just the way they were in the old days. The election and promises of God are intended for a community just as they were in the times of her beginnings.[101] The Deuteronomist endeavors to cross the expanse of time in order to make the traditions relevant once again. Deuteronomy 6:20–21, for example, reveals the instructional motive that encourages the adoption of the views of reality expressed through Israel's traditions into the new situations confronted by the community.[102] As McBride states, the

Deuteronomist desired to present the kingdom of God, grounded in the history of Israel, as a living and continuing reality to be experienced in the present.[103]

The persistent emphasis on the word "today" is the common denominator of Deuteronomic homiletics as a whole (9:1). The effect of this literary device is to create a sense of immediacy for the events being recalled.[104] The events of Israel's traditions are not experiences of the past that have lost their relevance for the present life of the community. In the effective recollection of Israel's past, both aspects of the positive, illustrated by God's care and loyalty, and the negative, revealed in Israel's rebellions, are actualized. By making Israel's past relevant for the present, the function of kerygma is revealed as both affirming the fidelity of God to the people and appealing to the fidelity of the people toward Yahweh.

The wilderness traditions also contribute to the emphasis in Deuteronomy on the important role of the law in the life of the community. The wilderness traditions assume the presence of the laws of God as the guiding principles which are critical to the survival of the people. Because the laws of God are firmly rooted in Israel's beginnings in the wilderness, the book of Deuteronomy seeks to revive obedience to divine law which had constituted the nation (5:22). The one constitutive event of significance for Deuteronomy is Horeb. The Horeb experience and the giving of the law are fundamental in the establishment of the relationship between Yahweh and the community. The community's experience at Horeb offers an example for life in Israel, due to the fact that the laws of Horeb have been with the people throughout their life as a community.[105] The Deuteronomist establishes an unbroken continuity between the first generation in the wilderness period and the generation of the future who will experience the same trials and temptations.

Deuteronomy chapter 8 incorporates the care and guidance of God in the wilderness period with the rule of God's laws. The wilderness period is a time of learning whereby the community would come to depend on their God, and that dependence takes the form of more than material welfare. In effect, the text encourages and affirms a close relationship between the community and Yahweh through appreciation of the grace of God and the laws given for their benefit. The relationship of the law to the traditions, as well as their obedience and faithfulness to God, is found in 8:11, "Take heed lest you forget Yahweh your God by not keeping his commandments and his ordinances and his statutes which I command you this day." Likewise, the reference to the wilderness traditions in 6:16, interpreted within the context of the sermon itself, affirms the presence of God among the people by the community's faithful obedience to the laws of God. Furthermore, the illustrative use of the exodus and the wilderness traditions in 11:1–7 supports the call to obedience to the laws of Yahweh (11:8).

According to Deuteronomy, Israel had no other option, for Israel could either obey and follow Yahweh or become lost in the world.[106] The alternative to following Yahweh, illustrated within the repeated warnings against the idolatrous and presumptuous living in the land, is without compromise because the land would have competitive elements that would corrupt the relationship just as other situations had done during the community's life in the wilderness. Like the tragic consequence of the wilderness period, the only other alternative for a rebellious community is absolute destruction, and by this consequential outcome the community is purged of the disobedient. Seen in this respect, the wilderness experience portrays the seriousness of the command to be faithful to God and the laws. The task and ultimate goal of Deuteronomy 6:4–5, for example, is to effect the corporate identity of the community as a people of God.

The law remained the central focus when the traditions of the wilderness period are recalled in Deuteronomy.[107] The role of the wilderness traditions is to provide the context for the Deuteronomic law at Horeb. During the wilderness period, the law was an important element as a mode of guidance. The rebellions of Israel in the wilderness may be understood as the breaking of the laws of God (Deut. 9:8).[108] Viewing the wilderness traditions in the context of the role of the law in the life of the community, the law is inseparably linked to God's care and guidance from Egypt to the entrance into the land, especially *in the land*. The frequent use of "word" (דָּבָר) in 1:19–46 is a further illustration of the significance of obeying the word of God. Yahweh had commanded the people in the wilderness through the "words of his mouth" (8:3). The commandments of God are the continuing words of God appropriate for the survival of the community as a Yahwistic people. Therefore, the ultimate goal of the various exhortations to obedience is the survival of the community in the world.

The wilderness traditions also contribute to the affirmation of God's fidelity to the promises of the fathers (chapter 9).[109] The fulfillment of the promises and fidelity to the covenant are the primary motivating forces in God's actions. The care and guidance in Israel's beginnings and the graciousness of God's judgment are influenced by Yahweh's honor to the promises (chapters 9, 32).

Regardless of a wilderness setting or in the land, the sins and rebellion of the people do not invalidate the faithfulness of God to the covenant.

Insofar as the dangers of the land pose a threat to the faithful obedience to God by the community, two points are evident. First, the potential sins of the people after they enter the land involve the disregard or forgetting of their origins and, therefore, the loss of their faith and trust in God. Sin of this nature violates the relationship established between Yahweh and the community; in short, the community breaks the covenant. Deuteronomy calls for a renewal or revival of the community's identity as a faithful follower of God. In Wolff's kerygma schema, the Deuteronomic historian calls for a return (שׁוּב) to their covenant relationship with God.[110] Second, Israel's religious traditions, rooted in the wilderness experience, present Israel's God as a forgiving sovereign who permits a remnant to survive the judgment on the first generation of the wilderness. Yahweh's commitment to the people, motivated by Yahweh's honor and loyalty to the promises made to the fathers, stands above all other situations that develop in the community as obstacles to the fulfillment of the promises. The consistent reminder of the community's rebellious and unfaithful nature, juxtaposed to Yahweh's faithfulness, enhances the unrelenting grace of God toward the community. The kerygma of Deuteronomy makes an appeal to the community's fidelity to God out of gratitude for what God has done for Israel, and out of fear for the alternative.[111]

In Deuteronomy 12:32, as von Rad observes, the focus is upon the maintenance of Deuteronomy as a canonical book for the community. Deuteronomy also never loses sight of its religious opponent, the Canaanite natural religion.[112] These two points indicate the constitutive sensitivity of the book. For the community the book reminds, calls, and challenges the faith of those who have ventured away from their true identity, now seen as threatened because they have no longer adhered to the laws of God. Deuteronomy draws the community to its origins in the wilderness period (32:10; 33:1–5), for the community will find continuity as the people of God in the Mosaic traditions and institutions.[113] The trials of the desert produced situations that resulted in rebellion and apostasy, and the wilderness traditions provide examples for each future generation that might neglect or leave the heritage which constituted its identity. The trials in the land are of equal, if not more serious, concern as they will influence the future of the community.

Notes

[1]Brevard S. Childs, *Introduction to the Old Testament as Scripture* (Philadelphia: Fortress Press, 1979), p. 211.

[2]Ronald E. Clements, *Deuteronomy* (Sheffield: JSOT Press, 1989), p. 18. S. R. Driver, *Deuteronomy*, The International Critical Commentary (Edinburgh: T. & T. Clark, 1902), p. i.

[3]Ernest W. Nicholson, *Deuteronomy and Tradition* (Philadelphia: Fortress Press, 1967), p. 46.

[4]Julius Wellhausen, *Prolegomena to the History of Ancient Israel* (Gloucester, Mass.: Peter Smith, 1983), p. 269; Carl Cornill, *Introduction to the Canonical Books of the Old Testament*, trans. G. H. Box (New York: G. P. Putnam's Sons, 1907), p. 47.

[5]Martin Noth, *The Deuteronomistic History* (Sheffield: JSOT Press, 1981), p. 14 *(Überlieferungsgeschichtliche Studien I*, 1957*)*. For a detailed analysis of the occurrence of the second person singular and plural in Deuteronomy see H. G. Mitchell, "The Use of the Second Person in Deuteronomy," *Journal of Biblical Literature*, 18 (1899), 61–109; G. Minette De Tillese, "Sections 'tu' et sections 'vous' dans le Deutéronome," *Vetus Testamentum*, 12 (1962), 29–87. Nicholson, *Deuteronomy and Tradition*, p. 31–32, concludes that Deuteronomy 1–4 and 31–34, as well as the majority of plural passages within chapters 5–30, are the work of the Deuteronomistic author. The singular passages contained in chapters 5–26 probably represent the original work that has been incorporated into the historian's work.

[6]Nicholson, *Deuteronomy and Tradition*, p. 20. For comprehensive analysis of the structure and unity of Deuteronomy see pp. 18–36.

[7]C. R. Driver, *Deuteronomy*, The International Critical Commentary (Edinburgh: T. & T. Clark, 1902), p. xix.

[8]Ibid., p. ii.

[9]Rolf Rendtorff, *The Old Testament: An Introduction*, trans. John Bowden (Philadelphia: Fortress Press, 1986), p. 150.

[10]Gerhard von Rad, *Old Testament Theology*, vol. 1, trans. D. M. G. Stalker (New York: Harper & Row, Publishers, 1962), p. 220.

[11]Gerhard von Rad, *The Problem of the Hexateuch*, trans. E. W. Trueman Dicken (London: SCM Press, Ltd., 1984), p. 27.

[12]Clements, *Deuteronomy*, p. 13.

[13]C. R. Driver, *Deuteronomy*, p. xv, concludes there is no doubt that the writer of Deuteronomy used the earlier material of the Pentateuch. Even where the Yahwist (JE) and the Priestly Writer cross each other repeatedly in the course of a few verses, the retrospect in Deuteronomy follows uniformly the parts belonging to the Yahwist and avoids those belonging to the Priestly Writer.

[14]Clements, *Deuteronomy*, pp. 13–14.

[15]The outline follows, in part, that presented by Clements, *Deuteronomy*, p. 34.

[16]W. Gunther Plaut, "Deuteronomy," *The Torah* (New York: Union of American Hebrew Congregations, 1981), p. 1317.

[17]Gerhard von Rad, *Deuteronomy: A Commentary*, The Old Testament Library, trans. Dorothea Barton (Philadelphia: The Westminster Press, 1966),p. 39; Noth, *The Deuteronomistic History*, p. 28.

[18]Peter C. Craigie, *The Book of Deuteronomy* (Grand Rapids: Wm. B. Eerdmans, 1976), p. 94.

[19]A. D. H. Mayes, *Deuteronomy* (Grand Rapids: Wm. B. Eerdmans Publishing Company, 1979), p. 121.

[20]Moshe Weinfeld, "The Emergence of the Deuteronomic Movement: the Historical Antecedents," in *Das Deuteronomium: Entstehung, Gestalt und Botschaft*, ed. Norbert Lohfink (Leuven: Leuven University Press, 1985), p. 93. Also Mayes, *Deuteronomy*, p. 56, points out that the community exhibits two of the three elements in the promises of Abraham, land and posterity. Driver, *Deuteronomy*, p. xxxi, also suggests that Yahweh's favor is limited to the people whom God has chosen.

[21]Mayes, *Deuteronomy*, p. 122.

[22]Eugene E. Carpenter, "Literary Structure and Unbelief: A Study of Deuteronomy 1:6–46," *Asbury Theological Journal*, 42 (1987), 77–84, identifies two paradigms or models of the community's response to Yahweh, one positive and the other negative. Deuteronomy 1:26–28 provides the departure from the positive pattern of response in 1:6–25, while "After verses 26–28, the 'hope' and the positive thrust of verses 6–25 are transformed into frustration and failure" (p. 79).

[23]Noth, *The Deuteronomistic History*, p. 28.

[24]John D. W. Watts, "Deuteronomy," in *The Broadman Bible Commentary*, vol. 2, ed. Clifton J. Allen (Nashville: Broadman Press, 1970), p. 194. See his "The Deuteronomic Theology," *Review and Expositor*, 75 (1977), pp. 321–332.

[25]See Patrick D. Miller, Jr., "The Gift of God: The Deuteronomic Theology of the Land," *Interpretation*, 23 (1969), 451–465, for an analysis of the role of the land in Israel's life. Two perspectives on the people's relation to land in the Old Testament include: the mobile community, seen in the example of Abraham; and the Deuteronomic picture of a good land as a gift from God. Deuteronomy 8:7–10 contains the fullest expression of the notion.

[26]Refer to the previously established murmuring motif in the Yahwist account in Numbers 13–14. In Deuteronomy, as well as in the Yahwist account of the rebellion, the nature of the murmuring is the community's despite for Yahweh; attitude toward the land itself is not the central issue. George W. Coats, *Rebellion in the Wilderness* (Nashville, Abingdon Press, 1968), p. 194, concludes that the rebellion motif in verse 28 is more in accord with the Yahwist account in Numbers 13–14.

[27]Carpenter, "Literary Structure and Unbelief," p. 79, identifies this division.

[28]Mayes, *Deuteronomy*, p. 129, identifies in 1:26–28 the reverse imagery of holy war. Further reverse imagery includes the confessions of Yahweh's attributes ascribed to their enemy (4:38; 7:1; 9:1f.; 11:23). See W. L. Moran, "The End of the Unholy War and the Anti-Exodus," *Biblica*, 44 (1963), 333–342.

[29]George W. Coats, "An Exposition for the Wilderness Traditions," *Vetus Testamentum*, 22 (1972), 288–295.

[30]Ibid., pp. 289–290.

[31]Mayes, *Deuteronomy*, p. 131. The Septuagint, apparently recognizing the problem, has ὁδηγῶν ὑμᾶς, thus making the use of the traditions parallel in content.

[32]Lothar Perlitt, *Deuteronomium (1:19-2:23)*, Biblischer Kommentar Altes Testament, vol. 2 (Neukirchen-Vluyn: Neukirchener Verlag, 1991), p. 112.

[33]Cf. Ian Cairns, *Word and Presence: A Commentary on the Book of Deuteronomy* (Grand Rapids: Wm. B. Eerdmans Co., 1992), p. 35, who interprets the actions of Moses as free of guilt and exemplified by an implicit trust in Yahweh's promises. Such an assessment would shift the cause of the crisis away from the expedition itself and focus almost entirely upon the rebellious response of the people to the positive report by the spies; a view more in keeping with the Numbers account than the recollection in Deuteronomy.

[34]G. Ernest Wright, "The Book of Deuteronomy," in *The Interpreter's Bible*, vol. 2, ed. George A Buttrick (Nashville: Abingdon Press, 1953), p. 339.

[35]George W. Coats, *Moses: Heroic Man, Man of God* (Sheffield: JSOT Press, 1988), p. 153.

[36]Ibid.

[37]Craigie, *The Book of Deuteronomy*, p. 105.

[38]Mayes, *Deuteronomy*, p. 179.

[39]Von Rad, *Deuteronomy*, p. 64.

[40]Driver, *Deuteronomy*, p. 95.

[41]Clements, *Deuteronomy*, p. 35.

[42]Brevard S. Childs, *Memory and Tradition in Israel* (Naperville: Alec R. Allenson, Inc., 1962), p. 78.

[43]D. L. Christensen, "Form and Structure in Deuteronomy 1–11," in *Das Deuteronomium: Entstehung, Gestalt und Botschaft*, ed. Norbert Lohfink (Leuven: Leuven University Press, 1985), p. 142.

[44]Robert H. O'Connell, "Deuteronomy VIII 1–20: Asymmetrical Concentricity and the Rhetoric of Providence," *Vetus Testamentum*, 40 (1990), 327–452.

[45]Patrick D. Miller, "The Gift of God," p. 458.

[46]Dennis J. McCarthy, "Notes on the Love of God in Deuteronomy and the Father-Son Relationship between Yahweh and Israel," *The Catholic Biblical Quarterly*, 27 (1965), 144–147.

[47]Ulrich Mauser, *Christ in the Wilderness* (Naperville: Alec R. Allenson, Inc., 1963), p. 35.

[48]Ibid.

[49]Von Rad, *Old Testament Theology*, vol. 1, p. 282.

[50]See Raymond C. Van Leeuwen, "What Comes out of God's Mouth: Theological Wordplay in Deuteronomy 8," *The Catholic Biblical Quarterly*, 47 (1985), 55–57, who states that given the emphasis in Deuteronomy 8:1–17 on keeping the commandments (מִצְוָה in 1:2, 6, 11 and צָוָה in 1:1, 11) as a requisite for life, it appears that מִצְוָה is to be seen as the final member of a chain of theological puns, all of which reveal the מוֹצָא פִּי יְהוָה as the only and ultimate source of life (e.g., מצוה/מוציא/מוצא).

[51]Duane L. Christensen, *Deuteronomy 1-11*, Word Biblical Commentary (Waco: Word Books, 1991), p. 176.

[52]Jacob M. Myers, "The Requisites for Response: On the Theology of Deuteronomy," *Interpretation*, 15 (1961), 14–31.

[53]Childs, *Memory and Tradition in Israel*, p. 77.

[54]Ibid., p. 78.

[55]Edward P. Blair, "An Appeal to Remembrance: The Memory Motif in Deuteronomy," *Interpretation*, 15 (1961), pp. 41–47.

[56]Childs, *Memory and Tradition*, p. 78.

[57]Craigie, *The Book of Deuteronomy*, p. 194.

[58]Noth, *The Deuteronomistic History*, p. 104.

[59]Driver, *Deuteronomy*, p. 113.

[60]Von Rad, *Deuteronomy*, p. 77.

[61]Driver, *Deuteronomy*, p. 112.

[62]Anthony Phillips, *Deuteronomy* (Cambridge: Cambridge University Press, 1973), p. 69, attributes this purpose to the Deuteronomic historian.

[63]Von Rad, *Deuteronomy*, p. 77.

[64]Coats, *Rebellion in the Wilderness*, p. 197, states that the close relationship between the prayer of Moses in vv. 26–28 and Exodus 32:11–13 indicate a common source behind the texts.

[65]Christensen, *The Book of Deuteronomy*, p. 190.

[66]Phillips, *Deuteronomy*, p. 70; Paul D. Hanson, *The People Called: The Growth of Community in the Bible* (San Francisco: Harper & Row, Publishers, 1986), p. 173.

[67]Samuel E. Balentine, "Prayer in the Wilderness Traditions: In Pursuit of Divine Justice," *Hebrew Annual Review*, 9 (1985), 53–74.

[68]Jacob Liver, "Korah, Dathan and Abiram," in *Scripta Hierosolymitana*, vol. 8, ed. Chaim Rabin (Jerusalem: The Magnes Press, 1961) pp. 189–217, proposes that Deuteronomy 11:1–7 and other texts, such as Psalm 106, provide evidence for two traditions that constitute the rebellion story of Numbers 16.

[69]Cairns, *Word and Presence*, p. 113.

[70]Ronald E. Clements, *God's Chosen People* (London: SCM Press, Ltd., 1968), p. 44, and *Deuteronomy*, p. 14; Norbert Lohfink, "Der Bundesschluss im Land Moab. Redaktionsgeschichtliches zu Dt. 28,69–32,47," *Biblische Zeitschrift*, 6 (1962), 32–56. See Nicholson, *Deuteronomy and Tradition*, p. 21–22, for a brief discussion on the nature of Deuteronomy 29–30 as a covenant ceremony; A. D. H. Mayes, *The Story of Israel between Settlement and Exile* (London: SCM Press, Ltd., 1983), p. 36.

[71]Noth, *The Deuteronomistic History*, p. 35. See C. J. Labuschagne, "The Song of Moses: Its Framework and Structure," in *De Fructu Oris Sui: Essays in Honour of Adrianus Van Selms*, ed. A. Van Selms (Leiden: E. J. Brill, 1971), pp. 85–98, for a survey of the scholarly views regarding the structure of the epilogue in Deuteronomy 31–34.

[72]Von Rad, *Deuteronomy*, p. 195. Clements, *Deuteronomy*, p. 14.

[73]Labuschagne, "The Song of Moses," p. 86.

[74]G. Ernest Wright, "The Lawsuit of God: A Form-Critical Study of Deuteronomy 32," in *Israel's Prophetic Heritage: Essays in Honor of James Muilenburg*, ed. Bernhard W. Anderson and Walter Harrelson (New York: Harper & Brothers, Publishers, 1962), pp. 26–67.

[75]Ibid., p. 44.

[76]Herbert B. Huffmon, "The Covenant Lawsuit in the Prophets," *Journal of Biblical Literature*, 78 (1959), 285–295.

[77]Wright, "The Lawsuit of God," p. 35.

[78]Craigie, *The Book of Deuteronomy*, p. 380.

[79]Von Rad, *Deuteronomy*, pp. 197–198.

[80]Driver, *Deuteronomy*, p. 356.

[81]*BDB*, p. 106.

[82]Mayes, *Deuteronomy*, pp. 385–386.

[83]Clements, *Deuteronomy*, p. 46.

[84]W. F. Albright, "Some Remarks on the Song of Moses in Deuteronomy XXXII," *Vetus Testamentum*, 9 (1959), 339–346.

[85]Labuschagne, "The Song of Moses," p. 96

[86]Driver, *Deuteronomy*, p. 370.

[87]Ibid., p. 371; John A. Thompson, *Deuteronomy* (London: Inter-Varsity Press, 1974), p. 301.

[88]Walter Zimmerli, *Man and His Hope in the Old Testament*, trans. Gilbert W. Bowen (London: SCM Press, Ltd., 1971), p. 76.

[89]Joel D. Heck, "A History of Interpretation of Genesis 49 and Deuteronomy 33," *Bibliotheca Sacra* 147 (1990), 16–31.

[90]For a survey of the priesthood in Deuteronomy, see J. G. McConville, *Law and Theology in Deuteronomy* (Sheffield: JSOT Press, 1984), pp. 124–153.

[91]Von Rad, *Deuteronomy*, p. 206.

[92]Raymond Abba, "Priests and Levites," *The Interpreter's Dictionary of the Bible*, ed. George A. Buttrick (Nashville: Abingdon Press, 1962), pp. 876–889.

[93]Cross, *Canaanite Myth and Hebrew Epic*, p. 197. See also Wellhausen, *Prolegomena to the History of Ancient Israel*, p. 135, from whom Cross also draws his information.

[94]Thompson, *Deuteronomy*, p. 310.

[95]Eissfeldt, Otto, *The Old Testament: An Introduction*, trans. Peter R. Ackroyd (New York: Harper & Row, Publishers, 1965), p. 228, points out that the blessing of Moses is from a time prior to the tragedies of the Northern and Southern Kingdoms. Such a time is perhaps prior to the development of the tainted picture of the community portrayed by later biblical writers who saw in the first generation an example of unfaithfulness.

[96]Noth, *The Deuteronomistic History*, p. 98.

[97]Ibid., p. 91.

[98]Hanson, *The People Called*, p. 172.

[99]S. Dean McBride, Jr., "The Yoke of the Kingdom: An Exposition of Deuteronomy 6:4–5," *Interpretation*, 27 (1973), 273–306.

[100]Ibid., p. 294.

[101]Gerhard von Rad, *Studies in Deuteronomy*, trans. David Stalker (London: SCM Press, Ltd., 1953), p. 70.

[102]Walter Brueggemann, *The Creative Word: Canon as a Model for Biblical Education* (Philadelphia: Fortress, 1982), p. 15.

[103]McBride, "The Yoke of the Kingdom," p. 305.

[104]Von Rad, *The Problem of the Hexateuch*, p. 28.

[105]Ibid., p. 29.

[106]McBride, "The Yoke of the Kingdom," p. 296.

[107]Thomas B. Dozeman, "Horeb/Sinai and the Rise of Law in the Wilderness Tradition," *SBL Seminar Papers*, (1989), 282–299.

[108]Ibid., p. 284. According to Martin Noth, *A History of Pentateuchal Traditions*, trans. Bernhard W. Anderson (Atlanta: Scholars Press, 1981), p. 58, the wilderness traditions provided the connecting link between the exodus and the conquest traditions. Noth excludes the law as a major factor in the development of the wilderness traditions, thus separating the law from the guidance motif.

[109]See John Van Seters, "Confessional Reformulation in the Exilic Period," *Vetus Testamentum*, 22 (1972), 448–459, for a discussion on the reference "promises of the fathers" in Deuteronomy. Van Seters writes that like Jeremiah and Ezekiel, the Deuteronomist refers to the promises of the fathers in Egypt instead of the patriarchal promises, which are a later reformulation during the exile.

[110]Han Walter Wolff, "The Kerygma of the Deuteronomic Historical Work," trans. Frederick C. Prussner, in *The Vitality of Old Testament Traditions*, 2nd. ed., ed. Walter Brueggemann and Hans Walter Wolff (Atlanta: John Knox Press, 1982), pp. 81–100.

[111]McBride, "The Yoke of the Kingdom," p. 301.

[112]Gerhard von Rad, "Deuteronomy," *The Interpreter's Dictionary of the Bible*, vol. 1, ed. George A. Buttrick (Nashville: Abingdon Press, 1962), pp. 831–838.

[113]Heck, "A History of Interpretation of Genesis 49 and Deuteronomy 33," pp. 22–23.

Chapter Four

The Wilderness Traditions in the Prophets

The Pentateuch has as its major setting Israel outside the land and primarily in the wilderness, and, of course, a wealth of material related to the wilderness period is contained therein. The abundance of material referring to the wilderness period is lacking in the Prophets. Table 7 records the more obvious occurrences of the wilderness traditions in the Prophets. The book of Joshua is the primary source exhibiting a distinct usage of the wilderness traditions as they occur in the Pentateuch. The presence of the wilderness traditions in Joshua, though scarce indeed, is perhaps due to the book's close relationship to the Pentateuch. Elsewhere in the Former Prophets, the recitation of the so-called credo elements might provide an occasion for the appearance of the wilderness traditions; however, this is not the case. In 1 Samuel 12:6–18, for example, the recollection of the saving acts of God in the farewell address of Samuel does not include events from the wilderness traditions.

Some of the references to the wilderness traditions in the Former Prophets are very brief and provide little or no information that would assist in establishing the writers' use of the traditions from the Tetrateuch. In Judges 11:12–28, for example, the wilderness traditions provide only the context for the explanation of the purpose of the Israelites' journey through the lands of Edom, Moab, and the land of the Amorites. With the exception of Joshua, the Former Prophets are virtually silent in their use of the early traditions of Israel's life in the wilderness. The books of 1 and 2 Samuel, on the other hand, have more to say about the traditions from the period of the settlement recorded in the book of Judges, than the period immediately prior to the conquest.

In the Latter Prophets, the wilderness traditions appear in a more creative manner through prophetic language and imagery. The book of Hosea is among the most creative in its use of wilderness imagery (cf. 2:14; 9:10; 13:5), but its connection with the actual wilderness traditions of the Pentateuch is difficult to confirm.[1] Jeremiah 2, like Hosea, is also an example of the use of the wilderness imagery, but, in this text, the rebellion motif is utilized significantly, thus requiring an investigation into the kerygma of Jeremiah's message.

Table 7

THE WILDERNESS TRADITIONS IN THE PROPHETS

Joshua	
5:1–12	Num. 13–14, Forty years in the wilderness; Exod. 16, manna
14:6–15	Numbers 13–14
24:1–28	The Wilderness Experience
Judges	
11:12–28	Num. 20:14–21; 21:10–35, Wilderness wanderings
I Samuel	
4:5–11	Exodus/wilderness traditions
II Kings	
18:1–8	Num. 21:4–9, the Bronze Serpent
Isaiah	
48:20–21	Exod. 17:1–7; Num. 20:2–13, Water in the wilderness
Jeremiah	
2	The Wilderness Experience
31:2–6	The Wilderness Experience
Ezekiel	
20:1–38	See the Detailed Outline, p. 168.

In summary, the Latter Prophets, as in the Former Prophets, are basically silent in their reference to the wilderness period, though Ezekiel 20 is certainly an exception. Table 7 lists the more prominent occurrences or applications of the wilderness traditions in the Prophets.

LITERARY ANALYSIS OF THE WILDERNESS TRADITIONS IN THE FORMER PROPHETS

The book of Joshua is divided into three basic sections, 1) 1:1–12:24 the conquest of Western Palestine under the leadership of Joshua, 2) 13:1–21:42 the division of the conquered land between the tribes, 3) 21:43–24:33 the farewell speeches of Joshua and the covenant at Shechem.[2] Each of the three sections contain references to the wilderness traditions. The three prominent occurrences are the Passover festival at Gilgal (5:1–12), the allotment of Hebron to the tribe of Caleb (14:6–15), and the covenant at Shechem (24:1–28).

The book of Joshua is believed by some to be both a Deuteronomic book and a book showing affiliation with the sources of the Pentateuch, though a distinction is often made between the two relationships.[3] As a Deuteronomic book, Joshua shows no connection with the sources of the Pentateuch (JEP).[4] The conquest traditions in Joshua 1–12 would then reflect the work of the Deuteronomistic historian.[5] Joshua 24 and Judges 1:1–2:5 are considered perhaps to be later additions that are distinct from the Deuteronomistic historical work. The relationship between Deuteronomy and Joshua is indicated further, according to Wenham, by the presence of five theological leitmotifs: the holy war of conquest; the distribution of the land; the unity of all Israel; Joshua as the successor of Moses; and the covenant.[6] Deuteronomic law is also reflected in Joshua. The theme expressed in Joshua is similar to Deuteronomy: maintain loyalty to God and the covenant, and live; go astray after other gods, and perish off the land.[7]

The view that Joshua shows relationship to the sources of the Pentateuch is also evident in Joshua 1–12, which contains elements of the Yahwist through the common emphasis, for example, on the giving of the land in fulfillment of the promises (Gen. 12 and 15).[8] Joshua 1–5 is also, according to Coats, an exposition or introduction to the conquest theme that begins in Chapter 6. The introduction connects Joshua with the credo elements in the Pentateuch that begin with God's promise of land to Abraham's seed and conclude with the conquest in Joshua.[9]

JOSHUA 5:1–12

Joshua 5:2–9 is an etiological narrative concerning Gilgal, while 5:10–12 records the celebration of the passover in the plains of Jericho. Joshua 5:2–12 exhibits probably its closest association with Pentateuchal traditions through its references to the wilderness traditions. The short narrative that follows in 5:13–15 is apparently connected with a holy place that is probably close to Gilgal.[10] Joshua 5:13–15, whose interpretation remains dubious, may also serve to authenticate Joshua's leadership role since the passage is similar to that of the appointment of Moses (Exod. 3:5).

In Joshua 5:4, the "men of war" who died in the wilderness has its parallel account in Deuteronomy 2:16. The people who were born in the wilderness had not yet been circumcised (5:5). This implies that the practice was discontinued during the wilderness period. The forty years in the wilderness (5:6) reflect a period of time similar to both Numbers and Deuteronomy; a time when those who rebelled at Kadesh-barnea died while in the wilderness. According to the book of Joshua, the rebellion or disobedience of the community is interpreted as a refusal to listen to the voice of Yahweh (Num. 14:22 [J]). The sworn oath of Yahweh (5:6) is also reflected in the Yahwistic account in Numbers 14:23 and the Deuteronomy recollection (Deut. 1:35).

Joshua 5 may be a *rite de passage* in the sense that it connected the crossing of the Jordan with the departure from the desert, which represents a land of darkness and death, and an entrance into the land of blessing and fruitful living.[11] Understood in this respect, the ritual of Joshua 5 could be seen as a ceremony of purification and sanctification. The ritual of circumcision, according to Coats, is not necessarily a part of the transition from wilderness to conquest. But in the present context, the ritual has been incorporated into the transition because the generation of the wilderness period were not circumcised. Thus, the wilderness period is over, and the ritual act of circumcision is renewed. As Coats suggests, the ritual process, that includes the circumcision and the celebration of the passover, establishes the beginning of the conquest by the people's "effective participation in the ritual."[12] The distinctiveness of the Israelites among the inhabitants of the land is perhaps emphasized through the ritual of circumcision and the Passover festival.[13] Circumcision also can be interpreted as a divinely ordained act of dedication prior to the occupation of the Promised Land.[14]

The transition from the wilderness period to the conquest of the land is indicated by the immediate realization of the gift of the land of promise (5:6), the circumcision of the generation born in the wilderness (5:7), the celebration of the passover (5:10), the eating of the fruit of the land of Canaan (5:11), and the cessation of the manna (5:12). Two changes occurred with the entrance into the land. First, with the death of the men of war and the circumcision of the new generation, the reproach of Egypt is lifted and, in essence, is left behind in the wilderness period.[15] Second, the divine care of the people, symbolized by the miraculous provision of manna, is displaced by the fruit of the land.

How does one interpret אֶת־חֶרְפַּת מִצְרַיִם (5:9)? Boling submits that the precise referent to חֶרְפָּה "reproach" (5:9) is uncertain. He states that the elimination of the "reproach" perhaps has to do with the freedom from the scorn and indignity of slavery.[16] The "reproach of Egypt," according to this interpretation, refers apparently to the status of the Israelites in Egypt, who were not yet a religious community; a status overcome with the covenant at Sinai.[17] According to one interpretation, the fact that the Egyptians were not circumcised created an atmosphere of scorn toward the Israelites.[18] In this respect, the interpretation of reproach is connected to the act of circumcision, that is, the act of circumcision made the reproach of Egypt disappear. But the full meaning of the "rolling away" of the reproach must involve more than circumcision itself.

When חֶרְפָּה occurs in other contexts, the implications have a wider interpretation than the ones cited above. For example, in Nehemiah 5:9, "reproach" refers to the taunts of Israel's enemies, the nations, which are created by the conduct of the Israelites. The righteous conduct of Israel, motivated by the reverent fear of the Lord, will prevent the ridicule of the nations. Micah 6:16 also speaks of the people's scorn or reproach for the desolated wicked city of Jerusalem caused by the judgment of God. In Ezekiel 36:15 life in general is scorned due to the fact that Israel is not dwelling in the land. Israel's reproach will be overcome, therefore, when they again inhabit the land as in the former times (Ezek. 36:11). In Isaiah 25:8 the reproach of Israel is related to the spread of the knowledge of God among the people. The reproach of God's people is taken away because of God's self revelation. Finally, in Isaiah 54:4 the reproach of Israel is related to Israel's despondent situation. Her reproach will be taken away when she regains her place in the world.

To summarize the points for interpreting the "Reproach of Egypt," the following considerations are in order. First, חֶרְפָּה appears to refer to Israel's status as slaves, without identity as a nation. The covenant at Horeb provides their constitution as a people. Second, the reproach of Egypt is related to the possession of a homeland. The sovereignty of God is affirmed through the exodus and guidance through the wilderness. Considered in regard to Israel's landless condition as slaves in Egypt, the fulfillment of the promise through the possession of the land is the immediate concern in Joshua 5. The interpretation of חֶרְפָּה varies among scholars, but the interpretation is related to its function within the transition from the previous period in Israel's life, which is characterized as a dispossessed people in Egypt outside their promised land, to a new future in the promised land. A great change occurs when the people enter the land. The landless, Egyptian slaves now begin to find their place in the world.

The Israelites were circumcised at Gilgal and celebrated the Passover, but, from a kerygmatic perspective, the function of Joshua

5:1–12 extends beyond the historical facts cited.[19] Joshua 5 proclaims the transition from the wilderness period in Israel's history to the settlement in the land. First, the ill experience of the wilderness period, characterized among other things by Yahweh's judgment against the "men of war" (Josh. 5:6), has now passed and a new community, renewed with hope and expectation, proceeds to enter the land. The transition is similar to that proposed by Olson, who identifies in Numbers 26 the confirmation of the death of the old generation and the birth of the new generation who are destined to inherit the promised land.[20] Second, the transition is proclaimed through the goodness of the land. The manna in the wilderness was a tangible sign of divine providence that is no longer needed in the land. The cessation of the manna upon entering the land is rather significant, since the writer did not say the Israelites stopped eating the manna once they entered the land. The imagery utilized by the writer suggests that the miraculous provision of manna ceased completely only when the land began to provide for the people. The land began to provide the nourishment for the community that Yahweh had provided previously in the wilderness. Both the land, which is received in fulfillment of the promise, and the manna represent the miraculous care provided by Yahweh. The transition in Joshua 5, therefore, is also a transition from the care and guidance of God in the wilderness, symbolized by the giving of the manna, and the gift of the land, that is now a new means of care for the people.

The kerygma of the wilderness traditions expressed in Joshua 5:1–12 is at its highest mark in the proclamation that the manna ceased when Israel entered the land and began to take of its provisions. The proclamation of the fulfillment of the promise of land draws the wilderness traditions under its service as a means for its accomplishment. The care of God for the community during the wilderness period finds its meaning in the achievement of this goal. The major kerygmatic statement in Joshua 5 is that the time of promise, that is, the Israelite bondage in Egypt and the period of the wilderness, is complete and a new era of fulfillment begins.[21] However, as Bright points out, Joshua continues the cautious warning that obedience to the law and loyalty to God, the giver of the land, is the very condition of Israel's existence as a nation in the land.[22]

JOSHUA 14:6–15

In the second section of Joshua (13:1–21:42), the wilderness traditions are found in the account of the allotment of Hebron to Caleb (14:6–15). Joshua 14:6–15 disrupts the carefully organized presentation of the tribal allotments (Josh. 6–12). Miller notes that the text appears to have been inserted secondarily, when it should follow 11:21–23.[23] In 11:21–22 Joshua had already conquered the hill country of Hebron by eliminating the Anakim. Joshua 14:6–15, then, may have a different function other than simply accounting for the allotment of Hebron to the Calebites. Traditionally, Caleb is associated with the territory of Hebron, and the etiological text of Joshua 14:6–15 explains, in part, how it is that Caleb inherited Hebron.[24]

The role of Caleb in the spy narrative of the wilderness traditions is maintained consistently throughout the sources (Num. 14:24 [J], Num. 14:38 [P], Deut. 1:36 [D], and Josh. 14:6 [JE]. The spy tradition associates Caleb's possession of Hebron with his faithfulness and courage at Kadesh-barnea in the initial effort in taking the promised land. The Caleb stories show that the Calebites were a tribe with military zeal and aggressive attitudes toward settlement in the land.[25] The faith and courage of Caleb stands as an example to encourage like-minded obedience to Yahweh and the commandments.[26]

Through the Priestly Writer, both Joshua and Caleb are united in the spy expedition under this motif of obedience (Num. 14:38). The character of Caleb in the book of Joshua illustrates the tendency of tradition toward making Caleb dependent on the character Joshua.[27] In Joshua 14:6, which some scholars assign to the JE strand, Caleb addresses his inquiry to Joshua by reminding Joshua of the promise made to both Joshua and Caleb.[28] According to the Priestly Writer in Numbers 14, both Joshua and Caleb would be "kept alive" to enter the land (Num. 14:38; cf. Josh. 14:10). The theme of God's providence in the wilderness is expressed in the term חָיָה; a verb used in the Hiphil perfect: "Yahweh has kept me alive" (Josh. 14:10).

The care and guidance of Yahweh is likewise revealed in the frequently used expression (Num. 14:38, Deut. 6:24; 8:3; 32:39), but the antithesis to the expression is found in Joshua 14:8. Joshua 14:6–15 exhibits the central motif for the spy tradition in Numbers 13–14 and Deuteronomy 1:19–46. The contrast between the obedience of Caleb and the disobedience of the people is stressed, though the sinfulness of the people in Numbers is perhaps exaggerated in order to explain the forty years of condemnation to wander in the wilderness.[29] Joshua 14:6–15, however, shifts the emphasis away from a lengthy exposition on the sins of the people (14:8) so as to focus upon the character of Caleb. Caleb reminds Joshua of the extreme difference between Caleb's own faithfulness to Yahweh and zeal for the land, compared to the contrary actions of the people, who reacted in fear to the report from the spies (Num. 13:32–33; Deut. 1:28).

Through such an emphasis, Caleb represents fulfillment of the divine plan for the community's existence in the land. The contrast is symbolized through a distinction between the heart of Caleb (Josh. 14:7) and the hearts of the people (14:8). Three terms are used in conjunction with the reference to the condition of the people that is illustrated through the metaphor "heart." Each of the terms (מוּג [Josh. 2:9, 24], מָסַס [Deut. 1:28; Josh. 5:1], מָסָה [Josh. 14:8]), can be translated "melt," thereby providing the usual translation "make the heart melt." In Joshua 14:8 the Israelites' hearts melt (מָסָה) because of the overpowering presence of the enemy in the land (Num. 13:32–33; Deut. 1:28). The reverse is stated in Joshua 2:10–11, when Rahab informs Joshua's spies that the hearts of the people in the land melt on hearing of the deeds of Yahweh at the Reed Sea. In 2:10–11, רוּחַ is connected with מָסַס in presenting the full effects upon the inhabitants in the land. Their hearts melt and therefore they no longer have any courage (רוּחַ). In Joshua 2:9 and 2:24, the helplessness of those who dwell in the land is caused by fear of the Israelites, expressed by the term מוּג. The fear is created through the knowledge of the acts of God, which calls for a recitation similar to that of Jethro in Exodus 18:10–11. In Joshua 5:1 the similar situation occurs when the kings of the Canaanites experience a melting of their hearts (מָסַס) because of the miracle of the drying of the Jordan by Yahweh and the presence of the people in the land. As a consequence, the people in the land who oppose the Israelites no longer have any רוּחַ. The fear and faint-heartedness of those who dwell in the land are attributed not to Israel's presence alone but to the actions of God (Josh. 2:9; 5:1).

Considering the relationship and implications of מָסַס (מָסָה, מוּג) and רוּחַ, a better understanding of Joshua 14:6–15 can be ascertained. The close relationship between Joshua 14 and Numbers 13–14 provides a clearer interpretation of the negative response of the people and the correct actions of Caleb. Joshua 14:7–8 makes an extreme distinction between the reactions of the Israelites, who rebelled out of fear (Num. 13–14), and the courageous actions of Caleb (Josh. 14:8). In Numbers 14:24 Caleb is afforded a different spirit (רוּחַ) or courage thus implying to the contrary that the people's hearts melted, though none of the terms for "melt" appears in the Numbers narrative (Cf. Deut. 1:28).[30] In Joshua 14:8 the contrasting element is "following" (מָלֵא), as opposed to "melting of the heart." Rebellion and disobedience are created by loss of courage and faint-heartedness. Caleb has a different heart compared to the weak courage of those who rebel (Josh. 14:7). The kerygma of the Caleb story in Joshua, which depends on stories of Caleb's unusual faith in the wilderness traditions, appeals to the people to mimic the nature of Caleb, for in him and his nature is found the precise formula for success in the land.

Joshua 14:6–15 also affirms the fidelity of God to past promises, while placing before the community the challenge to faithfulness. God is confessed as the giver of the land, and nothing Israel had done could permit any claims to ownership apart from God's gift (see Deut. 8, 32). Therefore, in Joshua's final speech (Josh. 23), this great address is not a victory speech, but, instead, Joshua's farewell address is given as a warning about the potential dark future for the people if they should forget their humility and faith.

JOSHUA 24:1–28

Joshua 24:2-13 can be divided into four themes, 1) the patriarchs, 24:2–4; 2) the exodus, 24:5; 3) the wilderness, 24:6–7; 4) the conquest, 24:8–13.[31] Coats finds evidence in Exodus 13:17–22, a text he identifies as an exposition for the wilderness theme, for including the Reed Sea tradition within the wilderness theme.[32] The book of Deuteronomy seems to distinguish between the Reed Sea event and the wilderness period (Deut. 11:1–7). By separating the Reed Sea event from the wilderness traditions, for example, as Childs proposes, then, Joshua 24:7b (יָמִים רַבִּים וַתֵּשְׁבוּ בַמִּדְבָּר) appears to be the only reference to the wilderness period in the confession of Joshua 24:2–13.[33]

Joshua 24 is a more elaborate recitation of the historical credo compared to Deuteronomy 6:20–23 and 26:5–9, but the contents are basically the same. The latter two do not mention the wilderness period. Yet, Joshua recognizes the period, but without substance. Sterling interprets רַבִּים יָמִים "many days" to possibly refer to the forty years spent in the wilderness.[34] The phrase is used in Deuteronomy 1:46 (2:1) to refer to the time spent at Kadesh following the aborted attempt to enter the land.

Further reference to the wilderness traditions occurs in another brief statement in Joshua 24:17 (וַיִּשְׁמְרֵנוּ בְּכָל־הַדֶּרֶךְ אֲשֶׁר הָלַכְנוּ בָהּ). In Deuteronomy 1:31–33 the kerygmatic element דֶּרֶךְ occurs in association with the care and guidance theme. The similarity in language between Joshua 24:17 and Deuteronomy 1:31–33 may indicate the common affirmation that Yahweh "bore" or "led" them along the "way." Sterling translates 24:17b, "who protected us throughout our entire journey," thus implying more the actions of God in relation to the deliverance from Egypt and the defense of Israel from her enemies than guidance in the wilderness.[35] The use of שָׁמַר can be translated "he preserved" or "he protected."[36] In this interpretation, Joshua 24:17 would imply a wilderness theme that reflects more a sense of protection than a care and guidance, though the two ideas are similar.

Joshua 24:2–13 recites the deeds of Yahweh almost always in regard to the deliverance of Israel from her enemies. The creed shows Yahweh's relationship with the people to be mainly as their divine protector. The creed contains no polemics against rebellion, in the sense found in other instructional uses of the wilderness traditions. Apart from the relatively brief statement of concern with idolatry (24:2, 23), Joshua 24 affirms the power of God against the enemies of the people, which, essentially, serves the divine plan and will for the people to possess the promised land. The creed can be abridged to demonstrate the deliverance theme. Basically, the creed states that Abraham is "taken" (לָקַח) by Yahweh from his family who worshipped other gods (v. 3); the fathers are delivered from Egypt (vv. 5–6); the people are then delivered at the Reed Sea (v. 7); the Amorites are defeated and Israel takes possession of that land (v. 8); Israel is delivered from the intended curse of Balaam (v. 10); and the Amorites, the Perizzites, the Canaanites, the Hittites, the Girgashites, the Hivites, and the Jebusites are defeated (v. 11). The confession concludes by affirming that God did this alone (v. 13).

Compared to the content of these elements, the wilderness period contains the least information. According to the purpose of the confession, God apparently did not perform an act of deliverance during the wilderness period. Perhaps 24:4b and 24:7b should be seen as parallel in function. Both statements, "Jacob and his children went down to Egypt" (24:4b) and "And you lived in the wilderness a long time" (24:7b) set up the subsequent actions of deliverance (24:5–6; 24:8). In Joshua 24:8a Israel is delivered from the wilderness (בוֹא) as they were from Egypt in 24:5b (יָצָא), though less dramatically.[37] Apart from this possible interpretation, the relevance of the statement in 24:7b to the confession remains ambiguous because each element in the creed contributes to the affirmation of God's power to deliver the people in order to fulfill the promise of the land.

In conclusion, Van Seters observes that certain confessional texts, such as Deuteronomy 6:20–25 and 26:5–9, have been shifted away from their confessional use to make the summaries the substance of a divine or prophetic speech and the basis for admonition.[38] This is true for the historical summary in Jeremiah 2 and the more elaborate recitation in Ezekiel 20. In Joshua 24:3–13 the historical summary has shifted into a divine speech, but the shift is different from the others cited above. The complete focus in Joshua 24:2–13 is on the notion of the deliverance and protection of Yahweh who has brought the Israelites to where they are at the present. The act of preservation (שָׁמַר v. 17b) is also the act of keeping them alive during the journey from Egypt (חָיָה Josh. 14:10). Likewise, the journey through the wilderness is expressed by the term דֶּרֶךְ (24:17a, Deut. 1:31). The immediate confession of the people in 24:18b is that since Yahweh has preserved or protected them along the way, to include the wilderness period, the people will therefore serve the Lord. The care and guidance theme of the wilderness traditions has been displaced by the protection theme. The displacement is due to the recession of the role of the wilderness traditions in the confession and the stress on the conquest.

Childs calls attention to the manner in which the book witnesses to the conquest. One should not be caught up in the unresolved tensions in the structure and traditions of Joshua.[39] Considering the notion of its testimony to God's saving acts, culminating with the conquest, the kerygma of Joshua 24 must be understood within that concluding act. Joshua 24 confesses the ultimate act of deliverance, an act that confirms in itself the divine purpose of God's actions from Abraham to Balaam. In Deuteronomy the problems confronting the people are almost entirely related to forgetting God. God and land have the potential of coming into conflict. In Joshua the potential problem is between God and the foreign gods in the land. Idolatry has been one of the problems confronting Israel in the wilderness period. The golden calf (Deut. 9) represents the basic problem in the wilderness. Baal Peor is different in that it occurs within the context of Israel's contact with other people. Since that contact is unavoidable, the challenge in Joshua is to obedience by serving the Lord instead of the foreign gods in the land.

I Samuel 4:5–11

Hertzberg draws a distinction between the events which precedes I Samuel 4:1b and those that follow.[40] Though nothing is mentioned directly about the sinfulness of Eli's sons, the continuation of the story of Eli and his sons in the Ark Narrative (I Sam. 4:1b–7:1) implies that, in its canonical context, the events that unfold are the consequence of the sins of the house of Eli. At this point in the writer's concern for presenting the history of the ark, the capture of the ark at Ebenezer is the last event in the life of Eli and his wicked sons (I Sam. 4:11, 18).

The wilderness traditions occur in a brief statement in I Samuel 4:8b. In comparison to the early Israelite traditions, I Samuel 4:8b illustrates a mixed use of the exodus and wilderness traditions:

הֵם הָאֱלֹהִים הַמַּכִּים	They are the gods who smote
אֶת־מִצְרַיִם בְּכָל־מַכָּה	the Egyptians with all sorts of plagues
בַּמִּדְבָּר	in the wilderness

The basic exodus tradition is present within the confused affirmations of the Philistines (cf. I Sam. 6:6, in which confusion is not apparent.). We do not know of any plagues or afflictions divinely imposed against the Egyptians in the wilderness. Divine judgments in the wilderness do, however, include plagues and other afflictions (cf. Num. 14:12; 11:33). Here, in I Samuel 4:8, a merging of traditions is apparent, much in the same manner that Deuteronomy 32:13 has a merging of traditions about the land and the wilderness.

The Philistines reacted in fear to the people's jubilant celebration of the entrance of the ark into the Israelite camp. Following the shout by the Israelites, the expected sequence of events dissolves into the unexpected. Instead of victory for the Israelites because of the presence of the ark, the victory was the Philistines'. Motivated by their fear of God, plus the thought of becoming slaves to the Hebrews, the Philistines fought with added courage. The same courage motivated by fear should have been exhibited by the Israelites.

Irony is implied in the response by the Philistines, when they are confused as to the correctness of the traditions of the exodus. Nevertheless, they gain strength for battle against the people, who possess the ark, as well as the correct versions of the exodus and wilderness traditions. Knowledge of the guidance and care of Yahweh for the people of Israel, obtained undoubtedly from Israelite traditions, has influenced the outcome of this great battle between the Israelites and the Philistines. Two confessional elements are evident in I Samuel 4:5–11: the fear of God and the sovereign will of God. The event of the capture of the ark by the Philistines provides the occasion for the purging of sin from Israel, which also contributes to the rise of Samuel in Israelite tradition.

II KINGS 18:1–8

One of the more popular references to the wilderness traditions in the Former Prophets is found in II Kings 18:4. The question remains hidden in mystery as to why Hezekiah destroyed the bronze serpent image that, supposedly, was made by Moses during the wilderness period (Num. 21:4–9). Noth suggests that the serpent image was a cultic object that had been taken over from the ancient Canaanite cult in Jerusalem.[41] Regardless of its traditio-historical explanation, why, considering the actions that could have been recorded of Hezekiah, was the incident of the bronze serpent mentioned? Perhaps the answer can be discovered through an analysis of its kerygmatic function.

The serpent was destroyed during the reform of Hezekiah in strictest observance of the commandments of Moses. Hezekiah's actions against the Canaanite religion and the Nehushtan are placed in direct parallel to his epitaph in II Kings 18. In verses 5–6, Hezekiah is venerated as a great king in Israel due to his faithfulness and obedience to the demands of Mosaic Yahwism. If his reform is judged as motivated by his zeal for Mosaic traditions, the practice of "burning incense" to the bronze serpent must be interpreted as a reflection of impure religious practices.[42] The name נְחֻשְׁתָּן might even be translated "piece of bronze" or "bronze god," which suggests an expression of contempt for the object.[43]

The kerygmatic idea surrounding the creation of the serpent in the wilderness is that life is sustained through faith in God. Hezekiah's actions illustrate the same theological point. The events that unfold in II Kings 18 contribute further to an understanding of the use of the incident of the serpent in the wilderness. The Northern Kingdom suffers its fate due to a lack of obedience to Mosaic Yahwism (18:9–12); whereas, in contrast, Hezekiah saves Jerusalem because of his faithfulness (18:13–19:37).

In much the same manner as Caleb in the wilderness traditions and in the book of Joshua, Hezekiah provides the example of obedience, courage, and faithfulness. The use of the wilderness traditions in II Kings 18 is for the encouragement of faith in later generations. In its canonical shape, II Kings 18:4 stimulates recollection of the initial purpose of the bronze serpent in the wilderness. Yahweh's purpose and will for the people can become distorted through disobedience and idolatry, resulting in the loss of continuity with Israel's religious heritage that goes back to the wilderness period.

The Kerygma of the Wilderness Traditions in The Former Prophets

The analysis of the kerygma of the wilderness traditions in the Former Prophets is restricted primarily to the period of pre-monarchical Israel. The community of faith now lives in the land,

and the life of the wilderness period is to be understood through Israelite traditions. The appropriation of the wilderness traditions in the book of Joshua is associated closely with their role in Deuteronomy. The community of faith in Joshua is also at a crossroad in its pilgrimage. The new beginning before the people represents the fulfillment of God's promises, in relation to acquiring the land. The contrast between the new setting in the land and the wilderness period is presented through the manna tradition. The manna tradition of the wilderness period is a multi-faceted metaphor. The manna represents the care and guidance of God while the community is outside the land. The reproach of such a state of life as a desert people is overcome by the possession of the land. Within the kerygma of the fulfillment of God's promises lies the subtle reminder that Israel is capable of a faint heart and a weak spirit. The weak character is due to the fact that the future, whether filled with prosperity or uncertainty, may find the community's spirit and faith tested.

Caleb provides the book of Joshua with its primary example of obedience, and such an example is derived from the wilderness traditions. The book of Joshua, unlike Deuteronomy, is relatively silent in regard to the community's history of rebellion and disobedience, although Joshua 5:6 and 14:8–9 state explicitly that Israel has a sinful history in the wilderness. In Joshua 23–24, where an exhortation to obedience is in true Deuteronomic style, Israel is cautioned to serve and obey Yahweh instead of the pagan gods in the land. The danger of apostasy and rebellion is the primary focus, but not one word of Israel's history of sin is found in the text. The fidelity of God to the covenant, presented in accordance with God's sovereignty in the divine plan for Israel, is the main confession. Because of God's fidelity to Israel, the people should examine themselves as to whether they will remain loyal to God.[44] For the Deuteronomic message in Joshua, there is always reserved jubilation over gaining the land.[45]

The care and guidance theme of the wilderness in Deuteronomy is transposed into an interpretation of the wilderness period as a time when God "kept alive" the faithful and "preserved" the people against Israel's enemies. The full impact of the Israelite traditions of God's leadership and protection of the people is evident in the Philistines' reaction to the presence of the ark of the covenant in I Samuel 4:5–11. A remnant of the care and guidance theme is found in the emphasis on the manna in Joshua 5 and God's leading in Joshua 24:17. The subtle shift from the care of Yahweh in the wilderness, symbolized by the manna, to the land's ability to provide is Deuteronomic (Deut. 8). But the motif is carried no further, since Joshua dwells upon the hazards of idolatry instead of the goodness of the land.

The books of Samuel and Kings rarely refer to the Pentateuchal traditions, especially the wilderness period. The two occasions discussed above stress the failures of community. The kerygma of the wilderness traditions in I Samuel 4:5–11 must be understood in relation to the sins of the house of Eli. As to the latter occurrence, II Kings 18:1–8 also alludes to the sins of the cult which were purged in the reform of Hezekiah. In both these incidents, the ancient traditions of Israel survive the threat from disobedience and address the issues of divine purpose, obedience, and faith. Basically, where the wilderness traditions are utilized by biblical writers in the Former Prophets, concern for the disposition of the community of faith lies at the heart of the texts.

Literary Analysis of the Wilderness Traditions in The Latter Prophets

In the book of Isaiah the wilderness traditions occur under various subtle forms. Isaiah 41:17–20, for example, is written as though the wilderness traditions were lying quietly in the background. The imagery is difficult to link with the Pentateuchal traditions of Israel's life in the wilderness. Isaiah 40:3 presents also the same problem of establishing a relationship between the prophet's language and imagery and the wilderness traditions. Isaiah 48:21 stands out as an example of a use of wilderness imagery associated with the Pentateuch. In the book of Jeremiah, chapter 2, with particular emphasis on verses 2–8, presents a brief recollection of the wilderness traditions. Ezekiel 20 represents the most extensive development in the appropriation of the wilderness traditions in the Latter Prophets.

Isaiah 48:20–21

Isaiah 48 is the conclusion to the Cyrus texts of Isaiah 44:24–48:22.[46] Four distinctive sections are identified in Isaiah 48. First, Isaiah 48:1–11 reveals the vindication of Yahweh's methods of revelation to Israel. The purpose of Yahweh's methods of revelation is to eliminate all evidence that would permit Israel or any other agent to claim credit for the actions of God in the past and in the present. Second, 48:12–16 stipulates that Yahweh's withholding of information is for the purpose of presenting something new. Third, 48:17–19 states that, though God wills good for Israel, Israel's disobedience has caused them to be cut off. Fourth, 48:20–22 concludes the chapter by proclaiming a new exodus and placing a challenge before Israel to depart from Babylon.[47]

Whybray questions whether the chapter should be treated as a unit or as separate passages (1–11, 12–16, 17–19, 20–22).[48] Two moods, according to Whybray, alternate in the chapter. One mood involves the comparison between the days of old and the new period that is to come for Israel. The prophecy of the new exodus, with God leading Israel back to the homeland, is expressed through the term חָרָבָה. The other mood contains harsh statements against Israel, which is uncommon to the texts of consolation in Isaiah 40–55. The charges against Israel claim that Israel's confessions are insincere; she lacks faith, commits idolatry, shows arrogance, and persists in rebellion. The anger of God is presented in relation to Israel's guilt of sin and her undeserved survival. Had it not been for God's concern for his own integrity, Israel would have no remnant; a motif similar to the traditions of Numbers 14:11–23, and its retelling in Deuteronomy 9.

Isaiah 48:20–21 is perhaps pivotal in the division of Isaiah 40–48 and 49–52. The former is concerned with Jacob-Israel, while the latter is concerned with Zion-Jerusalem.[49] In 48:20–21, the call to depart from Babylon is a reenactment of the exodus, in which the new exodus is given in the context of both a departure from Babylon and a wilderness journey.[50] McKenzie correctly interprets the event as a departure from bondage, but, then, why does the writer of Isaiah 48 mention the Meribah story? Is the proclamation of the event concerned with the exodus as a time of freedom (v. 20) or with establishing the nature of the exodus? Like the wilderness traditions of the Pentateuch, the kerygma of the event in Isaiah 48 calls for a commitment of faith in which the people will come to depend on God, who acts in the present just as in the days of old. Isaiah 48 is, therefore, concerned with the revelation of the truthfulness of God's word, as opposed to the corrupted understanding of the so-called revelations the people claim to know (vv. 3–5). God has disciplined the people through the past events, and now a new period in the life of Israel is proclaimed.

The wilderness traditions in 48:21 provide an illustration of God's gracious actions toward Israel. The memories evoked of the events of Exodus 17 and Numbers 20 are from Israel's distant past. "This recitation of past deeds becomes a joyous affirmation of faith in Yahweh's future care for the people."[51] The past is called upon to create hope for future actions of God. In order to accomplish this goal, Isaiah 48 transforms an ancient story from the wilderness traditions into a new proclamation. The proclamation of the new, within which the wilderness traditions provide a major service, is the key to the message of the entire chapter.[52]

In the present analysis, Isaiah 48:21 is understood to represent the wilderness period. Like Exodus 17, which affirms the presence of God, verse 21 encourages faith in God's presence at a time of national chaos. Various terms are used to refer to the notion of wilderness or desert in Isaiah 40–55 (מִדְבָּר, עֲרָבָה, אֶרֶץ צִיָּה, בִּישִׁמוֹן, צָמֵא, חֳרָבוֹת).[53] In Isaiah, מִדְבָּר seems to be the most frequent (40:3; 41:18, 19; 42:11; 43:19, 20; 50:2; 51:3) with עֲרָבָה occurring as well (40:3, 41:19; 51:3).[54] The use of חָרְבָּה, instead of the normal terms for wilderness or desert (מִדְבָּר and עֲרָבָה), provides a clue to the concerns expressed by the writer. The term חָרְבָּה implies the notion of waste places and ruins. In Isaiah 40–55 the term is used in reference to the waste places of Zion (49:19; 51:3), Jerusalem (52:9), and other cities of Judah (44:26). חָרְבָּה is used elsewhere in Isaiah in reference to places of ruin or waste (also 5:17, 58:12, 61:4). Only in Isaiah 48:21 is the wilderness called חָרְבָּה, which is not insignificant, considering the devastation of Jerusalem and the territory of Judah during the last days of the kingdom of Judah. Such imagery is certainly proper, and even adds to the notion of an exodus and God's care for Israel in the homeland. The term חָרְבָּה need not refer only to the wilderness as some secluded place. The text of 48:20–21 proclaims that, even in the ruins of Jerusalem, God will care for his people.

Further free adaptation of the Meribah tradition is revealed through the verbs נָזַל and זוּב. The former term נָזַל is used in Isaiah 40–55 to describe the flowing of water as streams (44:3; 48:21), while the latter term זוּב occurs only in 48:21. In 44:3, נָזַל refers to providing water to a dry land in order to save it and the people, but the reference is to the land and not the desert. The verb is also used to symbolize the salvation of God flowing down from heaven (45:8). Instead of נָזַל, יָצָא (in the Hiphil) is used in both accounts of the water miracle narratives in Exodus and Numbers (Exod. 17:6, Num. 20:8, 10; see 48:20). In Isaiah 48:21, the other verb זוּב is used in describing the land, for example, "flows with milk and honey" (Num. 13:27, 14:8). The language and imagery of God's miraculous transformation of the present situation in Judah is incorporated within the poetic description of the wilderness journey from exile.

Isaiah 48 presents a transition from the old to the new.[55] At crucial moments of change in Israel's history, Israel's ancient traditions, especially the exodus, were reappropriated to explain or create new horizons of expectations in Israel's religious life. In 43:18 the "old" refers to the exodus from Egypt, and the "new" implies the exodus from Babylon (48:20–21). As expressed in 43:18, Israel is no longer urged to look back to her past for the nation's "old" history of salvation, embodied in the story of the exodus from Egypt.[56] As Zimmerli explains "the greater 'new thing' simply surpasses the old, and this renders unnecessary any 'remembrance,' that is, the process of transmission of old tradition in the cultic 'memory.'"[57] Therefore, the call to no longer remember (43:18) is to be understood in relation to the proclamation of God creating something new. The new things to come are accomplished for the sake of God's honor, as in the judgment texts of the wilderness traditions in Numbers 14:11–23 and Deuteronomy 9 and 32.

The future of Israel finds its foundation in what happened in the past. That which is created new is not entirely new, as 48:21 indicates. Yet the past is forged into the new events of the future. Still, the hopes of Israel rest on her knowledge and faith in what God has done in the past. The theme of the wilderness experience in Isaiah 48:21 is linked to the wilderness traditions in Exodus and Numbers. The motif of God's care and guidance is revealed in 48:21. The imagery of Meribah is not one of deliverance as much as it is the sustaining and transforming power of God in the midst of unbearable situations, as the unusual use of חָרְבָה implies.

The use of חָרְבָה and זוּב is a brilliant management of contrasting terms to establish a sense of transition from the old to the new. The former term alludes to the disastrous condition of the homeland in Judah after 586 B.C.E. The latter term is used to describe the land of hope ("flowing with milk and honey"). The poetic use of the two terms, נָזַל and זוּב, creates a picture of a desert transformed by the miraculous provisions of water, similar to the other images in Isaiah 41:17–18, 43:19–20, and 49:10. The miraculous provisions in the wilderness are linked to the normative nature of God's care and guiding presence, established in the wilderness traditions in the Tetrateuch. Continuity with traditions is established with the recollection of the care and guidance by God for the Israelites in the first exodus and journey through the wilderness. The guidance theme is crucial within these unusual exodus/wilderness texts. The theme is established in 48:17 (אֲנִי יְהוָה . . . מַדְרִיכֲךָ בְּדֶרֶךְ תֵּלֵךְ). In Isaiah 63:14, the guidance theme appears only in brief, indicated by the poetic verb נָהַג (also, 49:10). As Simon observes, the restoration of Israel to the homeland, as well as the raising of the ruins of Judah, can only occur with God's guiding presence, just as God cared for and led them before.[58]

JEREMIAH 2

In the book of Jeremiah, the wilderness traditions are incorporated into the text of chapter 2:1–19. Following the prologue in 1:19, Jeremiah chapter 2 begins the poems and sermons against Israel (2:1–25:14).[59] Chapter 2 is divided as follows: 2:1–3 and 14–19; 4–13; 20–28; 29–32; and 33–37. Thompson proposes the structure of 2:1–19 to combine 2:1–3 and 2:14–19 under one section with 2:4–13 inserted secondarily.[60] Bright restructures 2:1–19 in the same manner to accommodate the ambiguous references to Israel in the second masculine plural (2:4–13) and the third feminine singular (2:1–3, 14–19).[61] The wilderness traditions are utilized in the two blocks of materials. In the second masculine plural section (2:4–13) the rebellious character of the fathers, and that of the present community, are placed in parallel. In the other block of material (2:1–3, 14–19) the fathers and the present community stand in contrast. The units that were originally separate have been combined to form an indictment against Israel, because of the people's rebellion.[62] The terminology in 2:4–13 is similar to that of a covenant lawsuit.[63]

An extreme contrast occurs between the seemingly perfect beginnings of Israel's relationship with God in the wilderness and the broken relationship between the fathers and Yahweh. The time of the rebellion of the community, clearly assigned to the wilderness period by most biblical writers, is not as clear in Jeremiah 2. In 2:5 the identity of the fathers who committed apostasy, for example, is unclear, and the reference could be either the contemporaries of Jeremiah or the exodus generation. The relationship between Yahweh and the community in the first days, which is given in the image of a marriage (כְּלוּלֹתָיִךְ, 2:2), is an allusion to the exodus generation. As Bright suggests, if Jeremiah 2:6 is a reference to the later fathers, then, the wilderness period occurred prior to the fathers' rejection of Yahweh.[64] Such a view is further indicated in 2:7, which places the time of the apostasy after the Israelites entered the land.

The indictment against the community claims they commit persistent apostasy and they, therefore, need a radical reform of their religious attitudes. The community's failure to pursue God resulted in the increased falseness of their religious beliefs.[65] The charges in chapter 2 reflect the failure to remember and the failure to appropriate the ancient traditions.[66] Israel's normal protected status as the chosen people of God is in jeopardy. The threat to that status, which is established here at the beginning of Jeremiah's oracles, underlies the events told throughout the book.[67] A contrast is then implied, on the one hand, between Israel's past and her present state of faithfulness and, on the other hand, the protection which Israel once enjoyed and her present weakness and defenselessness in the face of her enemies. Another contrast is evident between God's care and guiding presence long ago in the wilderness, made possible through Israel's devotion to God, and the absence of God's guidance in the present, due to her apostasy and unrepentant attitude. Underlying the obvious contrast is the fact that Jeremiah's community cannot recognize the change.

The merging of the wilderness journey and the "love motif" originated with Hosea.[68] With this merger, Jeremiah, like Hosea, deviates considerably from the Pentateuchal traditions and may not be dependent on that material. Usually, the wilderness traditions focus on the rebellious conduct of the community, but Jeremiah 2:1–3 is concerned with God's attitude and actions toward the people and not the people's actions toward God.[69] The actions of God shown to the second party to the relationship is expressed normally through the term חֶסֶד (2:2), and, here, חֶסֶד is used to express the love of the community for God. The context in which חֶסֶד occurs is the marriage covenant; a symbolic expression of the relationship between the community and its God.[70]

Further positive characteristics of the people in the wilderness contribute to the confession of Yahweh's leadership. Fox exegetes לֶכְתֵּךְ אַחֲרַי (2:2) in the figurative sense. When the phrase is used elsewhere, the reference is to one's loyalty to God with no specific location implied. Since the wilderness is the setting in 2:2, he concludes, "Now to say that Israel went after Yahweh in the desert is simply another way of saying that Yahweh went before Israel; that is, led her in the desert."[71] On the other hand, אַחֲרֵי is used in a similar manner in 2:5 to refer to the apostasy of Israel (וַיֵּלְכוּ אַחֲרֵי הַהֶבֶל וַיֶּהְבָּלוּ). So, when the people are accused of following after other gods (אַחֲרֵי) the implication is that the people worship in a cultic setting (Jer. 2:8).[72] According to the normal use of אַחֲרֵי, Jeremiah 2:2 suggests that the generation of the wilderness followed after Yahweh reflecting an obedient relationship to their God.

The inconsistencies between traditions of the Tetrateuch and their appropriation in the book of Jeremiah are found in their theological function and not their historical accuracy.[73] McKane attempts to reconcile the differences between the wilderness traditions of the

Tetrateuch and Jeremiah's positive views by interpreting the *contrast* between the perfect beginnings and the failure to maintain that relationship.[74] The kerygma of Jeremiah 2 is revealed through this contrast. In Jeremiah 2:1–3, for example, the important kerygmatic statement is the affirmation of God's relationship to the people and their dedication to God in the beginning. On the reverse, 2:6 reveals the nature of Israel's present relationship to God, which is more consistent with the wilderness traditions of the Tetrateuch. The kerygma exhorts the people to remember their ideal beginnings and return to that situation.

The one positive aspect that appears to be consistent with the wilderness traditions of the Pentateuch is the guidance motif.[75] The guidance theme is common to three sections of Jeremiah 2 (2:1–3, 4–13, 14–19), and the theme is identifiable through the repeated use of הָלַךְ (2:2, 2:6, 2:17).[76] הָלַךְ is found in the guidance theme of the wilderness exposition and is used in conjunction with לִפְנֵיהֶם (Exod. 13:17–22). The verb is one of the central kerygmatic elements in the wilderness traditions. The tribes depart from Egypt with Yahweh "going before them" (וַיהוָה הֹלֵךְ לִפְנֵיהֶם), symbolized by the pillars of cloud and fire. In Numbers 14:14, God "goes" before the people, and the theme is recited in Deuteronomy 1:31–33. When the ancient traditions state that God goes before them or is in the midst of them, they imply that Yahweh is present to lead them, even in battle. God's leading Israel in the desert is understood as both spatial guidance and as help.

The unusual appropriation of the wilderness traditions in Jeremiah is further enhanced through the merging of the two kerygmatic elements הָלַךְ and דֶּרֶךְ in Jeremiah 2. In verse 6, Yahweh led them through the wilderness, and, in verse 17, Yahweh led them in the right manner of conduct. In this respect, the interpretation of דֶּרֶךְ in 2:17 can imply an ethical leading. On the other hand, דֶּרֶךְ may be another way of saying "Yahweh brought us up," referring to the exodus and wilderness traditions wanderings.[77] For Israel's salvation history, דֶּרֶךְ refers to the route through the wilderness to the promised land. But Yahweh's דֶּרֶךְ appeals to the future conduct or manner of life for the people. If Israel *walked* in the *way* prescribed at Horeb, then, the community would live successfully in the land (Deut. 8:6f.).

Brueggemann interprets "They did not say" (2:6) to imply that the people of Israel no longer recited the salvation story.[78] The people no longer regarded the memory of their beginnings and therefore lost their election consciousness.[79] The core traditions in Israel's faith that comprise the covenant tradition include the exodus, wilderness wanderings, and the conquest. Israel's existence as a people depended on these divine acts of deliverance. Israel's election was a sign of divine grace, "ratified by the covenant to which it led, and crowned by the gift of the land of Canaan."[80] Within the prophetic writings, the covenant is the most widely used concept that expresses the nature of the relationship between the community and God. Jeremiah 2:2–3 reflects such an ideal relationship, while 2:4–13 charges the community for its departure from their historical bonding with Yahweh.[81]

The problems of forgetfulness and neglect of Israel's religious heritage has been established previously in the analysis of the confessional stance of the community in the Tetrateuch. The consequences of that non-confessional stance is the same for both the generations of ancient Israel and the present world of Jeremiah. The wilderness traditions play a crucial role in teaching the Israelites the essentials in successful community life. Deuteronomy expresses a concern for remembering Israel's religious heritage, for within her past lies her constitutive heritage (Deut. 8). The homiletic warnings of Deuteronomy against apostasy are rooted in the wilderness period from which God's fidelity to the community is revealed (cf. Hos. 13:5–6). Then, in Joshua the potential problems associated with living in the land are again combined with the stress on obeying the commandments of God in order to prevent apostasy from the faith (Josh. 24). The actions of God in Egypt and the wilderness testify to God's fidelity to the promises and the covenant. In the times of Jeremiah, that which is feared has come to pass with all the tragic consequences soon to be fulfilled. Considering the persistent calling of Israel to obedience in the Tetrateuch and the Deuteronomic history, the recitation of Israel's sacred history is the common practice, and, here, the recollection is used to establish the claims and indictment against Israel. If Jeremiah 2:6 and 2:8 refer to the problem of forgetting, which implies the community's failure to cling to Israel's religious heritage, as Brueggemann suggests, then, the cause of this failure is the same as expressed in Deuteronomy 8:11; the failure to obey and learn from the law results in presumptuous living in the land.[82]

The kerygma of the wilderness traditions in Jeremiah 2, therefore, contributes to the affirmation of the power of Israel's religious heritage, linked to obedience to the laws or Torah, which ultimately constitutes the people as a Yahwistic community. The community would then live under the guidance and protection of its

God (2:17). The kerygmatic appeal in Jeremiah 2 is for Israel to return to her God. The wilderness experience is understood as the period when Israel was taught the true nature of community (Exod. 15:25; Deut. 8:3). Jeremiah 2:2–3 appears to be the expression of an ideal, not in regard to the wilderness, but in regard to the relationship of the community to God.[83] The wilderness traditions in Jeremiah 2 are used, then, to address a community whose situation is not quite the ideal.

JEREMIAH 31:2–6

As part of the Book of Hope, Jeremiah 31:2–6 is a confession of God's great חֶסֶד for Israel, and reference to the wilderness traditions may be implied in the statement מָצָא חֵן בַּמִּדְבָּר (31:2). The oracles of hope were originally directed to the survivors of the Northern Kingdom of Israel.[84] Scholars suggest that the oracles originate from the early years of the prophet Jeremiah when Josiah, feeling relief from the pressure of Assyrian dominance, undertook a political and religious reform which extended Judah's territorial borders into the north.[85] Jeremiah 31:2–6 is therefore directed to the remnant of people from the Northern Kingdom. According to their canonical shape, the oracles of salvation, as a whole, refer to both the Southern Kingdom of Judah and the Northern Kingdom of Israel in its picture of the future restoration of the land (Jer. 31:23). In particular, the phrase לְכֹל מִשְׁפְּחוֹת יִשְׂרָאֵל in Jeremiah 31:1 seems to be inclusive.

Scholars suggest that Jeremiah 31:2 refers to the exile of the Northern Kingdom, in which many people died at that hand of the Assyrians. The identity of "Israel" in 31:2 depends on whether the passage is a recollection of the wilderness traditions or a symbolic reference to the tragedy of the exile of the Northern Kingdom.[86] In this segment in the oracles of salvation, the Southern Kingdom of Judah is not mentioned until much later (31:23). Bright's translation, for example, can suggest the latter context, "In the desert they've met with favor, the people escaped from the sword."[87] On the other hand, as the following discussion will reveal, Jeremiah 31:2–6 contains a statement about the past (vv. 2–3) and the future (vv. 4–6). The poetic use of חֵן and חֶסֶד unite the first passage under the primary theme of divine initiative toward the community during the wilderness. In the latter texts, the future restoration of the Northern Kingdom is anticipated through the repeated use of עוֹד, as a mirror of the past, in which God will once again act on behalf of the community.

The primary confession of the past is מָצָא חֵן בַּמִּדְבָּר עַם שְׂרִידֵי חָרֶב (31:2). The term חֵן appears to imply divine action by choice, in which God chose to show his love toward them, and divine favor is the correct implication of the action. One specific reference to the motif of divine favor in the wilderness is found in Numbers 11:11–15, but in this passage, חֵן is associated with Moses and his leadership. In Exodus 3:21 and 11:3, the favor that is given by God indicates a divine inclination toward the people of Israel which is witnessed by the Egyptians. The primary texts used by many scholars to link the wilderness period with the Jeremiah text is Exodus 33:12–17, and, here, the situation is associated with the Sinai tradition. At Sinai, God chose to be merciful toward the community, and the divine decision is significant, especially, since the sins of the people severed the covenant relationship. Divine favor in Exodus 33 is associated with Moses and his leadership of the people. Moses, however, is the representative of the people before God, and his intercession for them seals the agreement between Moses and God (cf. Exod. 33:1–4). The success and conclusion of Moses' intercession constitutes a restoration of the covenant promise, which allows the full renewal of the covenant to proceed, as recorded in Exodus 34. In this context, divine favor is shown by God's presence and the gift of the land as their place of rest. Such a relationship between the community and God indicates the distinctiveness of Israel among the peoples of the earth (Exod. 33:16).

Bozak apparently interprets the entire context of Jeremiah 31:2 as a reference primarily to the exodus.[88] Reference to the exodus is implied in the phrase שְׂרִידֵי חָרֶב (Exod. 5:21; 15:9; 18:4), but more is involved than simply remembering the miraculous deliverance. Thompson also interprets 31:2 as a reference to the exodus from Egypt, at which time Yahweh graciously provided and cared for the people in the wilderness.[89] The theme of Yahweh's guidance in the wilderness is perhaps implied, though inconclusively, in הָלוֹךְ לְהַרְגִּיעוֹ יִשְׂרָאֵל, since the experience remembered is assigned to the wilderness setting. The primary focus, nevertheless, is the divine חֵן that is shown toward the community. The expression of divine favor in 31:2 is placed in parallel with וְאַהֲבַת עוֹלָם and חֶסֶד in 31:3. The faithfulness of Yahweh to the people is an integral theme of the wilderness period, and the restatement of the theme in 31:3 is expanded by the promise of continued divine faithfulness through the repeated use of עוֹד in 31:4–5. Thus, the exodus, Sinai, and the wilderness traditions are utilized by the writer to express the kerygma. The setting is assigned to the wilderness where the relationship between the new community and Yahweh evolves.

By emphasizing the exodus experience, Bozak finds the message in Jeremiah 31:2–3 to be a reminder to the people in exile that Yahweh's power, displayed in the exodus, is still valid and can give hope in their present situation.[90] However, the stress in the verse is not on שְׂרִידֵי חָרֶב, which appears in construct relationship and can be translated as a relative clause (cf. Judg. 3:18), but on the main action of the sentence revealed in מָצָא חֵן בַּמִּדְבָּר עַם. The statement addresses the issue of the community's standing relationship with its God. The issue is repeated in 31:3 through the proclamation of God's love for the people and God's continued faithfulness to them. Such a confession is linked to the promises in 31:4–6, which confess that God will act again because of God's favor and steadfast love.[91] Even where Holladay suggests the subject of the verb מָצָא to be Yahweh instead of the people, he still recognizes the action of the statement to be an expression of the divine election of Israel in the wilderness; further comparing the statement with Hosea 9:10 and Deuteronomy 32:10.[92] Holladay's proposal to change חָרֶב to חֹרֵב, "Horeb," which would parallel בַּמִּדְבָּר, produces the translation "a people remnant from Horeb." The revision of the Hebrew also adds further credit to the suggestion that reference to divine favor is associated with the Sinai experience.[93]

In conclusion, the confession מָצָא חֵן בַּמִּדְבָּר עַם has profound significance for the kerygma of the passage. The favor or grace of Yahweh toward the community occurs in the wilderness after the incident of the golden calf at Sinai (Exod. 33:12–17). Brueggemann correctly links the recollection of the past experiences in the wilderness with Israel's present circumstances, with the purpose of correcting the belief that exile is "godless" and "graceless."[94] The parallel between the wilderness context, in which Yahweh shows divine favor and mercy instead of wrath, and the exilic period is evident. Sin and rebellion caused the crisis in both settings, and each situation is followed by a divine initiative to restore the community. The implication is exceptional: Yahweh's חֵן and חֶסֶד for the people are affirmed after a breach in the covenantal relationship. A reaffirmation of God's relationship to the community is proclaimed through the promise of restoration (31:3–5).

EZEKIEL 20:1–38

In the book of Ezekiel, the wilderness traditions occur predominately in 20:1–38. Within the composition of Ezekiel, chapters 15–20 make up sayings concerning sin, judgment, and responsibility: 15–16, sin and judgment of Israel; 17, sin and judgment of the monarchy; 18, responsibility and retribution; 19, Sin and judgment of the monarchy; and then chapter 20, sin and judgment against Israel.[95] Ezekiel 20:1–38 is an adaptation of the historical confession, which reveals Ezekiel's unusual interpretation of Israel's sacred traditions:[96]

20:5–9	Israel in Egypt
5	Election of Israel and revelation of Yahweh
7	Warnings against idolatry
8	Rebellion of Israel
9	The restraint of Yahweh
20:10–17	Israel in the wilderness
11–12	Provision of the laws and Sabbath observance
13	Rebellion of Israel
14	The restraint of Yahweh
15	Judgment preventing entrance into the land
17	Restatement of Israel's sins
18	Restatement of Yahweh's restraint
20:18–26	The next generation in the wilderness
18	Charge to obedience
19–20	Restatement of the laws and the Sabbath
21	Rebellion of Israel
22	The restraint of Yahweh
23	Future judgment of exile
24	Restatement of Israel's sins
25–26	The provision of the bad laws
20:27–32	Israel in the land
27	Israel blasphemes Yahweh
28	Israel commits idolatry
29	Etiological statement
31–32	Ezekiel rejects the elders
20:33–38	Israel returns to the wilderness from exile
33	Yahweh's oath to be Israel's king
34–35	The new exodus
36	Judgment in the wilderness
37	Promise of entrance into the land
38	Purging of sin from the community

One of the unusual characteristics of the recitation is Ezekiel's increased use of the historical judgments of Yahweh against Israel.[97] In 20:1–32 he shapes the history to show that even in Egypt the Israelites practiced idolatry. The purpose of such a presentation of history is to show that Israel was rebellious from the beginning.

Ezekiel's critical interpretation of Israel's exodus and wilderness traditions has contributed to his reputation as a religious zealot; and he has been called the first fanatic in the Bible.[98] Ezekiel's heart and mind are dedicated to Yahweh's purposes in the world. Therefore, the harshness of Ezekiel's attitude to Israel is revealed in his indictment of Israel as the "rebellious house" who must be punished.

Ezekiel interprets the destruction of Jerusalem and the temple to be the result of Israel's idolatry. Therefore, the most important message to be proclaimed is that God survives and that his honor is maintained in face of world opinion, also including the Israelite community, that would suggest the contrary. Cooke writes,

> Ezekiel feels acutely that Jahveh's honour has been outraged; he lays emphasis on *jealousy* as the motive which determines the divine action: it incites Jahveh to punish Israel, lest they should think that He overlooked their sin, it leads to their restoration, lest the heathen should imagine that He lacked the power.[99]

Pfeiffer also asserts that Ezekiel is filled with anger against the community's profanation of Yahweh's earthly abode, as well as other acts of insult against Israel's God.[100] Ezekiel 20:1–31 is a reformulation of ancient traditions stressing the radical sinfulness of Israel.[101] Israel's entire history, which is presented in Ezekiel 20, is not one of salvation but sin.[102]

An analogy is evident between chapters 8–11 and 14:1–11 with chapter 20 through the elders' inquiry of God and God's refusal to respond in a favorable manner.[103] Ezekiel 14 confronts the people's persistent sin of idolatry (14:6), which is the major reason for God's refusal to allow the elders to approach Yahweh with their inquiries. In the recitation of the salvation history, the new element which condemns Israel in Egypt is idolatry. The emphasis on idolatry, even at such an early stage in Israel's history in Egypt, seems to correspond to the sins of the people in Ezekiel's day. Idolatry, however, is not restricted to any one event, such as Mount Horeb or Baal Peor, and has been a problem from the beginning. Ezekiel's presentation of Israel's sinful history, which does not pre-date Egypt, is the prophet's original contribution to this unusual interpretation of Israel's beginnings.[104] Thus, in Ezekiel's interpretation of the wilderness traditions, the sin of idolatry permeates its entire scope.

The radical representation of the period from the exodus to the entrance into the land goes beyond the information available in early Israelite traditions.[105] The content of 20:1–38, therefore, shows the specific emphases of the prophet Ezekiel. Ezekiel's problems are more than that which is common to the wilderness traditions in the Pentateuch. Zimmerli points out that the normal positive mood of the historical credo, which recites the saving actions of God toward Israel, is replaced by a recitation of the sins of the people.[106] The strong nature of Ezekiel's reprimand indicates a problem of the failure of traditions to secure the people's obedience and faith. Perhaps due to this failure, Ezekiel is justified in radically adapting his message and recitation to his own context; a practice similar to the manner in which Isaiah 48:21 adapts the traditions to the return and restoration of Israel in the homeland.

Ezekiel's use of Israel's past experiences, though radical as they are, presents the kerygma of the wilderness traditions within three basic topics: the relationship between God and the people; the response of the people; and expectations for the future relationship between God and the community.

First, the establishment of the relationship between Yahweh and the community is motivated by the revelation of God to Israel and to the entire world. The confession of faith in God is affirmed through the revelation of God's activity in history.[107] In other words, where there is a profession of faith in God, that kerygmatic expression occurs with historical self-authentication. The purpose of Israel's history, illustrated for example by Ezekiel's adaptation of Israel's historical credo, is to express a knowledge of God, and within that knowledge is the affirmation of the sovereign power of God.[108] The revelation of the knowledge of God, according to Zimmerli, is expressed through the formula of acknowledgment: "know that I am the Lord."[109] This recognition statement usually occurs in association with a statement about God's actions.[110] The theme of the knowledge of God in Ezekiel 20 finds expression in the phrase, or its variation, אֲנִי יְהוָה אֱלֹהֵיכֶם (vv. 5, 7, 9, 12, 19, 20, 26, 38), which is particularly characteristic of the book of Ezekiel.

The role of the theme of the knowledge of God is equally developed in the wilderness traditions of the Tetrateuch, specifically within the exodus and wilderness narratives in the book of Exodus. The recognition formula, "that you know that I am Yahweh," is rooted in Moses traditions older than the Priestly Writer, which appear to be independent of Ezekiel. Zimmerli adds, however, that the present formula in the Moses traditions is based primarily on the Priestly writings, and the linguistic use is related to the subsequent use in Ezekiel.[111] Exodus 6:6–8, which is the first Priestly text to include the recognition formula, contains the recurring terms יָצָא and בּוֹא; and these exodus images appear in the second exodus material of Ezekiel 20:34–35. The recognition formula appears in association with the recitation of the miraculous actions of God. The correspondence and association of the two themes function to teach the community that God acts for the benefit of the people.[112] The implication of such a teaching is that a community that *knows* God does not commit idolatry and does not sin against its God.

The theme of the knowledge of Yahweh is expressed throughout the historical summary of Ezekiel 20:1–38. In 20:5 the election of Israel and Yahweh's self-disclosure are sworn acts that confirm Yahweh's fidelity to the community as their God, confirmed by the statement אֲנִי יְהוָה אֱלֹהֵיכֶם. The sworn statement in 20:5 connects the oath with the revelation of God to the community, and God binds himself to the oath.[113] Even the statutes and ordinances (20:11) support the proclamation that "I am Yahweh." Whatever occurs after Egypt must be understood as an amplification of this statement. The kerygma is, in effect, the knowledge of God emphasized in the statement of recognition, "I am Yahweh." In Exodus 6:6–8 a similar disclosure occurs, which is subsequently confirmed by the events of the deliverance from Egypt. Again in Ezekiel 20:7, though יָדַע does not appear, the recognition formula concludes another sworn statement by Yahweh (20:6a). The context of the confirmation is the promise to deliver them from bondage and to bring them into the land. In 20:7 the first conditional statement occurs in association with the recognition statement. The purification of the community of all idolatry is required, because Yahweh has established a divine relationship with the people.

At this juncture in the discussion of Ezekiel's emphasis on the relationship between the community and God, a summary of the function of the laws seems appropriate. In Ezekiel 20:1–31 the laws function in three ways: the recognition of Yahweh as in the previous discussion; as a leadership element in the guidance theme of the wilderness traditions; and as an element in the rebellion theme.

In Ezekiel 20:12, the recognition formula occurs as a concluding statement, thus establishing the relevance of the provisions of the laws of God and observance of the Sabbath for community life. In this respect, the laws are placed within the wilderness period and in conjunction with the exodus. Both the laws and the requirement to honor the Sabbath are given to confirm the knowledge of God, but with one additional element: the Sabbath is given as a sign that God sanctifies the community through their observance. Coats concludes that since the Sabbath plays a relatively minor role in Ezekiel as a whole, the Sabbath in Ezekiel 20 should be treated as a separate consideration, or an appendix, to the laws and commandments.[114] In respect to the kerygmatic function of laws and the observance of the

Sabbath, their value leads, however, to different conclusions. The observance of the Sabbath in Ezekiel 20 is the sign whereby the nations can recognize the relationship between God and the community. The laws and commandments function to constitute the community as well, by allowing the community to maintain or regain its self-identity and thus enjoy a productive life in community. The Sabbath, for Ezekiel, functions in the same manner as a witness to the nations, just as the exodus once did in the days of old. Observance of God's holy Sabbath contributes to the nations acquiring the knowledge of God.

A second manner in which the laws contribute to the development of God's relationship to the community is their function within the guidance theme (20:6).[115] The Pentateuchal traditions of the wilderness period are reflected in Ezekiel's statements about Yahweh's presence during the wilderness journey ("into a land that I searched out [תּוּר] for them," v. 6b; cf. Deut. 1:19–46) and allusions to the spy episode ("I will not bring [בּוֹא] them into the land," Ezek. 20:15, cf. Num. 13–14). Coats suggests that נָתַתִּי (Ezek. 20:15) can be changed to תַּרְתִּי which would parallel verse 6.[116] The language portraying Yahweh as a spy who searches out the land ahead of the people is similar to the kerygmatic statement in Deuteronomy 1:33.

Even when considering Ezekiel's dependence upon the traditions of the Pentateuch, the leadership of Yahweh theme in Ezekiel 20 is almost exclusively relegated to the function of the laws and commandments of God for the community throughout their history. Israel learns how to live (הָאָדָם וָחַי בָּהֶם v. 11) by faithful observance and implementation of the laws of God. The next generation in 20:18 are warned to not walk (הָלַךְ) or live in the wrong ways of their fathers. By presenting the role of the statutes and ordinances in such a manner, the guidance and leadership of God is presented as rigid and impersonal; compared to the miraculous nature of God's acts of guidance and provisions in the Yahwist's account of the wilderness period. Even the Priestly Writer, who is characteristically more impersonal than the Yahwist, has not separated Yahweh from the people to the extent Ezekiel has. The Priestly Writer in the Tetrateuch presents the guidance and leadership of Yahweh in the context of cult and its leadership, whose function is to provide the people access to their God. For Ezekiel, the laws of God and observance of the Sabbath provide the means whereby people can come to know God.

The second topic in relation to the kerygma of the wilderness traditions in Ezekiel 20:1–38 is the response or actions of the people.

The wilderness period in Ezekiel's short historical survey is not given the distinction as the time when sin, disobedience, death, and judgment destroyed the community of the wilderness. Rather, Ezekiel's shadowy picture of sin encompasses all of Israel's history. Basically, very little is said about the nature of the people, whereas in the Pentateuch the sins and actions of the people are considerable, and such a portrayal reveals the complex nature of the community and the environment of their life in the wilderness. Ezekiel's characterization of Israel is quite simple. The entire history of the community's relationship to God is one of brokenness and apostasy. The major motivating factors that cause the judgment of God are (1) the people's persistent tendency toward idolatry, (2) disobedience to the commandments of God, and (3) the persistent refusal to observe and sanctify the Sabbath.

Considering the truncated manner in which Ezekiel adapts the historical credo in Chapter 20, the kerygmatic appeal is nebulous. The quality of God's relationship to the community appears to be relegated to the sacral and the legal, such as that reflected from the Holiness Code.[117] The nature of the exodus from Egypt, as Zimmerli points out, is normally an expression of divine freely given love for the people.[118] Yet, in Ezekiel that intimate characteristic of God is subsumed by Ezekiel's determination to restore the community's relationship to Yahweh through obedience to the laws of God and honor of the Sabbath.

Through an understanding of Ezekiel's portrayal of Israel's sinful history, the prophet's response to the inquiry of the elders is revealing (20:3, 31). He accuses his contemporaries of being equally sinful as the generations of their ancestors. The audience of Ezekiel had not freed themselves of the rebellious nature of their fathers, which is another way of concluding that no generation learns from the previous, except to follow in their disobedient steps. Due to this crisis in Ezekiel's contemporary setting, the kerygma calls the present generation to return in faithful obedience to God. A major distinction of Ezekiel's presentation of the wilderness traditions, compared to other appropriations of the wilderness traditions, is the absence of positive examples that are utilized to encourage imitation by his audience. In Jeremiah's unusual interpretation of the wilderness traditions, the loyal generation of the wilderness period provides the antithesis to the present rebellious community. In the Pentateuch and the book of Joshua, Caleb and Joshua provide the examples of faithfulness. Ezekiel, on the other hand, recalls none of these individuals from Israel's history. Darr correctly points out that human intercession is not used because the text affords grace solely to God, which is perhaps why Moses is not mentioned in Ezekiel 20.[119]

The call to repentance, implied in the historical recitation, is dependent on the rigid details of the laws, guided by the demands to abolish idolatry, and the strict demands to observe the Sabbath. These three elements provide the norm for life and identity as the people of God. The three elements, one might conclude, correspond to the basic problems existing within the community of Ezekiel, which were apparently placing their survival in jeopardy as a Yahwistic community during the crisis of the exile. The future relationship between Yahweh and the community is also understood in regard to the resolution of these problems.

Klein recognizes the increased emphasis on the laws (20:25–26) as a provision in the judgment upon the community.[120] The contrasting notion is that the provision of the laws and the survival of the community are inseparably linked. In the book of Deuteronomy, for example, the laws provide life for those who obey them, for in so doing the community is "listening" to the words of God and following their God. In Ezekiel the people are given "bad" statutes (לֹא טוֹבִים, 20:25), and as a result, the people cannot live by them successfully (לֹא יִחְיוּ, v. 25). The goodness of God is revealed in the contrast between the life-giving nature of the good laws and the death that bad statutes and ordinances produce. Klein admits that the saying in 20:25–26 is difficult because it presents a harsh picture of God. However, the sovereignty of God, revealed through the honor of God's name, is to be understood when all events and practices come under the power of God in the world and work for the purposes of God. Ezekiel 20 strives for the sanctification of God's reputation, revealed through God's acts of judgment, and all that occurs in the world and throughout history is brought under that sovereignty. God allows, and, in fact, wills that some things occur, in order to maintain God's integrity among the nations of the world.

The theme of God's honor permeates the wilderness traditions of both the Pentateuch and Ezekiel 20. The intercessory passages of Exodus 32, Numbers 14, and Deuteronomy 9 indicate that God acts according to divine integrity regarding God's promises and loyalty to the covenant. In these passages, the actions of God provide an apologetic for God's show of mercy for the rebellious Israelites and God's righteous judgments. In Ezekiel 20 the apologetic is also understood in regard to divine mercy and justice. Ezekiel 20 attributes the events in Israel's past, with specific emphasis on the tragedy of 586 B.C.E., to the will and actions of God. One of the concerns that links Ezekiel to Pentateuchal traditions is the honor of God in the events of the world. God withholds punishment in the wilderness because of the threat of misinterpretation of divine actions by the nations (20:8–9, 13–14, 21–22). Ezekiel's message to his community affirms the divine sovereignty over the events in Israel's history and in her present world.

The kerygma of the wilderness traditions contributes in a third way to Ezekiel 20:1–38 by generating expectations for a future restored relationship between Israel and Yahweh in the land. The primary texts in which the wilderness traditions are used by Ezekiel are 20:33–38. The traditions of Israel's past are reformulated to speak of the future through the images of the new exodus, the new encounter with Yahweh in the wilderness, and the entrance into the land.[121]

The judgment scene in 20:33–38 is the first stage in Ezekiel's scene of the future restoration of Israel. Ezekiel 20:33–38, 39–42, and 43–44 serve as a counterbalance to the three stages in Israel's history recited in 20:1–31.[122] The new exodus in Ezekiel 20:33–38 is not described as a return directly to the promised land.[123] Verses 27–29 are separated from the content which precedes. Since the setting for Ezekiel's oracle is the exile, the return is through the wilderness a second time, with an eventual second entrance into the land. The return to the wilderness is a symbolic antitype to the wilderness of the Egyptian deliverance, where the Israelites are first given the statutes and ordinances.[124]

In Ezekiel 20:36, a return to the period of the first encounter between Israel and Yahweh, where God gives the statutes (חֹק) and ordinances (מִשְׁפָּט), suggests that the laws of God are reinstated for the good (Cf. vv. 25–26). Thus we might conclude that, for Ezekiel, the early period in their history, understood within the context of the wilderness period, is a time when the leadership of God is provided through the statutes and ordinances and intended for the good of the community. Ezekiel idealizes the future relationship between God and the community in terms of effective obedience through their adherence to the demands of God's commandments and statutes. The sanctification of the community can only be accomplished through the laws and the observance of the Sabbath (20:11–12). Because of Israel's repeated rebellion, Yahweh allowed the community to defile itself through laws that were appealing to them but unacceptable to God (vv. 25–26). The unique role of the law is indicated through the repeated terminology (חֹק and מִשְׁפָּט vv. 11, 18), which distinguishes between the laws intended for the good (20:11) and those which became harmful (20:18).[125] Before the people enter the land, they must return to the wilderness to fulfill the original intentions for the community's relationship to God (20:36). Perhaps the only positive aspect found within Ezekiel's harsh treatment of Israel's history is the affirmation of hope for the future relationship between the community and Yahweh that is expressed in sacral and legal terms.

Ezekiel 20:36 appears to be a general statement reflecting the condition and context of the situation to be experienced by the people, once they return to the wilderness from exile. Verses 37–38 expresses, in more detail, what the judgment situation will entail. The difficulties associated with the interpretation of verse 36 indicate the nebulous nature of the statement. Zimmerli suggests that the reference to judgment might reflect a judgment in the nature of the spy narrative in Numbers 14 and expressed in Ezekiel 20:15–16.[126]

Israel's rebellions in the wilderness may be understood as disobedience against the statutes and ordinances of God, which are intended to guide and teach Israel how to live. Thus to return to the wilderness and enter into judgment again is the same as suggesting that the full force of the statutes and ordinances of God will once again be revealed in the community of faith. The righteous judgments of God constitute the measuring rod for those who shall be allowed to enter the land.

Ezekiel's picture of the future entrance into the land is dependent upon his understanding of the outcome of the first wilderness wandering. Both entrances are the same in content: 1) the exodus event is transposed into a deliverance from exile,[127] and 2) those who rebel will not enter the land (Num. 14:21f.) Greenberg summarizes the effect of the parallel between the first and the second exodus,

> Vv. 37f. ––telling how God will make them pass under the rod, enter the obligation of the covenant, and purge them of rebels––related tersely and in fresh terms the future equivalent of events in the wilderness told at length in vv. 11–26.[128]

Thus, Ezekiel calls the people back to obedience with the hope of passing through the "purge" in the wilderness in the future. Likewise, he affirms the role of the statutes and ordinances as a crucial guide for reconstituting Israel after the exile. The kerygmatic appeal must be understood in light of the critical role that the laws of God takes in providing divine guidance for the community while outside the land. So, the call to the people is to obedience to God's laws, which are originally intended for the good of the community. The kerygma affirms the sovereignty and justice of God which the community will ultimately come to know. Eichrodt states the kerygmatic point correctly: "The purgative judgment, despite all its horrors, proves beyond all shadow of doubt that Yahweh stands by his people still and will have his way with them in the end."[129]

THE KERYGMA OF THE WILDERNESS TRADITIONS IN THE LATTER PROPHETS

In Isaiah 48:21 the wilderness traditions call for commitment of faith that finds its expression through dependence upon God. Kerygma in Isaiah 48, and Ezekiel 20, is understood within the expectation of the second exodus. In Isaiah, God will once again protect and provide for the community as they journey through the wilderness. The wilderness for Isaiah is not as narrow a term as used in the Tetrateuch. For the exilic community, the wilderness is much more than the dry arid places of the desert, and, through the use of חָרְבָה, has deeper implications for the community. The adaptation of the wilderness traditions in Isaiah 48:21 is intended to address the crisis associated with the restoration following the exile, which depends upon a response by the community similar to that of the first exodus. Isaiah's second exodus portrays a situation in which the community once again owes its existence solely to divine grace.[130] The wilderness setting describes the experiences confronting the community who returns to the ravaged land of Canaan. The kerygma of 48:21 is therefore not historically restricted, nor is it only futuristic; for the message remains relevant to the present crisis.

For Jeremiah 2, through the use of the wilderness setting, a contrast is created between the ideal beginnings of Israel in the wilderness and the present crisis in the community's relationship to God. Perhaps due to Jeremiah's desire to stress the extraordinary condition of the community's unfaithfulness, the prophet gives an equally unusual picture of Israel's ideal beginnings in the wilderness. A change has occurred within the community of Jeremiah, and the security of the community has come under threat because of their failure to trust in divine guidance. The theme of rebellion in the wilderness is transformed to apply to Jeremiah's community who is guilty of rebellion and apostasy. Jeremiah's view of Israel's early life in the wilderness therefore deviates considerably from the Pentateuchal traditions. The central theme that remains consistent with the Pentateuch is the guidance of Yahweh in the wilderness. Apart from this element, Jeremiah, like Hosea, stands outside the normal presentations of the wilderness traditions.

Jeremiah 31:2–6, like Jeremiah 2, is difficult to align with the wilderness traditions of the Pentateuch. The kerygma of the text should be understood in association with the continuing relationship of the community to its God. Jeremiah 2 stresses the failure of relationship because of the community's unfaithfulness, but Jeremiah 31 addresses the problem of relationship from a different perspective. The kerygma of Jeremiah 2 appeals for a return to a relationship grounded in Israel's beginnings. Jeremiah 31 affirms a continuing relationship that appears to be in doubt. In both contexts, the wilderness period is that period in which the community enjoyed divine favor, and God committed himself to the community through his steadfast love. Implied in the message of Jeremiah 31:2–6 is the restoration of Israel in the Northern country and the veneration of Zion as the abode of God. The future response of the community to divine initiative might be understood in the call of 31:6 for the people to go to Zion to worship God.

Ezekiel 20 represents the most extensive appropriation of the wilderness traditions in the Latter Prophets. Hanson observes that the future community of faith in Ezekiel is a purified community, guided by the statutes and ordinances, through whom the glory of God is revealed.[131] Likewise, individual responsibility for sin impinges upon the quality of community life. The glory of God can only return to the community when the community's sanctity is restored.[132] Yahweh had sanctified Israel in the wilderness through the giving of the statutes, ordinances, and the Sabbath as a sign of that sanctification (v. 12). A return to the wilderness also suggests a refocus upon and the reestablishment of this aspect in community life.

Ezekiel's view of Israel's history was not the "good old days," as might be implied in Jeremiah's recollections.[133] Whether in the land of Egypt or in the land of Canaan, the problem of Israel's rebellious nature persists. The confession of the saving acts of God in Ezekiel 20 is overshadowed by Ezekiel's concern for proper life in the community of faith. Ezekiel's message to the community in exile was to proclaim an unconditional "No!" to all hopes of restoration of the former life in Jerusalem.[134] The execution of God's judgment upon Israel, as Zimmerli suggests, meant the end of the old order of life as the Israelites knew it to be prior to 586 B.C.E. The harshness of the judgment matches Ezekiel's harsh interpretation of Israel's history. Since there is no possibility of returning to any state of existence prior to the exile, then, Ezekiel does not provide a model to which they could return. For Ezekiel, the model for community life is entirely futuristic. Understood as such, Ezekiel differs from Hosea, Isaiah 40–55, and Jeremiah, who prophesied hope of a restoration deeply seated in the memory of Israel's past. For Ezekiel, the corruption of Israel is rooted in Israel's past, a past that cannot be restored.[135]

Coats interprets the message in 20:23 as being directed to the community in exile. He writes, "Israel in exile is just as rebellious as Israel in the wilderness. The judgment then holds the exile generation responsible for its own rebellion."[136] The recitation of the events of the wilderness traditions responds to the claim that the fathers in the land caused the present situation for the people, and, therefore, the exilic community cannot control their fate. Fishbane proposes that the deferred judgment of exile (20:23) caused the succeeding generations to live under the curse of their fathers' sins.[137] The exilic community perhaps believed that their relationship to God was an indirect relationship because they were being punished for the sins of their fathers before them.[138] Israel's experience of the wilderness, on the other hand, addresses the problem of sin by establishing its origin at the beginning in the wilderness, where the problem has remained a thorn in their lives since Egypt. For Ezekiel, the giving of the statutes in the wilderness is a compelling act creating responsibility to God (2:11).[139] In effect, the wilderness traditions provide the setting for the claim to individual responsibility: each generation is called to obedience and faith.

In essence, the wilderness traditions have relinquished some of their characteristic role as the primary period depicting the evils of the community. To be sure, no period in Israel's history escapes the charges of sin and idolatry. The future return to the wilderness (20:33–38) testifies to the claim that each person is judged according to one's own walk (הָלַךְ) in life. In the gathering of the people from exile, they shall remember their evil ways (דֶּרֶךְ vv. 43–44). Rebels will be condemned to the wilderness and not allowed to enter the land. Those who rebel against God will not avoid the experience of the wilderness. The wilderness traditions also come full circle to embrace the theology of Numbers 13–14: only the faithful enter the land and those who rebel are doomed to the wilderness to die. In this respect, Ezekiel remains in the mainstream of Pentateuchal theology, though he transforms the details for his own situation.

In each text discussed from the Latter Prophets, the wilderness traditions contribute to the creation of an image of the restoration; whether pictured as a second exodus (Isa. 48:21; Ezek. 20:33–38), the revival of an exilic people (Jer. 31:4–5), or an appeal for the return of a disobedient nation (Jer. 2). Each writer utilized the wilderness traditions as an antithesis to the community's present crisis. When the beginnings of Israel are remembered in a positive light, the recollections contrast the sinfulness of the prophet's contemporary society (Jer. 2). However, the rebellious and sinful experiences of the wilderness generation can also be placed in parallel to the present generation's actions, whereby the kerygma makes an appeal for corrective actions by the community (Ezek. 20). The primary consistent theme that occurs in each recollection of the wilderness traditions is God's gracious acts of love toward the people in the past, present, and the future.

Notes

[1]James Luther Mays, *Hosea* (Philadelphia: The Westminster Press, 1969), p. 175. Hosea describes Israel's relationship to God through the language of covenant (אֲנִי יְדַעְתִּיךָ בַּמִּדְבָּר, 13:5a); and the wilderness provides the setting for the beginning of that relationship. Cf. Jeremiah 2; 31:2–6.

[2]Aage Bentzen, *Introduction to the Old Testament*, 5th ed. (Copenhagen: G. E. C. Gad Publisher, 1959), p. 82; John Gray, *Joshua, Judges and Ruth*, The Century Bible (London: Thomas Nelson and Sons, Ltd., 1967), p. 16.

[3]John Bright, "Joshua," *The Interpreter's Bible*, vol. 2 (Nashville: Abingdon Press, 1962), pp. 541–673.

[4]Martin Noth, *The Deuteronomistic History* (Sheffield: JSOT Press, 1981), pp. 4–11.

[5]Robert G. Boling, *Joshua*, The Anchor Bible (Garden City: Doubleday & Company, Inc., 1982), p. 56.

[6]Gordon J. Wenham, "The Deuteronomic Theology of the Book of Joshua," *Journal of Biblical Literature*, 90 (1971), 140–148.

[7]Bright, "Joshua," p. 548.

[8]Ibid., p. 544.

[9]George W. Coats, "An Exposition for the Conquest Theme," *The Catholic Biblical Quarterly*, 47 (1985), 47–54, and his "The Book of Joshua: Heroic Saga or Conquest Theme," *Journal for the Study of the Old Testament*, 38 (1987), 15–32. Leonard L. Thompson, "The Jordan Crossing: *Ṣidqot* Yahweh and Word Building," *Journal of Biblical Literature*, 100 (1981), 343–358.

[10]Georg Fohrer, *Introduction to the Old Testament*, trans. David E. Green (Nashville: Abingdon Press, 1968), p. 200. According to Fohrer Joshua 5:2–9 and 5:13–15 belong to the Yahwist with verses 4–7 from a Deuteronomistic recension. Bright, "Joshua," p. 546, assigns Joshua 5:10–12 to a Priestly gloss. Also, Boling, *Joshua*, p. 58, suggests the significance of the cessation of the manna is a Priestly concern.

[11]Porter, "The Background of Joshua III–V," p. 17.

[12]George W. Coats, "The Book of Joshua," p. 19. Circumcision functions as a preparation for the Passover observance (Exod. 12:43–49). See J. Alberto Soggin, *Joshua*, The Old Testament Library, trans. R. A. Wilson (Philadelphia: Westminster Press, 1972), p. 74.

[13]Margnus Ottosson, "Tradition and History, with Emphasis on the Composition of the Book of Joshua," in *The Production of Time: Tradition History in Old Testament Scholarship*, ed. Knud Jeppesen and Benedikt Otzen (Sheffield: The Almond Press, 1984), pp. 81–106.

[14]John Gray, *Joshua, Judges and Ruth*, The Century Bible (London: Thomas Nelson and Sons, Ltd., 1967), p. 70.

[15]Coats, "An Exposition for the Conquest Theme," p. 51.

[16]Boling, *Joshua*, p. 190.

[17]Gray, *Joshua, Judges and Ruth*, p. 70.

[18]Soggin, *Joshua*, p. 72.

[19]See J. R. Porter, "The Background of Joshua III–V," *Svensk Exegetisk Årsbok*, 36 (1971), 5–23, for a discussion of the various tradition-historical interpretations of Joshua 3–5 from the pre-Israelite status of the sanctuary at Gilgal to its cultic nature in their present form. Frank M. Cross, *Canaanite Myth and Hebrew Epic: Essays in the History of the Religion of Israel* (Cambridge: Harvard University Press, 1973), p. 103, for example, proposes that Joshua 3–5 illustrates the use of the "ritual Conquest" as a movement in the cultus. The features of the festival are 1) the sanctification of the people for holy war, 2) the Ark of the Covenant is carried in solemn procession to the sanctuary at Gilgal, 3) the Jordan plays the role of the Red Sea with Gilgal as the battle camp of the Conquest, 4) the twelve stones are set up at Gilgal as a memorial of the twelve tribes united in the festival.

[20]See Dennis T. Olson, *The Death of the Old and the Birth of the New*, (Chico: Scholars Press, 1985).

[21]Thompson, "The Jordan Crossing," p. 355.

[22]Bright, "Joshua," p. 548.

[23]J. Maxwell Miller and Gene M. Tucker, *The Book of Joshua* (Cambridge: Cambridge University Press, 1974), p. 117.

[24]R. F. Johnson, "Caleb," *The Interpreter's Dictionary of the Bible*, vol. 1, ed. George A. Buttrick (Nashville: Abingdon Press, 1962), pp. 482–483.

[25]A. Graeme Auld, *Joshua, Moses and the Land* (Edinburgh: T. & T. Clark, 1980), p. 89.

[26]Walter Beltz, *Die Kaleb-Traditionen im Alten Testament*, Beiträge zur Wissenschaft vom Alten und Neuen Testament, fünfte Folge, vol. 98 (Stuttgart: Verlag W. Kohlhammer, 1974). pp. 93–101.

[27]James Flanagan, "History, Religion, and Ideology: The Caleb Tradition," *Horizons*, 3 (1976), 175–185.

[28]S. R. Driver, *An Introduction to the Literature of the Old Testament* (New York: Meridian Books, 1956), p. 109, assigns Joshua 14:6–15 to JE.

[29]Flanagan, "History, Religion, and Ideology," p. 180.

[30]Dennis J. McCarthy, "Some Holy War Vocabulary in Joshua 2," *The Catholic Biblical Quarterly*, 33 (1971), 228–230, observes that מוּג and מָסַס are vocabulary common to holy war. The absence of the term in Numbers 13–14 does not dismiss the imagery since מָסַס appears in Deuteronomy 1:28. Boling, *Joshua*, p. 357, points out that הִמְסִיו is pointed in Aramaic (*GKC*, p. 215).

[31]Coats, "The Book of Joshua," p. 17.

[32]George W. Coats, "The Traditio-Historical Character of the Reed Sea Motif," *Vetus Testamentum*, 17 (1967), 253-265.

[33]Brevard S. Childs, "A Traditio-Historical Study of the Reed Sea Tradition," *Vetus Testamentum*, 20 (1980), 406-418.

[34]S. David Sterling, "Joshua 24 Re-Examined," in *Hebrew Union College Annual*, 58 (1987), 119-136.

[35]Sterling, "Joshua 24 Re-Examined," p. 130. Gerhard von Rad, *Old Testament Theology*, vol. 1, trans. D. M. G. Stalker (San Francisco: Harper & Row, Publishers, 1962), p. 281, briefly suggests that 24:7b reflects the guidance or leading theme.

[36]*BDB*, p. 1036. Robert G. Bratcher and Barclay M. Newman, *The Translator's Handbook on the Book of Joshua* (New York: United Bible Societies, 1983), p. 309, translate Joshua 24:17b "He kept us safe wherever we went among all the nations through which we passed." The translation excludes the wilderness traditions as part of the דֶּרֶךְ and places Israel directly in the lands of the nations. The "protection" (שָׁמַר) would then refer to Israel's encounters with the nations east of the Jordan. The conjunction (וּבְכֹל) is important to separate the two periods, otherwise, they would be correct to imply that the wilderness period is overlooked in 24:17.

[37]Bratcher and Newman, *The Translator's Handbook on the Book of Joshua*, p. 30, place 24:7b with verse 8, indicating that the events on the east side of the Jordan should be understood in relation to Israel's departure from the wilderness period.

[38]J. Van Seters, "Joshua 24 and the Problem of Tradition in the Old Testament," in *In the Shelter of Elyon: Essays on Ancient Palestinian Life and Literature*, ed. W. Boyd Barrick and John R. Spencer (Sheffield: JSOT Press, 1984), pp. 139-158.

[39]Brevard S. Childs, *Introduction to the Old Testament as Scripture* (Philadelphia: Fortress Press, 1979), p. 252.

[40]Hans Wilhelm Hertzberg, *I & II Samuel: A Commentary*, trans. J. S. Bowden (Philadelphia: Westminster Press, 1964), p. 46.

[41]Noth, *A History of Pentateuchal Traditions*, p. 121.

[42]Jesús Asurmendi, "En Torno a la Serpiente de Bronce," *Estudios Biblicos* 46 (1988), 283–294.

[43]Karen Randolph Joines, "The Bronze Serpent in the Israelite Cult," *Journal of Biblical Literature* 87 (1968), 245–256.

[44]Wenham, "The Deuteronomic Theology of the Book of Joshua," p. 148.

[45]Boling, *Joshua*, p. 51.

[46]John D. W. Watts, *Isaiah 34-66*, Word Biblical Commentary (Waco: Word Books, Publisher, 1987), p. 147.

[47]John Skinner, *Isaiah Chapters XL-LXVI* (Cambridge: Cambridge University Press, 1929), p. 87.

[48]R. N. Whybray, *Isaiah 40-66*, The New Century Bible (London: Oliphants, 1975), p. 126.

[49]Anna Katheryn Pfisterer Darr, "Breaking through the Wilderness: References to the Desert in Exilic Prophecy" (Ph.D. dissertation, Vanderbilt University, 1984), p. 356.

[50]John L. McKenzie, *Second Isaiah*, The Anchor Bible (New York: Doubleday & Company, Publisher, 1968), p. 96.

[51]Darr, "Breaking through the Wilderness," p. 357.

[52]Ibid., p. 355. Darr at first proposes that, since the majority of scholars claim that verses 20–21 are distinct form-critically and bear little relationship with the balance of the chapter, she is justified in focusing only on verse 21 without considering the rest; but, then, she concludes that the text is crucial for the message of Isaiah 40–55.

[53]Ibid., p. 353.

[54]Shermaryahu Talmon, "Wilderness," *The Interpreter's Dictionary of the Bible*, suppl. vol. ed. George A. Buttrick (Nashville: Abingdon Press, 1962), pp. 946–948, confirms the dominant use of the two terms.

[55]C. R. North, "The 'Former Things' and the 'New Things' in Deutero-Isaiah," in *Studies in Old Testament Prophecy*, ed. H. H. Rowley (Edinburgh: T. T. Clark, 1950), pp. 111–126.

[56]Aage Bentzen, "On the Ideas of 'the old' and 'the new' in Deutero-Isaiah," *Studia Theologica*, 1 (1948), 183–188, suggests the 'new' is a new cult practice which is the new exodus. He bases this change on the interpretation of זָכַר, which can mean, in addition to the basic remembering of past traditions, to remember them in the creative process of the cult.

[57]Walther Zimmerli, "Prophetic Proclamation and Reinterpretation," in *Tradition and Theology in the Old Testament*, ed. Douglas A. Knight (Philadelphia: Fortress Press, 1977), pp. 69–100.

[58]Ulrich E. Simon, *A Theology of Salvation* (London: SPCK, 1953), p. 162.

[59]Robert P. Carroll, *The Book of Jeremiah*, The Old Testament Library (Philadelphia: Westminster Press, 1986), p. 113.

[60]J. A. Thompson, *The Book of Jeremiah* (Grand Rapids: Wm. B. Eerdmans Publishing Company, 1980), p. 161.

[61]John Bright, *Jeremiah*, The Anchor Bible (Garden City: Doubleday & Company, 1984), p. 9.

[62]Ernest W. Nicholson, *Jeremiah: Chapters 1-25* (London: Cambridge University Press, 1973), p. 28.

[63]Herbert B. Huffmon, "The Covenant Lawsuit in the Prophets," *Journal of Biblical Literature*, 78 (1959), 285–295.

[64]Bright, *Jeremiah*, p. 17.

[65]Ibid., p. 123.

[66]William McKane, *A Critical and Exegetical Commentary on Jeremiah*, Vol. 1, I–XXV, The International Critical Commentary (Edinburgh: T. & T. Clark, 1986), p. 33.

[67]Carroll, *The Book of Jeremiah*, p. 120.

[68]Shermaryahu Talmon, "The 'Desert Motif' in the Bible and in Qumran Literature," in *Biblical Motif: Origins and Transformations*, ed. Alexander Altmann (Cambridge: Harvard University Press, 1966), pp. 31–63.

[69]Michael V. Fox, "Jeremiah 2:2 and the 'Desert Ideal,'" *The Catholic Biblical Quarterly*, 35 (1973), 441–450.

[70]Douglas Rawlinson Jones, *Jeremiah* (Grand Rapids: William B. Eerdmans Publishing Company, 1992), p. 83.

[71]Ibid., p. 446.

[72]F. J. Helfmeyer, הָלַךְ, *Theological Dictionary of the Old Testament*, vol. 3, ed. G. Johannes Botterweck and Helmer Ringgren, trans. John T. Willis, Geoffrey W. Bromiley, and David E. Green (Grand Rapids: Wm. B. Eerdmans Publishing Company, 1978), pp. 388–403. Von Rad, *Old Testament Theology*, vol. 1, p. 56,

identifies the motif in 1 Kings 19:19–21 where Elisha is recognized as the disciple who follows after Elijah.

[73]Carroll, *The Book of Jeremiah*, p. 121.

[74]McKane, *Jeremiah*, vol. 1, p. 28.

[75]Michael DeRoche, "Jeremiah 2:2–3 and Israel's Love for God during the Wilderness Wanderings," *The Catholic Biblical Quarterly*, 45 (1983), 364–376.

[76]Ibid., p. 368. DeRoche identifies הָלַךְ in Jeremiah 2 to refer to either a "following" in the Qal stem with Israel as the subject or in the Hiphil with God as the subject.

[77]Klaus Koch, דֶּרֶךְ, *Theological Dictionary of the Old Testament*, vol. 3, ed. G. Johannes Botterweck and Helmer Ringgren, trans. John T. Willis, Geoffrey W. Bromiley, and David E. Green (Grand Rapids: Wm. B. Eerdmans Publishing Company, 1978), pp. 270–292.

[78]Walter Brueggemann, *To Pluck Up, To Tear Down: A Commentary on Jeremiah 1-25* (Grand Rapids: Wm. B. Eerdmans, 1988), p. 35. Also, Prescott H. Williams, "The Fatal and Foolish Exchange: Living Water for 'Nothings': A Study of Jeremiah 2:4–13," *Austin Seminary Bulletin: Faculty Edition*, 81 (1965), 22–24.

[79]R. E. Clements, *Prophecy and Covenant* (London: SCM Press, Ltd., 1965), p. 51; Williams, "The Fatal and Foolish Exchange," p. 23.

[80]Clements, *Prophecy and Covenant*, p. 121.

[81]Ronald E. Clements, *Old Testament Theology: A Fresh Approach* (London: Marshall, Morgan & Scott, 1978), p. 96.

[82]Brueggemann, *To Pluck Up, To Tear Down*, p. 33.

[83]DeRoche, "Jeremiah 2:2–3 and Israel's love for God," p. 375.

[84]Childs, *Introduction to the Old Testament as Scripture*, p. 351.

[85]Bright, *Jeremiah*, p. 284.

[86]John Skinner, *Prophecy and Religion: Studies in the Life of Jeremiah* (Cambridge: Cambridge University Press, 1963), p. 304.

[87]Bright, *Jeremiah*, p. 273.

[88]Barbara A. Bozak, *Life 'Anew': A Literary-Theological Study of Jer. 30-31* (Rome: Editrice Pontificio Istituto Biblico, 1991), pp. 72–73.

[89]John A. Thompson, *The Book of Jeremiah* (Grand Rapids: Wm. B. Eerdmans Publishing Co., 1980), p. 566.

[90]Bozak, *Life 'Anew'*, p. 77.

[91]Jones, *Jeremiah*, p. 384.

[92]William L. Holladay, *Jeremiah 2* (Minneapolis: Fortress Press, 1989), p. 181.

[93]Holladay, *Jeremiah 2*, p. 181.

[94]Walter Brueggemann, *To Build and To Plant: A Commentary on Jeremiah 26—52* (Grand Rapids: Wm. B. Eerdmans Publishing Co.), p. 59.

[95]Fohrer, *Introduction to the Old Testament*, p. 412.

[96]Johan Lust, "Ez., XX, 4–26 Une paradie de l'histoire religieuse d'Israel," *Ephemerides Theologicae Lovanienses*, 43 (1967), 488–527, slightly rearranges Ezekiel 20:5–26 into four strophes (5–9, 10–14, 15–22, 23–26), each strophe marked by an oath (נָשָׂאתִי אֶת־יָדִי). The oath indicates an action depicting the power of God. Also, see Johan Lust, "'Gathering and Return' in Jeremiah and Ezekiel," in *Le Livre de Jérémie: Le prophète et son milieu, les oracles et leur transmission*, ed. P. M. Bogaert (Uitgeverij Peeters: Leuven University Press, 1981), pp. 119–142, and *Traditie, Redactie en Kerygma Bij Ezechiel* (Brussel: Paleis der Academiën, 1969), pp. 95–112.

[97]Fohrer, *Introduction to the Old Testament*, p. 416.

[98]Robert H. Pfeiffer, *Introduction to the Old Testament* (New York: Harper & Brothers Publishers, 1941), p. 543.

[99]G. A. Cooke, *The Book of Ezekiel*, The International Critical Commentary (Edinburgh: T. & T. Clark, 1936), p. xxix.

[100]Pfeiffer, *Introduction to the Old Testament*, p. 543.

[101]Walther Zimmerli, "The Message of the Prophet Ezekiel," *Interpretation*, 23 (1969), p. 145.

[102]Walther Eichrodt, *Ezekiel: A Commentary* (Philadelphia: Westminster Press, 1970), p. 280

[103]Walther Zimmerli, *Ezekiel 1*, ed. Frank M. Cross, Klaus Baltzer, and Leonard J. Greenspoon, trans. Ronald E. Clements, Hermeneia (Philadelphia: Fortress Press, 1979), p. 404.

[104]Pfeiffer, *Introduction to the Old Testament*, p. 545.

[105]Zimmerli, *Ezekiel 1*, p. 405.

[106]Ibid., p. 407.

[107]Rolf Rendtorff, "The Concept of Revelation in Ancient Israel," in *Revelation as History*, ed. Wolfhart Pannenberg (New York: Macmillan Company, 1968), pp. 25–53.

[108]Ibid., p. 43.

[109]Walther Zimmerli, "Knowledge of God According to the Book of Ezekiel," trans. Douglas W. Stott, in *I am Yahweh*, by Walther Zimmerli, ed. Walter Brueggemann (Atlanta: John Knox Press, 1982), pp. 29–98.

[110]G. Johannes Botterweck, יָדַע, *Theological Dictionary of the Old Testament*, vol. 5, trans. David E. Green, ed. G. Johannes Botterweck and Helmer Ringgren (Grand Rapids: Wm. B. Eerdmans Publishing Company, 1986), pp. 448–481.

[111]Zimmerli, "The Knowledge of God According to the Book of Ezekiel," p. 42, works on the assumption that the Priestly writings were written in the post-exilic period.

[112]Ibid., p. 44.

[113]Walther Zimmerli, "I Am Yahweh," trans. Douglas W. Stott, in *I Am Yahweh*, by Walther Zimmerli, ed. Walter Brueggemann (Atlanta: John Knox Press, 1982), pp. 1–28.

[114]George W. Coats, *Rebellion in the Wilderness* (Nashville: Abingdon Press, 1968), p. 235.

[115]Zimmerli, "I Am Yahweh," p. 11.

[116]Coats, *Rebellion in the Wilderness*, p. 236. *BHS* points out that other manuscripts insert לָהֶם to read the same as verse 6.

[117]Pfeiffer, *Introduction to the Old Testament*, p. 547, concludes that Ezekiel's ethical code closely resembles the Holiness Code. As a rule Ezekiel did not arrive at his indictment drawing from personal experiences but from reading and meditation. Further, 20:23 (זָרָה, a favorite term for Ezekiel, 5:10, 12; 6:5; 22:15; 29:12) may reflect Ezekiel's understanding of Leviticus 26:33. However, see Deuteronomy 4:27 and 28:64 (פוּץ). From a redactional standpoint, 20:23 points to 20:32f.

[118]Zimmerli, *Ezekiel 1*, p. 410.

[119]Darr, "Breaking through the Wilderness," p. 180.

[120]Ralph W. Klein, *Ezekiel: The Prophet and His Message* (Columbia: University of South Carolina Press, 1988), p. 77.

[121]Zimmerli, "Prophetic Proclamation and Reinterpretation," p. 91.

[122]Adrian Graffy, *A Prophet Confronts His People: The Disputation Speech in the Prophets* (Rome: Biblical Institute Press, 1984), p. 72.

[123]Lust, "'Gathering and Return' in Jeremiah and Ezekiel," pp. 119–142, states that verses 27–29 were later additions provided to reconcile Ezekiel's survey that placed Israel outside the land when sent into exile. Cf. also Zimmerli, *Ezekiel 1*, p. 404.

[124]Graffy, *A Prophet Confronts His People*, p. 70.

[125]Ibid., p. 411. Zimmerli identifies the distinction in the change from the feminine חֻקּוֹתַי in verse 11 to the masculine בְּחוּקֵּי in verse 18.

[126]Ibid., p. 416.

[127]The basis of this assessment is the similar language in 20:33–35 to 20:6 (יָצָא), Exod. 3:10–11; 6:13, also cf. Isa. 48:20.

[128] Moshe Greenberg, *Ezekiel 1-20* (Garden City: Doubleday & Company, 1983), p. 379.

[129]Eichrodt, *Ezekiel*, p. 281.

[130]Paul D. Hanson, *The People Called: The Growth of Community in the Bible* (San Francisco: Harper & Row, Publishers, 1986), p. 237.

[131]Ibid., p. 217.

[132]Ibid., p. 222.

[133]Klein, *Israel in Exile*, p. 79.

[134]Zimmerli, "The Message of the Prophet Ezekiel," p. 142.

[135]Ibid., p. 143.

[136]Coats, *Rebellion in the Wilderness*, p. 237.

[137]Michael Fishbane, "Sin and Judgment in the Prophecies of Ezekiel," *Interpretation*, 38 (1984), 131–150.

[138]James Luther Mays, *Ezekiel, Second Isaiah* (Philadelphia: Fortress Press, 1978), p. 50.

[139]Darr, "Breaking through the Wilderness," p. 177.

Chapter Five

The Wilderness Traditions in the Writings

The use of the wilderness traditions in the Writings occurs predominantly in the Psalms. Unlike the Prophets, with the exception of Ezekiel, when the wilderness traditions are recited in the Writings, they appear in a rather comprehensive manner, and in relation to other events in Israel's sacred history. Psalm 95 is not very comprehensive, though important themes are emphasized that are similar to the more detailed recitations. Some of the other references to the wilderness period, such as Psalm 136:16, are extremely brief and highly focused on some aspect of the wilderness traditions. Psalm 136, for example, recalls the wilderness experience (136:16) within a series of experiences that are recited to express thanksgiving for the great חֶסֶד of God. I Chronicles 21:29 refers to Moses and the tabernacle in the wilderness, and II Chronicles 24:9, where Moses is said to have imposed a tax upon the community in the wilderness, uses the wilderness traditions, of course, to add credence to the taxation imposed by King Joash.

Literary Analysis of the Wilderness Traditions in the Writings

The following discussions focus upon the more comprehensive and prominent occurrences of the wilderness traditions in the Writings. Psalms 78, 95, 105, 106, and Nehemiah 9 constitute the most extensive applications of the wilderness traditions in the Writings, and will therefore govern the analysis of the Writings.

Psalm 78

Psalm 78 is classified traditionally as a psalm of praise; that is, a descriptive hymn that praises the Lord of history.[1] The Psalm is part of the Psalms of Asaph (Pss. 50, 73–83), contained within the larger collection of the Elohist Psalter (Pss. 42–83).[2] Mowinckel concludes that Psalm 78, as well as Psalms 105 and 106, is non-cultic.[3] Fohrer supports this distinction, and assigns the Psalm the role as a psalm of instruction within the community, exhibiting the form similar to wisdom and didactic poetry.[4] The Psalm is divided into two sections (1–8 and 9–72) with section 2 divided further into two recitals (vv. 9–64, the rejection of Israel, and 65–72, the election of Zion and David).[5] The structure of the Psalm can be outlined as follows, with particular emphasis on the wilderness period:

- 1–8 Confession and call for commitment
- 9–11 The sins of Ephraim
- 12–55 Historical recitation
  - 12–13 The fathers in Egypt and the Reed Sea
  - 14–42 The fathers in the wilderness
    - 14–16 The good deeds of God
    - 17–20 The rebellion of the fathers
    - 21–33 The wrath of Yahweh
    - 34–37 The deceptions of the fathers
    - 38–39 The compassion of Yahweh
    - 40–42 The rebellions of the fathers
  - 43–55 The fathers in Egypt and the Reed Sea
  - 43–51 The plague traditions
  - 52–53 The Reed Sea (Guidance theme, v. 52)
  - 54–55 The conquest
- 56–64 Ephraim in the land
- 65–67 The rejection of Ephraim
- 68–72 The election of Zion and David

The purpose of the Psalm is stated in the introduction (78:1–8) by revealing riddles from old that describe the irrational quality of history.[6] The concern expressed, according to Weiser, is the encouragement of future generations to remember and not forget God's nature and will (v. 5) and the commandments (v. 7), which is the human tendency. The knowledge of God and reliance upon the law constitute the living force for the people.[7] Psalm 78:5 establishes a link between the laws and commandments or, in broad terms, the ancient traditions in Torah and the perpetuation of Israelite heritage. The introduction teaches that Israel can come to know Yahweh in two ways: the laws and the historical confessions of the actions of God.[8]

The wilderness traditions appear in the historical section contained in verses 12–55. The pivotal section is verses 38–39, which affirms the mercy of God (רַחוּם) as the reason that God did not destroy Israel in the wilderness (see. Neh. 9:17).[9] The mercy and forgiveness of God in verses 38–39, which are motifs characteristic of the wilderness period, are presented in contrast to the tragedy of Shiloh (vv. 59–64). A new recital begins in verse 40 by restating the rebellion motif. The account of God's saving history is told from the focal point of the wilderness period (vv. 40–42). The exodus traditions are represented by the plague traditions (vv. 43–51), which are used to illustrate the good deeds of Yahweh performed for the sake of Israel. The guidance theme in Psalm 78 is the common element that unites the exodus and the wilderness traditions (v. 14). The guidance theme employs the traditional term נָחָה "he leads," (see vv. 52–53) as well as reference to the cloud and fire (Exod. 13:21–22). The guidance theme appears again in verses 52–53. Nasuti points out that, in the Psalms of Asaph, the term נָסַע (v. 52), occurring in the Hiphil, only appears with God as the subject (Ps. 80:9).[10] In other passages, such as Exodus 15:22 Moses is the one who leads. However, with the exclusion of Moses in the recitation, the guidance theme stresses the community's dependence on God.

The purpose of the historical review (vv. 9–72) is to show how God's grace is ever present with Israel, but eventually divine grace is turned away from the original bearer of God's promises. The reference to the Ephraimites is inserted within the historical review to speak directly to the sinful and disobedient ways of the Northern Kingdom. The Southern Kingdom of Judah (Zion and David) is chosen, instead, to carry on the redemptive work of God (vv. 68–72).[11] The Psalm, then, draws a polemic against the tribes of Joseph (Ephraim, v. 9) in favor of Judah. Coats finds the polemic to imply that "only in Zion could the legitimate worship of God be found and only in Judah (or David) could the rightful heir to his election be seen."[12] He further concludes that the polemic in verses 67–72 gives rise to the murmuring tradition in the wilderness traditions of the Tetrateuch.[13]

The Psalm stresses the importance of memory in regard to the survival of the ancient traditions and the perseverance of faith in the community. Psalm 78 and Psalm 106, along with Nehemiah 9:6–38, have a common emphasis on the remembrance of the historical confession of God's saving acts (cf. Deut. 9:7).[14] Nehemiah 9, for example, portrays a fast with a public ceremony of confession, in which the ancient historical traditions are recited. The stimulation of memory functions as a prompt for change in the community. Understood in this manner, the psalmist does not simply wish to recall events from Israel's distant past for history's sake, but to motivate the community toward new directions.[15] Psalm 78 is one of the most distinctive texts where change is explicit in its message. The wilderness traditions assist the function through the recollection of the rebellions of Israel, which are used to support the choice of David as the new bearer of the covenant, since Ephraim has been rejected.[16] The community is encouraged to remember, and not forget, the past as the foundation for their new covenant loyalty.[17]

Psalm 78 is characteristically a theodicy, in which the psalmist tries to defend the actions of God as justified (also Ezek. 20).[18] Because Psalm 78 is a didactic hymn, its material is drawn from the history of Israel. The purpose of the didactic hymn, according to Mowinckel, is to testify to the faithfulness of Yahweh to the community. Likewise, the Psalm stresses the failure of the people to remain loyal to God, so illustrated by Israel's breaking of the covenant. The disaster that has come upon the community in the North is therefore understood as justified punishment from God.

As a didactic hymn, Psalm 78 also provides the occasion for the confession of sin or a prayer for restoration by the community. The occasion for confession is also common to other Psalms such as the combination of Psalm 105 with Psalm 106.[19] The recitation of the historical acts of God provides the foundation for the indictment and punishment of Israel for her sins against God.[20] In Psalm 78 the actions of God are achieved through an enemy of Israel (Also Deut. 32; Ps. 106; Neh. 9), and the defeat of Israel appears to be the reason for the composition of the Psalm. According to this interpretation, the Psalm may function in part as a national confessional.

In addition to the didactic function, the Psalm can be a liturgical celebration of God's merciful choice of Zion and David.[21] The new choice of Zion permits the continuation of the worship of Yahweh, once practiced at Shiloh. The celebration of the exodus, wilderness, and conquest traditions are now united with the new religious traditions of Davidic Zion. Clifford adds that the Psalm warns against continued efforts to worship at Shiloh, because God has rejected Shiloh as a legitimate place and replaced it with the central sanctuary at Jerusalem.[22] The rationale is that further loyalty to the old location will be understood as an act of rebellion against Yahweh's purpose that has as its goal the election of David and Jerusalem. In essence, the ancient traditions of God's relationship with the community of faith are now appropriated through Judah.

In regard to the role of the wilderness traditions, Psalm 78:32 illustrates the theme of God's guiding presence in the wilderness. In spite of all that God has done for the people, they persistently fail to believe. The psalmist recalls that God provided water miraculously as a compassionate act. The water miracles (vv. 15–16), like the traditions of Massah-Meribah in the Tetrateuch, retain a positive mood, while the manna and quails depict an incident of rebellion (vv. 17–31). The two events represent the extreme contrast between the gracious leadership of Yahweh, illustrated through the miraculous provision of water from the rock (vv. 13–16), and the ungratefulness of the people (vv. 17–20), illustrated by the craving for food (v. 30). The probing statement in verses 20–21 calls upon the goodness of God's actions in the past to force God to act again. The fact that the question calls upon the goodness of God, intended to create a sympathetic response to their present needs, indicates that the water miracles represented the goodness of the wilderness experience.[23]

The wilderness traditions in the Tetrateuch are separated basically into two periods: one reflecting the period from Egypt to Sinai, to include the exodus from Egypt; and the other more complex period in the book of Numbers, characterized by divine response to the murmuring of the people through acts of judgment. The Sinai narratives (Exod. 19:1–Num. 10:11) separate the two periods, but in the recitation of the wilderness traditions in Psalm 78, the Sinai experience is not mentioned, though the events at Sinai may be implied in association with the provision of the laws in the introduction (v. 5).[24] In Isaiah 48:21 the exodus and the wilderness traditions, represented by the water miracles, appear in a positive confession, used to generate faith in the future guidance and care provided by Yahweh. In Psalm 78, the two traditions also appear together and represent the goodness of God's actions on behalf of the community.[25] The manna and the quails traditions, on the other hand, indicate a different aspect of Israel's beginnings. In Psalm 78:21–30 the entire episode of the miraculous provision of food is conveyed under divine wrath. Both the manna, which in the Tetrateuch retains a positive nature (Exod. 16; cf. Num. 6f.), and the quails are associated with the ungrateful attitude of the people.

In regard to the ungrateful response by the people, Coats argues that the community's spiteful "testing" is the cause of the punishment.[26] He concludes that since the reference in the narrative is no longer to meat but to food (v. 30 אָכְלָה), the text reflects a combination of the two murmuring incidents; the manna and the quails stories. The interpretation is further suggested by Tate's translation of verse 18a, "They willfully put God to the test" and in verse 19b "Is God able?", indicating a rebellious and dishonorable attitude toward

God. The image contributes to the purpose of the recitation as a whole, which shows that Ephraim, who is like their forefathers, is no longer worthy of possession of the ancient traditions.[27]

The sin of craving is an essential element dependent upon Numbers 11 (אָוָּה Num. 11:34; תַּאֲוָה Ps. 78:30). Two points are similar in both Numbers 11:33 and Psalm 78:30. The first similarity is the fact that judgment comes, while the food is still in their mouths (בֵּין שִׁנֵּיהֶם, Num. 11:33a; בְּפִיהֶם, Ps. 78:30b). The second correlation stresses that judgment occurs before the food was consumed (יִכָּרֵת טֶרֶם, Num. 11:33a; לֹא־זָרוּ מִתַּאֲוָתָם, Ps. 78:30a). In Numbers 11, the narrative contains an etiological statement, indicating that the sin of craving is the motivating factor for judgment (11:34), but, in Psalms 78:30, the craving element is not etiological, but descriptive of the event. Tate adds that לְנַפְשָׁם (v. 18) can be translated "for themselves," which, in the context of food, relates to appetite, thus indicating undisciplined appetites.[28] The testing motif is associated normally with the positive water traditions, but here, the motif is a primary factor in motivating divine judgment. The craving motif of Numbers 11 provides an inclusive frame (vv. 18 and 30) that establishes the context for both the testing and the punishment.

The kerygma of Psalm 78 exhorts the community in Judah to adhere to the traditions of old, as a possession of their own.[29] Ephraim had lost its proprietorship of the sacral traditions of the past. Her unworthiness is demonstrated by her history in the wilderness and in the land. Therefore, two affirmative statements are implied: 1) the transfer of the guardianship of the traditions, and 2) the new election of Judah. The wilderness traditions function as a witness to the unworthiness of Ephraim, and they also validate God's motives for the rejection of Ephraim.

Another element in the kerygma of Psalm 78 is revealed in the psalmist's use of the water miracle story.[30] The water miracles reveal the divine initiative toward Israel and the gracious consideration of her (vv. 12–16). In a play on words, the sin of Ephraim in 78:35 is her forgetting that God was her "rock." The rock imagery expresses the notion of God's loyalty, reliability, protection, and stability.[31] The Psalm, therefore, calls for each generation to put their confidence and trust in Yahweh by not forgetting the deeds of God and by obeying the commandments.[32]

Due to the nature of the recitation as didactic, the emphasis on the future of Judah suggests that an oath of obedience is taken (78:1–8), and the pledge is critical in order to guard against a similar fate as Ephraim. The polemic against Israel can also be understood as one against Judah, who may be in jeopardy of the same judgment.[33] In this respect, the Psalm does not necessarily affirm the monarchy of David, while opposing Israel as an idolatrous nation rejected by God. Instead, the concern is with the recognition of the righteous acts of God performed to guard divine integrity against the sins of Ephraim.

The dual nature of kerygma is, on the one hand, the affirmation of the good deeds of God in the wilderness traditions, given almost always as a validating witness to God's loyalty to the community. On the other hand, kerygma almost always appeals to the loyalty of the nation to their God. The demonstration of the correct response of the community is found in adhering to the call to obedience in the introduction (78:1–8). The contrasting response is remembered as the rebellious actions of the past fathers in the wilderness and in the land. Ephraim's example as a failure calls the present community to obedience, since failure continues as a potential threat to the community in Judah (cf. Jer. 7:12–15).

PSALM 95

Psalm 95 is a hymn of praise, which is balanced with a song of exultation (95:1–7a) and prophetic admonition (vv. 7b–11), calling the community to worship God as the king and ruler over all creation (95:1–4). The Psalm is identified within the special category of the enthronement psalms contained in Psalms 93–100. Mowinckel interprets Psalm 95 as a covenant renewal (95:6f.), connecting the formula of the epiphany in Psalm 81:11 with the events following the covenant as mentioned in 95:8.[34] Kraus suggests that the parallel between Psalm 81 and Psalm 95 helps in the interpretation of the reason the wilderness traditions are recalled. Since Psalm 81 is associated with the Decalogue, then Psalm 95:8–11 is perhaps referring to the law of God and the people's refusal to obey.[35] The imagery of hardness of heart (95:8) and an erring of the heart (95:10) would, then, be understood in relation to the law. The admonitions of 95:7b–11 prepare the community for the proclamation of the commandments as the order of the covenant.[36]

The psalmist remembers the people in the wilderness as rebellious and without faith. Both the wilderness traditions of the Yahwist and the Priestly Writer are utilized to build the prophetic case against the tendency toward unfaithfulness. The water traditions of Massah and Meribah (Exod. 17:1–7; Num. 20:2–13) are recalled in 95:8. The connection is also evident in 95:9, since both accounts of the water stories in the wilderness traditions and their recollection in Psalm 95 have the people contending with Yahweh, instead of the reverse. The verb רִיב, which usually describes the contention between the people and God, does not appear in the Psalm, except by implication in the name Meribah. Instead, בָּחַן, "examine," or "try," is used to express the similar notion of contention. The verb is also used in reference to God's testing individuals (cf. Pss. 26:2; 66:10), especially in Psalm 81:8 where, in that context, the translation may suggest that God tests the people.[37]

The interpretation of the water stories is stated in 95:9 through the notion of testing (נִסָּה) and proving (בָּחַן), but the language also suggests the basic interpretation of the spy tradition (Num. 13–14). 95:9b may allude to the Yahwist account of God's judgment in Numbers 14:22. Kraus interprets פָּעֳלִי, "my work," as the saving activity of God, but the term can also refer to God's acts of punishment.[38] Dependence on the spy tradition is further suggested by the reference to the period of the forty years (P) in the wilderness (95:10). The sins of testing and proving are common motifs of the water traditions and the spy tradition in the Tetrateuch, as well as in the present Psalm. Allusions to the spy tradition are further suggested in the statement of God's anger and God's refusal to allow the people to enter into rest, that is, the promised land (95:11; cf. Num. 14:23, 30).[39] Recollection of the spy tradition has remained very close to the tradition in Numbers 14, and, perhaps the negative characterization of the people in the spy tradition has influenced the psalmist's interpretation of the water traditions. The water traditions of the Tetrateuch do not characterize the people with hardened hearts, nor is the anger of God shown toward the people, because of their contentions with God. Without a doubt, the nature of the wilderness community as a whole is rebellious. The people have seen the works of God, and, yet, they have put the Lord to the test (95:9b); and because of this, God has had to endure the rebellious community for forty years. Such a picture is utilized by the psalmist to encourage the faithful worship of God (95:1–7). The community is called to decide which course it shall take; one is that of faithfulness, which has its reward in the rest of God, while the alternative course leads down a path similar to that of the wilderness community.

Psalm 119:158 associates קוט with those who do not keep the commandments of God. Likewise, in Psalm 139:21 the term is used in parallel with שָׂנֵא, thus expressing hatred by the psalmist for the wicked who do not love the Lord. The plea in 139:24 is for God to recognize the psalmist's zeal for following the ways of God. A similar disgust for the community in the wilderness is expressed in 95:10, because they possess a "wandering" heart (תֹּעֵי לֵבָב), which is characterized by a disregard for the ways of God (cf. Isa. 53:6). The psalmist in Psalm 119:176 describes his own situation through the imagery of sheep wandering aimlessly (also תָּעָה); yet, the psalmist claims loyalty to the commandments of God, believing that such devotion justifies his supplications to God. Thus, the period of the forty years of wandering in the wilderness is restated as a wandering of the heart that is closed and inaccessible to God's word and instruction.[40] One might conclude that the ways of God are understood in association with the laws of God, though the Psalm is not as explicit in that association as Psalm 139.

Apart from the Psalm's connection with the covenant ceremony, the function of the Psalm is a call to obedience, and the outward sign is shown in worship. The particle אִם (95:7b) sets the balance of the Psalm apart, and in contrast to the first section. The proper attitude demonstrated by worship is the opposite of that which is characteristic of the wilderness community.[41] If the context for the Psalm is the covenant renewal, then the community in the present is called to recommitment to faith, which will allow them to remain in their rest.[42] However, the combination of the call in 95:7b and the recitation of the sinful past of the wilderness generation seems to strengthen the seriousness of the occasion, more than the implications of another covenant ceremony might suggest. In other words, the characterization of the wilderness community can also be an allusion to the situation within the psalmist's community.

The Psalm, and other enthronement psalms, may reflect the celebration of the fall festival in which the people made pilgrimages to Jerusalem.[43] The Psalm makes a subtle call for the community to come to Zion, but perhaps in much the same manner as Psalm 78 or Jeremiah 31:6. Since the imagery, in the recollection of the wilderness traditions, implies the crisis in the spy tradition of Numbers 13–14, the exhortation appears to be directed at the community which is outside Jerusalem, and perhaps Judah. In the spy tradition, the people failed not only in trusting God but also in claiming the land. Such an action resulted in the judgment of forty years of wandering in the wilderness, thus preventing them from entering the land (95:11). Along with the call to faith and obedient worship, the Psalm may make a subtle appeal for the community to embrace Jerusalem, or Zion; and by responding to the call, the community would not become guilty of a sin similar to that of the wilderness generation that prevented the community from finding its rest in the land. Thus, the Psalm addresses what is proper and correct in the community's relationship to God. The kerygma of the wilderness traditions in

Psalm 95 is understood within the context and setting of worship that centers upon praise, instead of contention, and faith, instead of strife.

PSALM 105

Psalms 105 and Psalm 106 are traditionally understood to be cultic hymns which appear in Book IV of the Psalter (Pss. 90–106). Both Psalms 105 and Psalm 106 contain elements that resemble wisdom poems.[44] Sabourin, on the other hand, proposes that Psalm 105, as well as Psalm 78, are didactic, though wisdom and the pedagogical function are not mutually exclusive.[45] Briggs adds that Psalm 105 and Psalm 106 were originally one psalm while others, such as Weiser, disagree.[46] As one unit, Psalm 105 would, then, recount the history of Israel from the beginnings with the Patriarchs down to the deliverance from Egypt, and Psalm 106 would have accounted for the balance of Israel's history through the period of the Judges. In their present form, Psalms 105 and Psalm 106 present the obverse or reverse of Israel's history, that is a history of God's kindness to Israel and a parallel history of Israel's ingratitude toward God.[47] Therefore, Psalms 105 and 106, as well as Psalm 78, in their present form, are poetic adaptations of narratives from Israel's sacred history.[48]

According to Ceresko, the structure of Psalm 105 is divided into two major historical periods: the period of the patriarchs and the Egypt–wilderness period.[49] The following outline reflects the structure suggested by Ceresko:

- 1–11 Introduction
  - 1–6 Call to worship
  - 7–11 Announcement of theme
- 12–22 The movement from Canaan to Egypt
  - 12–15 Wandering in Canaan
  - 16–22 The Joseph story
- 23 Israel enters Egypt (the "hinge" verse)
- 24–45 The movement from Egypt to Canaan
  - 24–38 The exodus story
  - 39–41 The desert
  - 42–45 The promise fulfilled

The content of the Psalm is associated with the covenant community, while the leading thought is Yahweh's faithfulness to his covenant and promise.[50] All of Israel is implied in the reference to Jacob (105:10) as the covenant community (cf. Ps. 78). The Psalm praises the covenant loyalty of God and the blessings of that covenant.

The entire Psalm is focused primarily on the patriarchal promise of the land.[51]

Childs stresses the important role of memory in the Psalm, and the view that Israel's history of salvation is the result of God's remembering his covenant.[52] Psalm 105, then, affirms faith in the "God who keeps his word."[53] Psalm 105, along with Psalm 78, is didactic in function and testifies to the faithfulness of God.[54] Unlike Psalm 78 and 106, the role of the people in Psalm 105 is not stressed significantly, except as beneficiaries to God's goodness. The wilderness traditions (vv. 39–41) illustrate the close intimate relationship that developed following the exodus from Egypt. From Egypt to Canaan, the people are characterized as joyful and obedient benefactors of the goodness of God's actions, and 105:45 reveals the goal of the community's response by obedience to the laws of God.[55]

The recitation of the events in Israel's sacred history stresses that all of those events in history come under God's divine will, and they are shaped according to the divine plan. The main theme of God's fidelity to the promises stresses the fulfillment of divine plans in spite of adverse human interference.[56] In Psalm 105, human interference originates entirely from outside the community of Israel. In this harmonious relationship, both the community and God contribute to the fulfillment of God's plans for the people, culminating in the possession of the promised land (v. 44).

Psalm 105:5 begins the recitation with a call to remember the saving acts of Yahweh. Verses 7–11 introduce the covenant theme, which establishes the motive for the sequence of actions that follow. The Psalm refers to the promise and fulfillment of the gift of the land (vv. 11, 44).[57] The promise of a great posterity is associated with the patriarchal period (vv. 12–15). God's protective love is underscored by the proclamation "Touch not my anointed ones, do my prophets no harm!" (v. 15). Kraus recognizes the ambiguity of the reference to the מָשִׁיחַ "anointed ones" and the prophets (נָבִיא) in verse 15. Perhaps the title of king is transferred to the patriarchs or borrowed from earlier references to Abraham such as Genesis 23:6.[58] Kirkpatrick and Dahood interpret 105:15 as a reference to the consecrated status of the patriarchs.[59] Behind this characterization lies the notion of undiminished purpose that the human element acquires within the framework of God's plans for Israel. Within this role, Israel enjoys divine protection that continues into the wilderness experience. Clifford links the protection of Israel by God throughout their history to the land as the fulfillment of the promise. He calls it the protection of the promise.[60]

In the wilderness traditions the manna and quails episode is retold with a distinct emphasis, compared to Psalm 78:24-29. In Psalm 105, the food is provided in respect to the gracious guidance of God without the motive for divine judgment, since the issue of rebellion is not developed.[61] The relationship between the positive traditions of the wilderness, illustrated by the water stories (v. 41), and the exodus is a recurring combination in the historical recitations, especially in the book of Exodus, or Isaiah 48:21, and Psalm 78:12–16. The motive for the guidance in the wilderness serves the primary theme of the Psalm, stressing the promise and fulfillment of covenant. God delivers Israel from Egypt (vv. 37–38) and leads her through the wilderness because God remembered the promise to Abraham (v. 42). The difficulties associated with the wilderness, normally utilized to illustrate the complex nature of the journey, are completely overshadowed by the guidance of God.

Both references to God's leading or delivering Israel from Egypt employ יָצָא (vv. 37 and 43).[62] The two verses at first appear to be parallel in message and content. In 105:37, the imagery of leading is linked with the exodus through the imagery of "gold and silver" (Exod. 11:2, 35–36). Coats identifies the motif of the spoils taken from Egypt as a primary ingredient in the traditions of the exodus from Egypt (Exod. 3:21f., 11:2f., 12:35f., and Ps. 105:37).[63] In 105:37, כּוֹשֵׁל, "stumbling," can be a reference to the removal of the booty from Egypt. Haglund argues that the notion of stumbling (v. 37) is not found in the Tetrateuch and therefore must be from other origins.[64] Nevertheless, the actions of the people are characterized by strength and exhilaration (vv. 37, 43). In verse 43 the leading forth is not specifically related to the exodus as such. The general mood of harmony and thanksgiving is shown through the language of praise.

Kraus, on the other hand, understands יָצָא in 105:43 to refer to the exodus event itself.[65] The reference to the exodus is in retrospect and adds a positive summary to that which has occurred prior to the conquest. The euphoric imagery of God leading, and Israel following obediently, provides a subtle influence on the nature of the conquest. Briggs perhaps has the correct interpretation. He isolates verses 42–44 as a concluding summary to the historical recitation.[66] In this construction, verse 42 is not the concluding refrain to the wilderness period in verse 41. The restatement of the exodus in verse 43, combining יָצָא with נָתַן in verse 44, is a confession of the fulfillment of the promise.

The wilderness traditions in 105:39–41 are therefore framed within the deliverance theme of the exodus from Egypt. The deliverance and guidance themes are identified by traditional images in the three segments of 105:37–44:

vv. 37–38 The exodus יָצָא
vv. 39–41 The wilderness עָנָן and אֵשׁ
vv. 43–44 The conquest יָצָא

Each segment reflects the three traditions of the Hexateuch, with each introduced and controlled by the deliverance and/or guidance themes. Both the exodus and conquest are emphasized by the term יָצָא. The term almost completely refers to divine deliverance from Egypt or from bondage of oppression or exile.[67] However, the guidance theme of the wilderness period appears under the imagery of the dual symbols of the cloud and fire (v. 39). Haglund is correct, in part, to imply the protective aspect in the symbolic notion of the cloud (Exod. 14:20).[68] Kirkpatrick interprets the symbolic cloud as a canopy to shelter the people from the heat of the desert. The notion of protection from the Egyptians has been transformed to protection from the threat of the wilderness.[69] The guidance theme of verse 39 reflects the exposition of the wilderness period in Exodus 13:21 (Deut. 1:33). Although הָלַךְ, a common term used in the guidance theme, is missing, verse 39 still represents the leading of God during the wilderness period (cf. Ps. 136:16). In the present context verse 39 provides the transition from the exodus to the wilderness.

The positive aspects of the wilderness traditions are further developed through the use of the manna, quails, and water miracle traditions.[70] The three episodes reveal a need/provision pattern that creates a contrast between the community's faithfulness (Ps. 105) and their rebelliousness (Ps. 78, 106). The stories begin with a request, "they asked" (v. 40a).[71] The request does not occur in the corresponding narrative in Exodus 16. Instead, the people murmur (לוּן) against Moses and Aaron. In the event recorded in Exodus 16, Moses does not intercede on their behalf. God responds to the complaint as though the murmuring is directed in the presence of God's hearing. לוּן (Exod. 16:2) and שָׁאַל (Ps. 105:40) are to be seen in direct contrast to what actually occurred in the Tetrateuch. Even in the tradition of Exodus 16, the murmuring motif gives the story a negative mood. In Numbers 11, the people also complain ("weeping" וַיִּבְכּוּ) about their food. Psalm 105, on the other hand, depicts a different relationship where need is expressed without complaint.

Another reversal of imagery is found in the word יַשְׂבִּיעֵם "and he caused them to be satisfied," or "he gave them . . . in abundance"

(v. 40b). The parallel episode in Psalm 78:29 states that the food was provided until the people were "over" filled (וַיִּשְׂבְּעוּ מְאֹד emphatic), suggesting that the miraculous provision matched or exceeded the people's craving. The episode in Psalm 78 is portrayed as the judgment of God who acted out of divine wrath against their rebellious attitude, but, in Psalm 105:40, the mood of the recollection is controlled by the use of שָׁאַל, which conveys the goodness of the wilderness experience, wherein the needs of the people were met by equal provisions. Instead of craving, which indicates a mood of dissatisfaction with the situation confronted by the people, Psalm 105 depicts a relationship between the community, its environment, and Yahweh as one of satisfaction (v. 40) and joy (v. 43).

The contrasting image of the wilderness experience is also depicted by the desert transformation in verse 41. Instead of מִדְבָּר, the psalmist inserts בַּצִּיּוֹת (pl. "lands of drought" or "dry places"). The image is one of dryness and absence of water that changes because God provides water abundantly for the dry places around the lands.

To conclude, with verse 5 the psalmist calls upon the community to remember what God has accomplished for the people in times past. God's actions and relationship to the community appear in the events in Israel's sacred history. The negative aspects of that history are not utilized since the goal of the psalmist is the affirmation of the goodness of God's relationship to the community and not the nature of people. The wilderness traditions provide a personal touch. They are the only traditions recalled that show God actually providing for the community and guiding them through their situation. God's gracious help to Israel provides the climax to the history recited. The praise and expression of joy, in verse 43, further illustrates the mood of the recitation. In the wilderness, harmony is expressed through the pattern of need followed by provision. Not only does the image of harmony apply to the wilderness traditions, but to the whole of Israel's sacred history, where the goodness of God strives to fulfill the promise with the gift of the land.

Psalm 106

Mowinckel suggests that Psalm 106 is a penitential psalm, since confession of sin is a key characteristic (v. 6).[72] Ringgren adds that Psalms 78, 105, and 106 are instructional in purpose because they do not appear to be real cultic hymns.[73] Both Psalm 105 and Psalm 106 reflect the common emphasis on the *Heilsgeschichte*, which indicates that they perhaps were once part of the same covenantal liturgy.[74]

The two Psalms are composed of a combination of historical recitation and exhortation. Psalm 105 and Psalm 106 present two views of history: the former presents history as an unbroken chain of divine acts of grace, while the latter provides examples of disobedience and punishment as warnings (Ezek. 20).[75] Psalm 105 is a hymn expressing thanksgiving for the saving acts of God, while Psalm 106, with its negative presentation of the community, can be compared to Psalm 78 as a hymn of praise, though Psalm 106 should be understood more as a national penitential lament.[76]

As the following outline of Psalm 106 reveals, the wilderness traditions constitute the most extensive portion of the recitation of Israel's sacred history. Then, one might assume that the kerygma of the wilderness traditions is understood within the message and purpose of the Psalm as a whole.

1–5	Call to testify
6	Confession of guilt
7–12	Israel in Egypt and the Reed Sea
13–33	The rebellions of Israel
13–15	Craving in the wilderness
16–18	Rebellion of Dathan and Abiram
19–23	Israel at Horeb
24–27	The spy tradition
28–31	Idolatry at Baal Peor
32–33	Waters of Meribah
34–39	Settlement in the land
44–46	Historical cycle of grace
47	Plea for deliverance
48	Doxology

Though neither Psalm 105 nor Psalm 106 begins its recitations with the same historical period, the historical sections of each are similar in purpose. In Psalm 105 the wandering of the patriarchs begins the recitation, while Psalm 106 begins with Israel in Egypt; however, the historical recitation of both Psalms has the receiving of the land as the primary concluding event (cf. Ps. 136). In addition to the events recited from Israel's sacred history, which can vary in content, new elements appear frequently, such as the response of the people. Dahood points out the paradox of Israel's history: the goodness of God's deeds performed on behalf of the community are accomplished in order to fulfill the promise. The history of the actions of the community are then set in opposition to the actions of God.[77] The response of the people, when presented as rebellious, functions to admonish and to warn the community against similar conduct in the present and the future.[78]

Psalm 106 begins with a call to praise God's goodness (חֶסֶד v. 1, 45).[79] Anderson interprets the prayer request זָכְרֵנִי (v. 4) as a plea for divine favor in regard to God's covenant loyalty.[80] The sentiments of Psalm 106 reflects Numbers 24:5, "How fair are your tents, O Jacob, your encampments, O Israel!" Such sentiments are expressed in 106:4–5 where the psalmist petitions God to restore Israel to her greatness. Such prosperity and gladness are signs of God's blessing.

In 106:6, the psalmist identifies the sins of the present generation with the sins of the past generations (Neh. 9:32–37; see Dan. 9:4–19). The present generation, who recites the rebellion history, accepts the blame for their sins and recognizes their unworthiness (v. 6).[81] Recognition of sin is the fundamental distinction between Psalm 78 and 106. In Psalm 78, the people of Zion apparently do not identify with the rebellion history, since Ephraim is accused of failure to follow and obey God. The psalmist in Psalm 106, on the other hand, speaks for the community by making a plea for divine consideration, which is not on the basis of Israel's past or present actions, although the sinful conduct of the people in the past and the present is openly confessed. Rather, the plea is for God to remember God's ancient relationship to the people. The history of Israel is viewed as "a history which takes place between God and the people."[82]

Psalm 106:27 establishes the context for the present situation for the community. The judgment against those who rebelled in the spy episode (vv. 24–27) is both death in the wilderness and dispersion among the nations (Ezek. 20:23).[83] The information in 106:46b–47 indicates that the community is currently in exile.[84] Combined with the confession of sin (v. 6) and the stress on the judgment from the spy tradition, the community apparently identifies their exile or dispersion as the divine judgment for Israel's sins. One might conclude that 106:27, therefore, presupposes the exile; but, as to which, the Assyrian or Babylonian, such a conclusion is difficult to ascertain.[85]

The kerygma of Psalm 106 points distinctly to the community's dilemma. Psalm 106:40–46 is a short recitation of a deliverance cycle that describes Israel's history as one of repeated rebellion, followed by judgment, wherein the people cry to God and God delivers them (cf. Judg. 2). In verse 46, the deliverance cycle is left open, thus portraying the generation in exile as a rebellious nation in exile yet to be delivered (cf. Ezek. 20:21–30). Psalm 106, as a whole, views Israel's sacred history as a deliverance cycle that begins in Egypt and continues through the period of the judges (vv. 34–46).[86] When the people cry to God for deliverance, the supplications include a looking back in history. For example, the vow of praise for the deliverance, which occurs in reference to the exodus tradition (v. 12), also concludes the Psalm in verse 47, thus anticipating a future deliverance. The massive content of the rebellion history, likewise, accentuates the magnitude of Israel's failure, as well as the belief in God's equal, if not greater, love (חֶסֶד) for Israel. Deliverance establishes the reason for praise, and also reminds God of the divine obligation to act once again according to past actions, because of the covenant relationship with the people.

The historical recitation begins with the people living in bondage in Egypt. They are epitomized as forgetful with complete disregard for the historical acts of God (v. 7). The acts of God reveal God's חֶסֶד that is intended for the benefit of the community. The epithet of the fathers in Egypt is different from that of Ezekiel 20, which specifically assigns the sin of idolatry to the people while in Egypt (Josh. 24:14). For the psalmist, idolatry is attributed to the two traditions of the Tetrateuch: Horeb (Exod. 32, Ps. 106:19–23) and Baal Peor (Num. 25, Ps. 106:28–31). Following the Reed Sea crossing, the people believed and sang praises (106:12). The expressed belief of the people in 106:12 sets up the contrast which follows in verse 13.[87] Upon entering the wilderness, the community soon forget their experiences under God's deliverance, and they depart from seeking counsel or understanding from God (v. 13). The verse is not insignificant to the events that follow, for the verse sets the tone for Israel's behavior during the rest of the historical recitation. לֹא־חִכּוּ לַעֲצָתוֹ (v. 13b) is translated "did not wait for his (יְהוָה) counsel." Kraus interprets עֵצָה to refer to God's plan of salvation.[88] Psalm 106:13, then, implies the community's refusal to learn and accept God's purposes behind the events in Israel's beginnings. The disbelief of the people causes them to forsake their confident expectations of the fulfillment of God's plan for the community. The community's numbness is further emphasized by the rejection of the land, which would have fulfilled the promise (v. 24). Psalm 106:13 characterizes the community as one of impatience and mistrust, which likewise calls the psalmist's audience to courage, patience, and faith.[89]

Coats points out that, in Psalm 106, the sin of forgetfulness is a new element for the rebellion theme associated with the sin of craving for food.[90] The distinction between 106:14–15 and Psalm 78:17–31 is found in the notion of testing. In Psalm 78 the testing motif controls the shape and message of the murmuring episode, but in Psalm 106, murmuring and testing carry the same weight and are subordinate to the sin of forgetfulness. In other words, the testing of God and their craving for food are the result of forgetting.

The rebellion of Numbers 16–17 is recorded in verses 16–18. The psalmist's account is an unusual mixture of Priestly and Yahwist material, which indicates that the psalmist utilized Pentateuchal traditions. Moses and Aaron mentioned together is a common practice of the Priestly Writer. Dathan and Abiram are borrowed from the Yahwist's account. The exclusion of Korah in verses 16–17 is thought by some to relieve the possible confusion over those particular psalms that are assigned to the "sons of Korah" (42–49; 84; 87–88).[91] The support for the leadership roles of Moses and Aaron is indicated by associating Dathan's and Abiram's jealousy with the divine response of judgment (Num. 16:30 [J]; also cf. 106:23a). In the Tetrateuch, the fate of Dathan and Abiram is not mentioned (Num. 16:31–35), but, in Psalm 106:17, the psalmist interprets their fate as the same as the fate of Korah, as recorded in Numbers 16.

The sin of the Horeb event is transformed to express the forgetfulness of the people. The sin of idolatry is attributed to their forgetting God, and reference to Sinai and the law are excluded. The Baal Peor event is placed within the wilderness traditions where the leadership role of Phinehas is central. In Numbers 25, Phinehas won God's favor because of his jealousy for God, whereby the jealousy of God, commonly aroused by idolatry (Deut. 32:21; Ps. 78:58; Num. 25:11, 13), is subdued, thus preventing the destruction of Israel. Interestingly enough, human intercession usually follows acts of idolatry (106:19–23 and 28–31), but in the last episode of idolatry in the land, no intercession occurs (vv. 34–39). The Psalm itself, then, must provide the intercessory function, as in 106:47.

In the spy record (vv. 24–27), a combination of materials from Numbers 14, Deuteronomy 1, and Ezekiel 20 appears. Coats recognizes the rejection of Israel in 106:24, but he does not link the idea with Numbers 14. The sin of the rejection of the promised land in 106:24a (וַיִּמְאֲסוּ בְּאֶרֶץ) is related to Numbers 14:31 (אֶת־הָאָרֶץ אֲשֶׁר מְאַסְתֶּם [P]), whereas, Coats adds that 106:25a relates to Deuteronomy 1:27.[92] Israel's failure to listen to God, a motif established already in 106:13, appears to reflect the Yahwist account of the divine oath in Numbers 14:21–23. The judgment requiring Israel to wander in the wilderness, which results in death in the wilderness, is borrowed from the Priestly account in Numbers 14:32. The judgment by exile (106:27) is entirely new to the wilderness traditions, though Ezekiel inserts the judgment motif (20:23), apparently to explain the reason for the exile and God's inactivity in that regard. In Psalm 106 the exile has come to be understood and accepted by the psalmist as justified punishment.[93]

The Meribah story provides the climax to the wilderness section of the historical recitation because, in this incident, the community causes Moses to become involved in her sins.[94] Numbers 20:2–13 is apparently the only water tradition implied. Perhaps in this retelling, though very brief as it is, the psalmist's interpretation of the Meribah incident is clearest in explaining the judgment against Moses. First, the people are the cause of their leader's sin, "They angered him (Yahweh, cf. v. 29)." Therefore, the community both angered Yahweh through their actions at Meribah and caused Moses to react sinfully. In 106:33a, Dahood understands רוּחוֹ, "his spirit," to refer to Yahweh.[95] Oesterley is perhaps more correct in attributing the "spirit" to Moses, thus translating the phrase, "because they were rebellious against his spirit."[96] If הִמְרוּ is emended as a Hiphil (הֵמֵירוּ), then the passage would read "for they caused his (Moses) spirit to be rebellious." In this interpretation, the result of the people's effect upon Moses must be assumed because the text only refers to the fate of Moses in a nebulous way (v. 32b). The retelling has Moses acting in a similar way as the people. In poetic parallelism, the manner of Moses's actions is revealed by בָּטָא (v. 33b), translated "speak rashly," "thoughtlessly," or "unadvisedly." The implication of Moses' actions is perhaps to be coordinated with the initial statement in 106:13b in regard to the community's tendency to shun the guidance and teaching of God.

Having established that forgetfulness is a central motif utilized by the psalmist to describe the community's rebellious disposition, the structure of Psalm 105 and Psalm 106 can now be addressed under the theme of memory and forgetfulness. The role of remembering is juxtaposed to forgetfulness, and the two motifs enclose Psalms 105 and 106.[97]

105:1 Summons to make known the deeds of God
5 Remember the works of God
8 Yahweh remembers the covenant[98]
42 Yahweh remembers the promise[99]

106:4 Remember me (Israel)[100]
7 Israel forgets in Egypt
13 Israel forgets in the wilderness
21 Israel forgets at Horeb
45 Yahweh remembers his covenant

The object of Israel's praise is Yahweh's faithfulness in remembering the covenant, and, in fact, Israel's entire redemptive history is the result of God's remembering the covenant.[101] Because Israel did not remember her history, the community is rebellious. The Psalm, then, begins with a call for the audience to make known the deeds and mighty or wonderful works. The historical recitation constitutes the memory of Israel's relationship with her God. Psalm 105:5 repeats the exhortation from 105:1 by calling on Israel's memory. Psalm 105:42 summarizes the historical recitation by claiming that all the works and good deeds accomplished by Yahweh were motivated by God's covenant loyalty.

In Psalm 106, the mood changes considerably, in regard to the emphasis on remembering the works and deeds of God. As Westermann observes, in periods of calamity, especially the 586 B.C.E. tragedy, Israel's worship changes to the lament.[102] Therefore, 106:4 makes a plea for Yahweh to remember the past in order that divine favor might be restored. The heart of Psalm 106 reveals the forgetfulness of Israel as the counterpart to remembering. The historical recitation clearly indicates that throughout Israel's history, within which God continuously strives to fulfill the promise, Israel persistently fails to understand and remember. Israel forgets in Egypt from the beginning, and the community forgets in the wilderness. Israel also forgets God at Horeb, which is most assuredly an allusion to Israel's breaking the covenant.

A conclusion may be drawn that in all instances in which the affirmation is made that God remembers, the text of Psalm 105 and Psalm 106 refers to the covenant. Further, in all instances where Israel is guilty of forgetting, the references are to the works and deeds of God. The kerygma of the wilderness traditions affirms that God remains loyal to the covenant made with Israel, within which the community's relationship with God is believed to be an on-going experience. The works of God include God's leading and guiding Israel through the wilderness, which validates that relationship. The kerygma of the wilderness traditions, on the other hand, appeals to the memory of the community so as to prevent repeating the sins of the past. Since the psalmist identifies the sins of the community with the sins of the exodus generation, their survival depends on God remembering the covenant. The community can claim no special privilege except to call on God to remember.

Westermann links the necessity of praising God to the prevention of forgetfulness.[103] In 106:12–13, which emphasize the contrast so clearly, the Psalm points directly to the problems of the community.

The Psalm not only calls upon God to hear their cry again, just as in the days of old, but calls upon the community to praise God and to remember; for in remembering the good works of God Israel would find her greatest hope of restoration. In Psalm 105, the close relationship between the community and God is almost idealistic, creating a hope from within the community that such a relationship may once again be restored. Kraus notes that the recitation of God's deeds and wonders are not merely in historical retrospect but, in worship, the sacred history is presented to the community as a present reality.[104] Yahweh's works are understood in this respect as present and not lost in Israel's past.

NEHEMIAH 9:6–37

Nehemiah 9:6–37 is an example of the Chronicler's use of scripture for exhortation and instruction.[105] In terms of its intentions, Nehemiah 9 is characteristically a lament, which may be indicated by 9:32–36.[106] Williamson suggests further that Nehemiah 9 is a penitential prayer.[107] The instructional approach of Nehemiah 9:6–37 is comparable to that of Pss. 78, 105, 106, and 136. Psalm 106 and Nehemiah 9 are similar in their thematic concerns. Fensham observes that historical psalms include psalms with a thanksgiving theme and psalms which have the penitential theme.[108] In Nehemiah 9, primary emphasis is placed upon the mighty deeds of Yahweh, and, like the psalmist in Psalm 106, Nehemiah identifies his community with the generations before them. The prayer of Ezra has the community in mind as much as it is an appeal to God.[109]

Chapters 8–10 are considered a unity, reflecting the closing of Ezra's administration. Myers notes the possible displacement of Nehemiah 8–10, which some believe should follow Ezra 10.[110] If chapters 9 and 10 are a literary unit, then Nehemiah 9 would be the antecedent history to Chapter 10, thus giving relevance to the phrase וּבְכָל־זֹאת (10:1).[111] Though a comprehensive treatment of the literary problems of Nehemiah 8–10 is beyond the scope of the present study, the placement of Nehemiah 9 within the context of the covenant ceremony in Nehemiah 8–10 is significant.

The following is an outline of the entire prayer in Nehemiah 9:6–37. The chronological order of events in the wilderness traditions of Nehemiah 9 (vv. 12–21) depart from the usual order as recorded in the Tetrateuch, perhaps in favor of the thematic concerns. Thematic sequence begins with divine providence (vv. 12–15), followed by the rebellion of Israel (vv. 16–18), concluded by renewed evidence of divine benevolence toward Israel (vv. 19–21).[112]

5b–6 Confession of God as creator
7–8 Election of Abraham
9–11 Israel in Egypt and the Reed Sea
12–21 Israel in the wilderness
22–25 The conquest and Israel in the land
26–31 The deliverance cycle
32–37 Confession of sin

Williamson proposes also the following scheme: (a) God's gracious provisions (vv. 12–15), (b) the people's ungrateful rebellion (16–18), and (c) God's continuing mercy (vv. 19–21).[113] The former sequence focuses on divine purpose in Israel's history while the latter emphasizes the sustaining care of God. Both approaches place the gift of the land at the pinnacle of God's purposes and provisions (v. 15b).[114] That which follows 9:15 reveals the problems encountered by God because of the community's faithlessness (vv. 16–21). Divine benevolence, described in terms of divine mercy (רְחוּם), however, permits the community to survive in spite of themselves.

The following discussion will analyze the individual elements in the wilderness traditions from the Pentateuch, such as the guidance theme, Sinai, the spy tradition, and the rebellion motif. The discussion will conclude with an analysis of the theme of the mercy of God. The more focused structure of the wilderness traditions in Nehemiah 9:12–21 contains the confession of God's guidance and care. The structure of 9:12–21 specifically highlights the kerygma in the wilderness portion of the prayer. In the recitation, the theme of God's mercy is pivotal.

- 12 Guidance in the wilderness
  - 13–14 God's provisions from Sinai
    - 15 God's provisions in the wilderness
      - 15b–17a Rebellion at Kadesh (Num. 13–14)
        - 17b–19a The mercy of God in the wilderness
      - 19b Guidance in the wilderness
    - 20a God's provisions of the laws
  - 20b God's provisions in the wilderness
- 21 Summary confessional of God's care

The guidance theme (v. 12) reflects the popular guidance theme in Exodus 13:21–22 (Num. 14:14; Deut. 1:30–33; Pss. 78:14, 105:39, 106:13). The verb נָחָה, "he led," and the noun דֶּרֶךְ, "way," function in a similar manner to describe the guidance theme.[115] The guidance theme links the exodus (vv. 9–11; cf. Exod. 13:21–22) with the wilderness period (vv. 13–21; cf. Exod. 15:22–18:27). In regard to the kerygmatic function of the guidance theme, biblical writers emphasize God's relationship to the community by reciting Exodus 13:21–22, or variations of its content. Whenever the theme is appropriated, for example in the present study in particular, the focus is upon God's purposes. Divine purposes are not only to successfully lead Israel in the wilderness but to fulfill the promise in the receiving of the land. God, as well as Israel, are therefore reminded of this purpose through the use of the guidance theme (Num. 14:14; Deut. 1:30–33).

Nehemiah 9:21 summarizes the wilderness period in an idealistic interpretation (cf. Deut. 2:7, 8:4). Ryle adds that verse 21 is "a proverbial description of Jehovah's protection of His people in the wanderings."[116] The forty years in Nehemiah 9 is used to illustrate the completeness of God's care (cf. Deut. 2:7). The time is not necessarily to be understood as a period of judgment, though an allusion to Numbers 14:34 is certainly possible. In the wilderness traditions, as recorded in the prayer of Nehemiah 9, no judgment is implied for that period. Instead, the focus is on the mercy of God upon which the survival of the people depends. Furthermore, the wilderness period is not presented as a threat to the life of the Israelite community, compared to the dangers and desert conditions recorded in the Tetrateuch. Like Psalm 105, the needs of the people are met with sufficient provisions from God. In Nehemiah 9 the real threat to the community's survival in the wilderness is attributed solely to the community's lack of trust and disobedience; nevertheless, God did not forsake them (v. 17b).

Mount Sinai (vv. 13–14) is a prominent place where the commandments were given. In Nehemiah 9, the name Sinai is used instead of Horeb, and 9:13 probably reflects Exodus 19:18–20 where God met Moses on Sinai.[117] The mention of the Sabbath in 9:14 perhaps indicates the supremacy of this particular law during the time of Ezra and Nehemiah.[118] The fact that Sinai is mentioned in connection with the provision of the law, indicates Nehemiah's peculiar use of the wilderness traditions in association with Sinai. Other passages outside the Tetrateuch also refer to the giving of the law (Ezek. 20), but only in regard to the wilderness in general. Such an association in Nehemiah 9, more than any other text, suggests a dependence upon the traditions of Sinai and the wilderness in the Tetrateuch.

Sinai occurs at the beginning of Israel's relationship with God, following the exodus. For Nehemiah, the Sinai event is the primary event that directs the life of the people in the wilderness and in the land. Understood in this respect, the guidance of God for the duration of the wilderness period is characterized by the influence of the Sinai event and the giving of the laws. The emphasis on the right ordinances, true laws, good statutes, and commandments is given in contrast to the rejection of the provisions by the community (vv. 13, 16–17; see Ezek. 20:25, לֹא טוֹבִים).[119] The description of the value of the provisions at Sinai is used to establish the basis for the description of the rebellions of Israel in the wilderness and in the land.

The guidance theme in verse 12 is also influenced by the provision of the law. The law given through Moses provides the means whereby Israel is taught and led (vv. 16–17, 20). Therefore any act of rebellion is the result of the community's refusal to be guided by God's laws. The guidance of Yahweh is now being replaced by the function of the law in the life of the community in the wilderness, and rebellion is understood as sin committed against the law.[120] Such an interpretation is very important for understanding the significant role that the law has now attained in God's leading of the community (cf. Ezek. 20).

Nehemiah 9:15b–17 is an adaptation of the Spy narrative from Numbers 13–14. Nehemiah 9:15b is a Deuteronomic expression "to go in and take possession of the land" (cf. Deut. 1:8; 9:5). Verse 15b "you lifted your hand" ("sworn") also recalls the Numbers spy traditions in which the fulfillment of the promise is set before the people (Num. 14:23, 30). The prayer does not mention a spy mission, though the disobedience is understood as the community's refusal to enter the land, which is consistent with the account retold by the Deuteronomist (1:19–46). According to Numbers 13–14, God commands the people to first scout the land prior to any attempt to enter. Because of the scouting report, the people rebel against the command to enter the land. In Nehemiah 9:17a, the forgetfulness of the people creates fear that results in their refusal to go in (Deut. 1:26–28). A rejection of the land (Num. 14:31) is also indicated when the community chooses a leader to return to Egypt. The rejection of the land, likewise, is associated with Israel's disobedience to God's laws and instructions. Reference to the spy tradition is therefore transformed in Nehemiah 9:16 to depict the disobedience of the community in terms of their refusal to obey God's commandments (מִצְוֺת) and their refusal to listen (v. 17a).

In 9:16 and 9:17, וַיַּקְשׁוּ אֶת־עָרְפָּם, "and they stiffened their neck," appears to be Deuteronomic (cf. Deut. 9:6, 13; 10:16; Exod. 32:9; 33:3; 34:9).[121] The phrase is associated in 9:17 with the selection of a leader by the rebellious people with the expressed intention of returning to Egypt. Ryle points out a possible optional reading of verse 17b, (וַיִּתְּנוּ־רֹאשׁ) to be "turned their attention," or "directed their thoughts," and literally, "set their head."[122] The language of selecting a leader to return to Egypt is similar to that of Numbers 14:4 (cf. נָתַן and שׁוּב). Coats interprets the desire to return to Egypt to be also an allusion to the rejection of Moses as the leader of the people. Nehemiah 9, as Coats observes, seems to be the only explicit reference outside the Pentateuch which mentions the rejection or denial of the exodus by the community.[123] Of course, this motif is common to the wilderness traditions of the Tetrateuch, and is contained within the rebellion theme.

Two significant elements are excluded from the spy narrative from Numbers 13–14, the sentence of death in the wilderness and the denial to enter the land. The use of the spy narrative in Nehemiah 9, instead, focuses upon the long-suffering and forgiveness of God, rather than divine wrath or judgment.[124] The only event attributed to divine judgment is the exile (v. 30; cf. Ezek. 20). Since judgment is not the primary issue, then the forty years of wilderness wandering (9:21; Num. 14:34) depicts the positive aspects of God's relationship to the community, especially the guidance theme.

The theme of the mercy of God is central to the kerygma of Nehemiah 9. Divine mercy can be understood as sympathetic love which is expressed outwardly in helping action.[125] The term can also suggest an act of forgiveness. In the Old Testament, God's mercy is understood as the continual regard for divine covenant loyalty, among other attributes revealing God's fidelity to the promises. In Nehemiah 9, חַנּוּן "graciousness" (v. 17, 31) and סְלִיחָה "forgiveness" (v. 17) contribute to the expression of God's covenant loyalty.[126] Likewise, Israel's dependence on Yahweh is linked to their understanding of Yahweh's covenant loyalty.[127] That loyalty is demonstrated by Yahweh's deliverance of Israel from their enemies (Neh. 9:27) and divine care for them during the wilderness period (Neh. 9:19).

The confession in verse 17b reveals the conventional attributes of God that are common in the prayers of Moses in the Pentateuch (Num. 14:18; also Deut. 33:19; 34:6, 7). At moments in which the divine wrath of God threatens, the confession counters divine intentions.[128] Williamson holds that verse 17b stands, therefore, at the center of the prayer itself.[129] The contrast created in 9:16–17 is between the people who are arrogant, stubborn, and rebellious, and God, who is forgiving, gracious, and merciful. God's benevolence and mercy are directly related to Israel's sinfulness (9:17, 19, 27, 28,

31[2]).[130] That relationship, when mercy and rebellion relate, originates with Israel in the wilderness, when the rebellion of Israel begins; not in Egypt as indicated by Ezekiel 20 and perhaps Psalm 106. Therefore, the mercies of God may not have an explicit relation to the exodus. On the other hand, since mercy is an expression of covenant loyalty, then the prayer begins with the Abrahamic covenant (vv. 7–8), and the mercy of God is shown perhaps in the exodus as well, though not specifically stated by the writer. Nevertheless, Nehemiah 9 refers explicitly to the mercy of God in regard to permitting Israel to survive, because, due to her sinfulness, she deserved to be lost in the wilderness.

In the wilderness traditions, the theology of mercy is developed and applied to the whole of Israel's history from Sinai to the restoration at the time of Ezra and Nehemiah (Neh. 9:6–31). The cycle of mercy originates in the wilderness alongside the rebellions of Israel. Following Sinai, the future of Israel is understood in regard to the mercies of God, though רְחוּם does not occur in the book of Numbers. For Nehemiah, the rebellion of Israel became more critical during the period of the monarchy. The people who live in the land during the monarchy are characterized in a similar manner as the generation of the wilderness (vv. 16, 29).[131] The sins of the people are overshadowed by the unfailing mercy of God. From the time Yahweh forms the community at Sinai, Israel acts presumptuously and disobeys the guidelines for effective community life set forth by Yahweh. In respect to the Tetrateuch, Nehemiah appears to interpret the book of Exodus in regard to the development of community through the guidance and instruction of the laws of God (vv. 13–14).

In conclusion, the kerygma of the wilderness traditions appeals to the loyalty of the community to the covenant and therefore its religious heritage. Israel's history is utilized to address the religious problems during the times of Ezra and Nehemiah.[132] The history of pre-exilic Israel serves as a warning to the post-exilic community. The community is called to obedience in regard to its faithfulness to the cult in order to avoid the fate of the pre-exilic community.[133] Blenkinsopp notes that unfaithful conduct by the community is caused by their forgetting the sacred traditions. The collective memory of her traditions that are preserved and expressed in the cult maintain the community's identity.[134] The law and the sacred traditions provide the continuity with the old community of faith. In Ezra and Nehemiah's community, the ancient traditions retained a dynamic quality that allowed them to be applied to new situations within the community, yet remaining rooted in the past.[135]

In regard to the affirmative aspects of the kerygma in Nehemiah 9:6–37, consideration must be directed to the condition of the community. In the confession of verses 32–37, disobedience (vv. 32–35) and the confession of faith (vv. 36–37) explain the current distress of the community, "Behold, we are slaves this day; in a land that thou gave to our fathers" (v. 36a).[136] The whole emphasis in Nehemiah 9, according to Ackroyd, centers around the land.[137] Prudence is therefore practiced by the psalmist to avoid conflict with the ruling Persian Empire.[138] Ezra and Nehemiah never lose sight of the foreign domination; and in the community's present situation of servitude under the Persian empire, Nehemiah understands political freedom as an expression of the fulfillment of the promises.[139] The prayer is concluded with reference to their present situation as slaves in their own land. The situation under Persian domination represents what Williamson interprets as "contradictory circumstances."[140] The ironic contrast is between the lands once given into the hands of Israel by God (v. 24) and the community's present situation of servitude (vv. 30, 36).[141] The deliverance theme is stressed in 9:9–11 through the recollection of the Egyptian bondage and the Reed Sea miracle. The kerygma of the wilderness traditions affirms God's mercy toward Israel, while appealing to that mercy by reminding God of the covenant and God's חֶסֶד, with the hope that they might be delivered and freed once again (v. 36).

THE KERYGMA OF THE WILDERNESS TRADITIONS IN THE WRITINGS

Of the Pentateuchal traditions that appear in Psalms 105, 106, 136 and Nehemiah 9, the wilderness traditions are among the common elements recited from Israel's sacred history. For example, references to Sinai (Neh. 9:13–14) or the patriarchs (Ps. 105:9–25; Neh. 9:7–8) do not appear in each historical recitation. The exodus from Egypt, the wilderness period, and Israel in the land of Canaan are recited in all texts.[142] Psalms 78, 106, and Nehemiah 9 reveal the dual nature of the wilderness traditions in recitations of Israel's sacred history. In the Writings of the Hebrew Bible, these three texts provide important examples of the positive views of Israel's experiences in the wilderness. When remembered in a positive way, the confession focuses on the guiding power of God, with limited reference to the disposition or receptive attitude of the community (Pss. 78:12–16; 105:39–41; Neh. 9:12–15). On the other hand, Psalms 78, 95, 106, and

Nehemiah 9 are greatly concerned with the actions and nature of the community in the wilderness. Each of these texts recites portions of the rebellion history. Psalm 95 and Psalm 106 do not emphasize the guidance theme, which is common to the other texts in the present survey (cf. Pss. 78:12; 105:39; Neh. 9:12; cf. Ps. 136:16). In most recollections of the wilderness period, the positive experiences are retold to provide contrast to Israel's rebellious actions. Psalm 78 and Nehemiah 9:6–37, for example, reveal the contrast between God's guiding presence and Israel's persistent faithlessness (cf. Ezek. 20).

The wilderness traditions in Psalm 78, and the historical summary as a whole, are used to legitimize the shift in the religious traditions in Israel. Psalm 78 summons the people to accept and appropriate the ancient traditions, that were once associated with the Northern Kingdom and Shiloh, in their new religious and political context in Jerusalem.[143] Used in this manner, the Psalm appears to separate the Judahite people from the ancient traditions. Unlike Psalm 106 and Nehemiah 9, Psalm 78 fails to identify its present community with the exodus generation, though the community most certainly included people from the north after the destruction of Shiloh.

Three summary points stand out in regard to the kerygma and the community of faith revealed in Psalm 105 and Psalm 106, as understood in relation to the wilderness traditions of the Tetrateuch. First, the two Psalms reveal the central problem of sin and its influence upon the community. In Psalm 106, the sins of the community, both the exodus generation and the present, involve the rejection of all aspects of Israel's sacred history, that is, those elements Israel came to understand to be constitutive. One of the functions of Psalm 105 and Psalm 106 is to overcome the abandonment of Israel's sacred heritage by utilizing the wilderness traditions as instructional illustrations that warn against similar behavior. The psalmist calls for a renewed confessional stance of the community.[144] Gratitude toward God's merciful actions stands at the center of Israel's life (Ps. 105).[145] However, ingratitude caused by forgetfulness, culminating in the lack of confession, constitutes rebellion. Each incident recorded of Israel's rebellious actions has as its central factor the people's blatant disregard for God and the divinely appointed leaders, with idolatry as the critical offense (vv. 19–23; 28–31; 34–39).

Brueggemann notes that laments or complaints of Israel are a counter-voice to Israel's ancient credo.[146] Yahweh's absence or indifference is challenged by the psalmist due to the present calamity that has come upon the community. The actions of God are recited not only to call the community to obedience, but to remind God of the great inconsistencies between the past and the present. In this respect, the community asks why there is still suffering, and they make their appeal for God's deliverance. The community calls upon the paradigm of the wilderness traditions where the mercy of God overshadows the sins of the people, for in this lies their hope.

Second, Psalm 105 is given in direct contrast to Psalm 106 so as to present a "Garden of Eden" picture of the ideal confessional stance of the community. The community ideal is characterized by memory, appreciation, and praise of Israel's religious heritage. Brueggemann states that the Psalm reflects theological innocence.[147] Psalm 106 would, then, be a polemic against those of opposite sentiment who still refuse to believe and embrace the ancient traditions. The fate of the wilderness generation, who is characterized by this opposing sentiment, is shared by the community in exile. The implications of repentance in 106:6, along with the cry of help in 106:47, indicate an attempt by the community to recover its place before God.

Third, the kerygma of the wilderness traditions in Psalm 106 and in the Tetrateuch are very similar, though the individual events recited in Psalm 106 are transformed to take on peculiar characteristics. Psalm 105 may reflect the ideal that lies behind the Tetrateuch, regarding the community's relationship to God, but Psalm 106 contains the failures of Israel. The community implied in the wilderness traditions of Psalm 106 is strikingly similar to that revealed in Exodus and Numbers. Of great significance is the point that the community of the psalmist identifies with the exodus or wilderness community. Sin and rebellion for the psalmist are revealed in the community's non-confessional stance, which undermines efforts and hopes for restoration. The loss of a confessional stance, for the psalmist, is caused by forgetting the ancient traditions that constituted the community as a chosen people of God. Psalm 105 and Psalm 106, when read as a unit, can therefore be interpreted as a plea for restoration. The use of the wilderness traditions, and the historical recitation as a whole, is to show why the community has come to accept their exile as just judgment for their sins. History, then, provides hope for deliverance through a new act of God.

In Nehemiah 9:6–37, the kerygma of the wilderness traditions appeals to faith, because of the belief that sin and rebellion have caused the community's present situation. A national confession of sin is given with a subtle plea for deliverance, and, in the context of the times of Ezra and Nehemiah, freedom is a political issue. The ancient traditions affirm the works of God as being motivated by the abiding mercy of God, upon which the community's deliverance depends.

Divine mercy and deeds are furthermore motivated by God's covenant loyalty.[148] Israel's history began in Egypt, and, now, the community lives in another form of bondage (v. 36). Therefore, the distinctiveness of Nehemiah 9 is in its use of the historical traditions to stress the extreme contradiction between the promise of land and the present foreign domination. Blenkinsopp notes that the land theme in Nehemiah 9 is a place of freedom.[149] As Blenkinsopp correctly observes, the fulfillment of the promise, which means freedom in the land, is not possible with foreign domination.[150]

All of the texts analyzed in the present chapter appeal to the community's memory of the ancient traditions. Psalms 105, 106, and Nehemiah 9 appeal to covenant loyalty, while Psalm 78 appeals to the community to embrace the ancient traditions. Psalm 95 appeals to obedient worship in Jerusalem. In many of the historical recitals in which the wilderness traditions appear, a phenomenon occurs in which a period of transition or change is being experienced by a community and its religious traditions.

Notes

[1]Claus Westermann, "Psalms, Book of," *The Interpreter's Dictionary of the Bible*, suppl. vol., ed. Keith Crim (Nashville: Abingdon Press, 1962), pp. 705–710.

[2]Robert H. Pfeiffer, *Introduction to the Old Testament* (New York: Harper & Brothers Publishers, 1941), p. 626.

[3]Sigmund Mowinckel, *The Psalms in Israel's Worship*, vol. 2, trans. D. R. Ap-Thomas (Nashville: Abingdon Press, 1962), p. 111.

[4]Georg Fohrer, *Introduction to the Old Testament*, trans. David E. Green (Nashville: Abingdon Press, 1965), p. 289. Compare Clifford's arguments below. Hans-Joachim Kraus, *Psalms 60-150: A Commentary*, trans. H. C. Oswald (Minneapolis: Augsburg, 1989), p. 125, points out that the words מָשָׁל and חִידוֹת (v. 2) reflect the language of wisdom.

[5]Anthony F. Campbell, "Psalm 78: A Contribution to the Theology of Tenth Century Israel," *The Catholic Biblical Quarterly*, 41 (1979), 51–79. Richard J. Clifford, "In Zion and David a New Beginning: An Interpretation of Psalm 78," in *Traditions in Transformation*, ed. Baruch Halpern and Jon D. Levenson (Winona Lake: Eisenbrauns, 1981), pp. 121–141, describes the structure of Psalm 78 as an introduction (vv. 1–11); the first recital (vv. 12–32) with a sequel (vv. 33–39); and a second recital (vv. 40–64) with a concluding sequel (vv. 65–72).

[6]Artur Weiser, *The Psalms*, trans. Herbert Hartwell (Philadelphia: The Westminster Press, 1962), p. 538.

[7]Ibid.

[8]Marvin E. Tate, *Psalms 51-100*, Word Biblical Commentary (Dallas: Word Books, Publisher, 1990), p. 288. In Tate's analysis of 78:1–8 (p. 289), he establishes the link between laws and actions as requirement for understanding of Yahweh.

[9]Augustine Stock, *The Way in the Wilderness* (Collegeville: The Liturgical Press, 1969), p. 60, writes "In Psalm 78 the Lord's acts of mercy provide the background against which the sins of the people stand out."

[10]Harry P. Nasuti, *Tradition History and the Psalms of Asaph* (Atlanta: Scholars Press, 1988), p. 89.

[11]Weiser, *The Psalms*, p. 540.

[12]George W. Coats, *Rebellion in the Wilderness*, (Nashville: Abingdon Press, 1968), p. 219.

[13]Ibid., p. 224.

[14]Brevard S. Childs, *Memory and Tradition in Israel* (Naperville: Alec R. Allenson, Inc., 1962), p. 49.

[15]Edward L. Greenstein, "Mixing Memory and Design: Reading Psalm 78," *Prooftexts*, 10 (1990), 197–218.

[16]Childs, *Memory and Tradition in Israel*, p. 49.

[17]Greenstein, "Mixing Memory and Design," p. 201.

[18]Sigmund Mowinckel, *The Psalms in Israel's Worship*, vol. 2, trans. D. R. Ap-Thomas (Nashville: Abingdon Press, 1962), p. 112.

[19]Ibid.

[20]G. Ernest Wright, "The Lawsuit of God: A Form-Critical Study of Deuteronomy 32," in *Israel's Prophetic Heritage*, ed. Bernhard W. Anderson and Walter Harrelson (New York: Harper & Brothers, Publishers, 1962), pp. 26–67. Compare Deuteronomy 32.

[21]Clifford, "In Zion and David a New Beginning," p. 137.

[22]Ibid.

[23]See Coats, *Rebellion in the Wilderness*, p. 78, who suggests that the water narratives are positive traditions of Yahweh's aid in the wilderness. In the three wilderness narratives of the water miracles (Exod. 15:22–27; 17:1–7; Num. 20:1–13), though the murmuring motif occurs, the judgment of God does not occur. In Numbers 20 the judgment is against Moses and Aaron and not the people.

[24]Erik Haglund, *Historical Motifs in the Psalms* (Lund: CWK Gleerup, 1984), p. 93, suggests that even though Psalm 78 contains the manna, quails, and the water stories, the writer is unfamiliar with the double traditions of the Pentateuch. Kraus, *Psalms 60-150*, p. 126, notes the terms תּוֹרָה (v. 5, 10) and בְּרִית (v. 10) suggest the connection with the Sinai tradition.

[25]Coats, *Rebellion in the Wilderness*, p. 201, interprets verses 12–16 to reflect a historical credo emphasizing the miraculous aide of God in the wilderness, instead of focusing on the people's response.

[26]Ibid., p. 215.

[27]Tate, *Psalms 51-100*, p. 278.

[28]Ibid., p. 282.

[29]Robert P. Carroll, "Psalm LXXVII: Vestiges of a Tribal Polemic," *Vetus Testamentum*, 21 (1971), 133–150.

[30]Tate, *Psalms 51-100*, p. 290.

[31]Ibid., p. 282.

[32]Ibid., p. 295.

[33]C. A. Briggs, *The Book of Psalms*, vol. 2, The International Critical Commentary (Edinburgh: T. & T. Clark, 1907), p. 185.

[34]Sigmund Mowinckel, *The Psalms in Israel's Worship*, vol. 1, trans. D. R. Ap-Thomas (Nashville: Abingdon Press, 1962), pp. 156–157.

[35]Kraus, *Psalms 60—150*, p. 248.

[36]Weiser, *The Psalms*, p. 627.

[37]Mitchell Dahood, *Psalms II: 51—100* (Garden City: Doubleday & Company, Inc., 1968), p. 265, translates בָּחַן (Ps. 81:8) in the passive, "I was provoked," since no alternative is available in the other references to testing in the wilderness traditions. The passive would permit the translation to correspond to the traditional interpretation of the water stories in which the people test God and not the reverse, as might be indicated in Psalm 81:8.

[38]Kraus, *Psalms 60—150: A Commentary*, p. 248. *BDB*, p. 821.

[39]Dahood, *Psalms II: 51—100*, p. 355.

[40]Hans-Joachim Kraus, *Theology of the Psalms*, trans. Keith Crim (Minneapolis: Augsburg Publishing House, 1986), p. 146.

[41]Haglund, *Historical Motifs in the Psalms*, p. 20.

[42]Weiser, *The Psalms*, p. 627.

[43]Bernhard W. Anderson, *Out of the Depths: The Psalms Speak for Us Today* (Philadelphia: The Westminster Press, 1983), p. 175.

[44]Otto Eissfeldt, *The Old Testament: An Introduction*, trans. Peter R. Ackroyd (Evanston: Harper & Row, Publishers, 1965), p. 125.

[45]Leopold Sabourin, *The Psalms: Their Origin and Meaning*, vol. 2 (Staten Island: Society of St. Paul, 1969), p. 306.

[46]Briggs, *The Book of Psalms*, vol. 2, p. 342. Cf. Weiser, *The Psalms*, p. 679.

[47]A. F. Kirkpatrick, *The Book of Psalms* (Cambridge: Cambridge University Press, 1951), p. 614.

[48]A. A. Anderson, *The Book of Psalms*, vol. 2, (Grand Rapids: Wm. B. Eerdmans Publishing Co., 1972), p. 726.

[49]Anthony R. Ceresko, "A Poetic Analysis of Ps. 105, with Attention to Its Use of Irony," *Biblica*, 64 (1983), 20-46.

[50]Kraus, *Psalms 60-150*, p. 308.

[51]Richard J. Clifford, "Style and Purpose in Psalm 105," *Biblica*, 60 (1979), 420-427.

[52]Childs, *Memory and Tradition*, p. 41.

[53]Anderson, *The Book of Psalms*, vol. 2, p. 725.

[54]Mowinckel, *The Psalms in Israel's Worship*, vol. 2, p. 212.

[55]W. O. E. Oesterley, *The Psalms* (London: SPCK, 1955), p. 448.

[56]Sabourin, *The Psalms*, vol. 2, p. 307.

[57]Walter Brueggemann, *Abiding Astonishment: Psalms, Modernity, and the Making of History* (Louisville: Westminster/John Knox Press, 1991), pp. 16-17.

[58]Kraus, *Psalms 60-150*, p. 311.

[59]Kirkpatrick, *The Book of Psalms*, p. 618; Mitchell Dahood, *Psalms III: 101-150*, The Anchor Bible (Garden City: Doubleday & Company, Inc., 1970), p. 55.

[60]Clifford, "Style and Purpose in Psalm 105," p. 424.

[61]Claus Westermann, *Praise and Lament in the Psalms*, trans. Keith R. Crim and Richard N. Soulen (Atlanta: John Knox Press, 1981), p. 241.

[62]Martin Noth, *Exodus: A Commentary*, trans. J. S. Bowden (Philadelphia: The Westminster Press, 1962), p. 105.

[63]George W. Coats, "Despoiling the Egyptians," *Vetus Testamentum*, 18 (1968), 450-457.

[64]Haglund, *Historical Motifs in the Psalms*, p. 27.

[65]Kraus, *Psalms 60-150*, p. 312.

[66]Briggs, *The Book of Psalms*, p. 348.

[67]H. D. Preuss, יָצָא, *Theological Dictionary of the Old Testament*, vol. 6, trans. David E. Green, ed. G. Johannes Botterweck and Helmer Ringgren (Grand Rapids: Wm. B. Eerdmans Publishing Company, 1990), pp. 225-250, like Noth, has יָצָא most frequently connected with deliverance, as in the exodus from Egypt.

[68]Haglund, *Historical Motifs in the Psalms*, p. 27.

[69]Kirkpatrick, *The Book of the Psalms*, p. 623.

[70]Dahood, *Psalms III: 101-150*, p. 62, וְלֶחֶם שָׁמַיִם is another term for manna (Psalm 78:24, וּדְגַן־שָׁמַיִם)

[71]שָׁאַל is emended by *BHS* to שָׁאֲלוּ to refer to the community. *BDB*, p. 981, implies that the request is in the mode of prayer.

[72]Mowinckel, *The Psalms in Israel's Worship*, vol. 2, p. 214.

[73]Helmer Ringgren, *The Faith of the Psalmists* (Philadelphia: Fortress Press, 1963), pp. 98–99.

[74]Weiser, *The Psalms*, p. 680.

[75]Eissfeldt, *The Old Testament*, p. 16.

[76]Weiser, *The Psalms*, p. 679.

[77]Dahood, *Psalms III: 101-150*, p. 67.

[78]Westermann, *Praise and Lament in the Psalms*, p. 242.

[79]For a brief discussion of the role of חֶסֶד in the book of Psalms see Kraus, *Theology of the Psalms*, pp. 43–45.

[80]Anderson, *The Book of Psalms*, vol. 2, p. 737. *BHS* notes that זָכְרֵנִי in verse 4 occurs as זָכְרֵנוּ in other manuscripts to be consistent with the plural in verse 3.

[81]Coats, *Rebellion in the Wilderness*, p. 224.

[82]Westermann, *Praise and Lament in the Psalms*, p. 246.

[83]*BHS* notes the similarity between וּלְהָפִיץ and וּלְהַפִּיל.

[84]Kraus, *Psalms 60-150*, p. 317, suggests the Babylonian exile. Weiser, *The Psalms*, p. 682, is reluctant to claim any definite setting. The exile could reflect a calamity in the Northern Kingdom.

[85]Coats, *Rebellion in the Wilderness*, p. 229.

[86]Westermann, *Praise and Lament in the Psalms*, p. 114.

[87]Ringgren, *The Faith of the Psalmists*, p. 79.

[88]Kraus, *Psalms 60-150*, p. 319.

[89]Anderson, *The Book of Psalms*, vol. 2, p. 740

[90]Coats, *Rebellion in the Wilderness*, p. 227.

[91]Dahood, *Psalms III: 101-150*, p. 71.

[92]Coats, *Rebellion in the Wilderness*, p. 228.

[93]Ibid., p. 229.

[94]Kirkpatrick, *The Book of Psalms*, p. 631.

[95]Dahood, *Psalms III: 101-150*, p. 74.

[96]W. O. E. Oesterley, *The Psalms, Book IV* (London: Society for Promoting Christian Knowledge, 1936), p. 68.

[97]Childs, *Memory and Tradition in Israel*, p. 41.

[98]Ibid., p. 49.

[99]*BHS* notes that a few manuscripts have the Qal imperative זִכְרוּ with Israel as the subject. Kirkpatrick, p. 617, argues that such an exhortation is out of place here. Also, Briggs, *The Book of Psalms*, vol. 2, p. 344.

[100]Literally, "He remembers his holy word." Dahood, *Psalms III: 101-150*, p. 62, translates, "his sacred pact" referring to דָּבָר in verse 8.

[101]Some manuscripts read זְכָרֵנוּ.

[102]Westermann, *Praise and Lament in the Psalms*, p. 270.

[103]Ibid., p. 246.

[104]Kraus, *Theology of the Psalms*, p. 35.

[105]David Noel Freedman, "The Chronicler's Purpose," *The Catholic Biblical Quarterly*, 23 (1961), 436–442.

[106]Westermann, *Praise and Lament in the Psalms*, p. 205.

[107]H. G. M. Williamson, *Ezra, Nehemiah*, Word Biblical Commentary (Waco: Word Books, Publisher, 1985), p. 272.

[108]F. Charles Fensham, *The Books of Ezra and Nehemiah* (Grand Rapids: Wm. B. Eerdmans Publishing Company, 1982), p. 228.

[109]Mark A. Throntveit, *Ezra-Nehemiah* (Louisville: John Knox Press, 1992), p. 103.

[110]Jacob M. Myers, *Ezra-Nehemiah*, The Anchor Bible (Garden City: Doubleday & Company, Inc., 1965), p. 165. For example, L. E. Browne, "Ezra and Nehemiah," *Peake's Commentary of the Bible*, ed. M. Black and H. H. Rowley (London: Nelson, 1962), pp. 370–380, structures his commentary according to this revised order. Also, Loring W. Batten, *The Books of Ezra and Nehemiah*, The International Critical Commentary (New York: Charles Scribner's Sons, 1913), p. 303.

[111]Klaus Baltzer, *The Covenant Formulary*, trans. David E. Green (Oxford: Basil Blackwell, 1971), p. 43.

[112]Joseph Blenkinsopp, *Ezra-Nehemiah: A Commentary*, The Old Testament Library (Philadelphia: The Westminster Press, 1988), p. 304.

[113]Williamson, *Ezra, Nehemiah*, p. 313.

[114]Peter R. Ackroyd, "God and People in the Chronicler's Presentation of Ezra," in *La Notion biblique de Dieu*, ed. J. Coppens (Leuven: Leuven University Press, 1976), pp. 145–162.

[115]Coats, *Rebellion in the Wilderness*, pp. 289–290.

[116]Herbert E. Ryle, *The Books of Ezra and Nehemiah* (Cambridge: Cambridge University Press, 1907), p. 259.

[117]Ibid., p. 256.

[118]Batten, *The Books of Ezra and Nehemiah*, p. 367.

[119]Myers, *Ezra-Nehemiah,* p. 160, has "reliable laws."

[120]Williamson, *Ezra, Nehemiah*, p. 306.

[121]Ryle, *The Books of Ezra and Nehemiah*, p. 258.

[122]Ibid.

[123]Coats, *Rebellion in the Wilderness*, p. 246.

[124]Ibid., p. 247.

[125]Elizabeth R. Achtemeier, "Mercy, Merciful," *The Interpreter's Dictionary of the Bible*, vol. 3, ed. George A. Buttrick (Nashville: Abingdon, 1962), pp. 352–354.

[126]Ibid., p. 352.

[127]Ibid., p. 353; F. Charles Fensham, "Covenant, Promise and Expectation in the Bible," *Theologische Zeitschrift*, 23 (1967), 305–322.

[128]James L. Crenshaw, *A Whirlpool of Torment* (Philadelphia: Fortress Press, 1984), p. 9.

[129]Williamson, *Ezra, Nehemiah*, p. 314.

[130]Martin Noth, *The Laws of the Pentateuch and Other Studies*, trans. D. R. Ap-Thomas (London: SCM Press, Ltd., 1966), p. 82.

[131]R. J. Coggins, *The Books of Ezra and Nehemiah* (Cambridge: Cambridge University Press, 1976), p. 117.

[132]Jacob M. Myers, "The Kerygma of the Chronicler," *Interpretation*, 20 (1966), 259–273.

[133]Ibid., p. 265.

[134]Blenkinsopp, *Ezra-Nehemiah*, p. 304.

[135]Paul D. Hanson, *The People Called: The Growth of Community in the Bible* (San Francisco: Harper & Row, Publisher, 1986), p. 295.

[136]Ackroyd, "God and People in the Chronicler's Presentation of Ezra," p. 156.

[137]Peter R. Ackroyd, *The Chronicler in His Age* (Sheffield: JSOT Press, 1991), p. 302.

[138]Fredrick C. Holmgren, *Israel Alive Again* (Grand Rapids: Wm. B. Eerdmans, 1987), p. 135.

[139]Blenkinsopp, *Ezra-Nehemiah*, p. 305.

[140]Williamson, *Ezra, Nehemiah*, p. 318.

[141]Roddy L. Braun, "Chronicles, Ezra, and Nehemiah: Theology and Literary History," in *Studies in the Historical Books of the Old Testament*, ed. J. A. Emerton (Leiden: E. J. Brill, 1979), pp. 52–72.

[142]F. Charles Fensham, "Neh. 9 and Pss. 105, 106, 135 and 136: Post-Exilic Historical Traditions in Poetic Form," *Journal of Northwest Semitic Languages*, 9 (1981), 35-51.

[143]Carroll, "Psalm LXXVII," p. 135.

[144]Ringgren, *The Faith of the Psalmists*, p. 79, explains the renewal in terms of the community's obligation to praise God for her deliverance.

[145]Brueggemann, *Abiding Astonishment*, p. 18.

[146]Ibid., p. 51.

[147]Ibid., p. 17.

[148]Achtemeier, "Mercy, Merciful," p. 352.

[149]Blenkinsopp, *Ezra-Nehemiah*, p. 304.

[150]Ibid., p. 305.

Chapter Six

THE KERYGMA OF THE WILDERNESS TRADITIONS IN THE HEBREW BIBLE

The analysis in Chapter 2 revealed that the structure and composition of the wilderness traditions in the Tetrateuch are truly complex. Noth suggests that the wilderness narratives in Numbers lacks unity.[1] On the other hand, Olson finds unity in the book's theological purpose as the title of his book indicates.[2] Outside the Tetrateuch, the wilderness traditions are equally complex. Biblical writers appropriate the traditions to accommodate each situation the community experiences. The writers are free to adapt and apply the traditions in a manner that will address the new situation faced by the community of faith. In essence, biblical writers are calling the community to remember the past in order to be able to survive a crisis in the present.[3] The best description of the social and religious context of the biblical community addressed by the traditions is the community that is struggling through a period of transition.

The kerygma of the wilderness traditions is revealed through the biblical writers' recollections of Israel's sacred history. The wilderness traditions are utilized in biblical texts in two basic ways. First, biblical writers recite the historical accounts of Yahweh's actions in the past, within which Yahweh interacts with the Israelite community (*Heilsgeschichte*). The exodus, the wilderness period, and the conquest are the primary events from Israel's past that are most frequently recited (Pss. 78; 105–106; Ezek. 20). Second, the wilderness period afforded biblical writers a wealth of language and imagery that reflect the events and experiences of Yahweh and the community (Isa. 48; Jer. 2, 31; Ps. 95). The use of the material from Israel's history, for example in the prophets, is not necessarily intended to recite history as such, but to express certain aspects of Yahweh's relationship with the community (Isa. 48:21).

From their historical context, of course, the wilderness traditions are recorded in the Tetrateuch. In the Hexateuch, the wilderness traditions appear within the context of historical accounts and their immediate recollection; and the wilderness period is still considered a part of the history of the present generation at that time (Num. 26–36, Deuteronomy, and Joshua). Numbers 26–36, for example, contain events in which the wilderness traditions are recalled within the current situation of the community following the wilderness period. Numbers 25 and 26 constitute the transition from the rebellious generation of the wilderness to the faithful generation who will soon be led into the land under the leadership of Joshua. Numbers 32 is the primary example of the successful application of the wilderness traditions, whereby specific events in the traditions are recalled to correct a potential problem relating to the conquest of the land.

In the book of Deuteronomy, the wilderness traditions are retold with the purpose of warning the people of the dangers of disobedience and forgetfulness in the land. Understood in this regard, the gift of the land, as fulfillment of the patriarchal promise, does not eliminate the problems that were indicative of the wilderness traditions. The prophetic exhortations against idolatry and disobedience to God's laws are supported by the various stories of the wilderness period. The kerygma of the wilderness traditions, then, focuses upon the relationship between the community and God, in order to correct a potentially distorted understanding of the community's relationship to the land. The nature of the community, above all else, is one whose orientation is that of God/community and not land/community. Considering the serious attention given to the nature of the community's relationship to God, the kerygma of the wilderness traditions, as well as the Yahwist's kerygma, attempts to correct the problem of secularization.[4]

In Deuteronomy, the wilderness generation is depicted as ungrateful, presumptuous, forgetful, and idolatrous; a foreshadowing of the nature of the people after they enter the land. The community's dependence on God in the wilderness is juxtaposed to the prosperity inside the land, and, because of the unfaithful tendencies of the community, possession of the land is a potential stumbling block. Idolatry and assimilation in the land are directly associated with the neglect of their religious heritage. The laws of God function to prevent such a neglect (Deut. 8:11). Therefore, Deuteronomy stresses obedience to God's laws by contrasting success in the land with the failure of those who were disobedient in the wilderness. The interpretive measures in Deuteronomy, and also in Numbers 26–36, are prophetic in nature; that is, they warn against disobedience or departure from Israel's close relationship to God.

The wilderness traditions are utilized in Joshua in a similar manner as in Deuteronomy and in Numbers 26–36, and, because of Joshua's historical link with the events in the Tetrateuch, the wilderness traditions maintain a direct association with the traditions of Numbers. Joshua 5:1–12 utilizes the wilderness traditions to establish the relevance of the ceremonial rites of circumcision and the passover, which are observed in preparation for entrance into the land. Joshua 14:6–15 links Caleb's role in the wilderness traditions to the land allotment of Hebron. The covenant ceremony in Joshua 24 mentions briefly the significance of the wilderness traditions to challenge the community to faith in and fidelity to the covenant at Shechem. The people are reminded that they owe their survival and constitution as a community of faith to the loyalty and protective guidance of their God.

I Samuel 4:5–11 and II Kings 18:1–8 are unusual applications of the wilderness traditions. Both events enhance the role of the ancient traditions within the history of the Israelite community. I Samuel 4:5–11, by mentioning only briefly the destruction of the Egyptians in the wilderness, stresses the reputation of God's relationship to the community in times past, and the traditions of Israel's past effect the furtherance of God's will for the community by influencing the defeat of Israel at the hand of the Philistines, thus purging the sins of Eli's sons and setting the stage for the arrival of Samuel on the historical scene. The destruction of the bronze serpent in II Kings 18:1–8 must be interpreted in light of the entire narrative of Hezekiah's reform. The initial function of the serpent in the wilderness is perhaps best understood as distorted during the times of Hezekiah. Hezekiah's corrective actions can reflect the knowledge of the symbolism associated with the bronze serpent in the wilderness, and the serpent tradition of the wilderness and the actions of Hezekiah address the issue of life and obedience in the community of faith.

The wilderness traditions in the Latter Prophets exhibit characteristics distinct from the traditions in the historical context of the Hexateuch. The writer's creative skill, for example, in Isaiah 48 is evident in the use of the term חָרְבָה for מִדְבָּר, building an image not of a desert setting for the second exodus, but a setting more compatible with the desolated homeland around Jerusalem. The guidance theme touches deeply the needs of the exilic community by reminding the people that God will lead and care for them. Jeremiah is equally effective in building images of the wilderness period. In Jeremiah, the contrast between the idealistic beginning of the community in the wilderness and the idolatrous realities of Jeremiah's contemporary situation is achieved in order to indict the community for their sins. Ezekiel 20 recalls the wilderness traditions by creatively interpreting the sins of the community and its punishment. The sins originate in Egypt prior to the exodus, and divine punishment by exile is foretold in association with the spy tradition. The second exodus is a return to the wilderness, where a purification process will take place so that they will be able to enter the land as a cleansed community.

In the Writings, in particular the Psalms and Nehemiah 9, the historical experiences from the wilderness period become more detailed and consistent with the traditions of the Tetrateuch. Psalm 78 contains a distinct perspective of Israel's sacred history, and the rebellion history of the exodus generation is completely attributed to Israel in the north. God's fidelity to the covenant and the community takes a theological and political shift along the path of Israel's history. The dual presentation of the wilderness period in Psalms 105 and 106 can be compared to Jeremiah 2 through a similar dramatic contrast between Israel's harmonious beginnings on the one hand (Ps. 105:39–41; Jer. 2:2–3) and the history of rebellion on the other hand (Ps. 106:13–33; Jer. 2:4–8). A major point in the message of Psalms 105 and 106 is the relationship between rebellion and the consequential fate of the community. The recognition of sin leads to repentance and, hopefully, deliverance. Therefore, Psalm 106 and Nehemiah 9 appeal to God's deliverance by asserting that the community identifies its sins with the exodus generation. In this regard, the grace of God is understood to be the reason the rebellious community survived in the past, and therefore God is called upon to act again. Psalm 106 and Nehemiah 9 are distinguished from Psalm 78 by the notion of the community's identification with the ancestors.

The wilderness traditions almost always appear in association with the recitation of Israel's sacred history. When biblical writers recite Israel's history as God's history, the wilderness traditions are remembered not simply as a period in Israel's history, nor were any other historical events treated so mildly by biblical writers, but from the perspective of kerygma, Israel's wilderness period is used to address situations confronted by the community. In that function, the wilderness traditions retained characteristics all their own, and no other event in Israel's history reveals a kerygma quite like that of the wilderness traditions. The one important element that distinguishes the wilderness traditions from other traditions is the close intimate relationship between God and the people, although the response by the community may suggest otherwise. Nevertheless, in the wilderness, the actions of God are personal. The guidance, protection, and miraculous provisions of God in the wilderness, plus God's confrontation with the people, provide an image unmatched in Israel's history. Although divine judgment was a tragic part of that relationship, the fact remains that the wilderness period was a time when leadership and instruction came from God, through the divinely appointed leaders.

One of the important themes that unites the recollections of the wilderness traditions in the Hebrew Bible is the fidelity of God to the covenant and, hence, the community as its beneficiary, which is characterized by divine incentive described as חֶסֶד. The underlying message is that the community owes its existence and survival to God's grace, even though the community rebelled against its God throughout the entire period in the wilderness. If the biblical writers drew upon positive traditions of Israel's beginnings in the wilderness, a renewal or a return to that ideal relationship was most certainly encouraged in times of crisis (Jer. 2; 31). However, when the wilderness traditions reflect the negative aspects of the wilderness narratives in the Tetrateuch, corrective actions are encouraged in order to avoid tragic consequences. In either case, the relationship between the community and its God is stressed.

In all the examples analyzed from the Hebrew Bible, with the possible exception of I Samuel 4:5–11, the wilderness traditions are utilized within the context of situations that occur in relation to issues involving the land.[5] Not wishing to oversimplify this conclusion, the land, nevertheless, is a major concern whenever traditions of Israel's past are recalled. Some of the concerns expressed by biblical writers even focus more specifically upon Zion or Jerusalem (Ps. 78; Jer. 31:2–6). The wilderness traditions of the Tetrateuch portray the exodus community existing outside the land, and failing to enter the promised land because of their rebellious actions. Deuteronomy incorporates the wilderness traditions within its exhortation to obedient living in the land in order to enjoy a prosperous and successful living in the land. The content of Joshua is without a doubt related to the land; the conquest and the faithful life in the land. Even Hezekiah's reform in II Kings 18 relates to the restoration of the land to a proper relation to God. The Latter Prophets, such as Isaiah, Jeremiah, and Ezekiel, address the problem of the community's relationship to the land; whether through affirming faith in God's guidance during the new exodus (Isaiah 48), appealing to renewal of the community's trust and obedience to God in order to avoid the inevitable consequences of apostasy (Jeremiah 2), affirming the continued relationship between the community and God (Jeremiah 31), or the unusual prophetic anticipation of the second exodus (Ezekiel 20).

In the Writings, Psalm 78 proclaims a change in the land which affects the future of the people in the land. Psalm 95 makes a firm call for renewed worship in the land. Psalm 105 and Psalm 106, after confessing the sinfulness of the community, conclude by making an appeal for God to "gather us from among the nations" (106:47a). Nehemiah 9 brings the community's experiences in full circle, from the wilderness period, to life in the land, to the period in exile, and now home again in the land, by praying, "We are slaves this day, in a land that you gave to our fathers" (9:36a). One can conclude that, considering the direct connection between the wilderness traditions and the problems associated with the land, the wilderness traditions receive their great impetus among the traditions of the Pentateuch because of the theological problems being addressed by biblical writers that were caused by the experience of exile, or a landless condition.

The kerygma of the wilderness traditions also exhorts the community to believe in God, which, in effect encourages the people to embrace the ancient Israelite traditions (Deut. 8; Josh. 24; Jer. 31; Pss. 78, 95, 105, 106; Neh. 9). By claiming the ancient traditions, and therefore affirming its faith in God, the community can avoid the tragic fate of the exodus generation. Numbers 13–14 establish the connection between the sin of rebellion and divine rejection in the Tetrateuch (cf. Deut. 1:19–46; Ezek. 20:14–16; Ps. 106:24–27). In the Tetrateuch, following the rejection of those who rebelled in Numbers 14, the transition to the next generation is revealed in Numbers 26. In the Psalms, Psalm 78 makes the clearest connection between rebellion and divine rejection.

The rebellious attitude of the exodus generation is demonstrated by their persistent refusal to believe and understand their situation in the wilderness as divinely initiated and motivated by God's loyalty to the covenant. The actions of the exodus generation have been interpreted in relation to the confessional stance of the community. Psalm 95 makes one of the more explicit appeals in calling the community to a confessional stance by proclaiming God as King, although the explicit call is to a revival in worship. Jeremiah 31:2–6 also address the problem of the continuing relevance of Israel's relationship to the God that was once revealed and understood in the ancient traditions. The wilderness community provides the contrast between the right and wrong attitude toward commitment. The community in the wilderness, it would appear, never gained a level of maturity in its faith and dependence upon God. Within this characterization of the wilderness community lies a polemic against future generations who refuse to embrace Israel's religious heritage. The similarity between the wilderness traditions of the Pentateuch and the Writings suggests a similar crisis within the Israelite community during the late period in Israelite history immediately prior to 586 B.C.E. and during the restoration. The constitutive effect of Israel's ancient traditions becomes acutely relevant in periods of transition when the community's identity as a Yahwistic community of faith is threatened.

Notes

[1]Martin Noth, *Numbers: A Commentary*, The Old Testament Library, trans. James D. Martin (Philadelphia: Westminster Press, 1968).

[2]Dennis T. Olson, *The Death of the Old and the Birth of the New* (Chico: Scholars Press, 1985).

[3]Gerhard von Rad, *Old Testament Theology*, vol. 2, trans. D. M. G. Stalker (New York: Harper & Row, Publishers, 1965), p. 130.

[4]Terrence E. Fretheim, "The Theology of the Major Traditions in Genesis-Numbers" *Review and Expositor*, 74 (1977), 301–320.

[5]For an analysis of the land, see Walter Brueggemann, *The Land* (Philadelphia: Fortress Press, 1977).

BIBLIOGRAPHY

Abba, Raymond "Priests and Levites." *The Interpreter's Dictionary of the Bible*, vol. 3. Ed. George A. Buttrick. Nashville: Abingdon Press, 1962.

Achtemeier, Elizabeth R. "Mercy, Merciful." *The Interpreter's Dictionary of the Bible*, vol. 3. Ed. George A. Buttrick. Nashville: Abingdon, 1962.

Ackroyd, Peter R. *The Chronicler in His Age.* Sheffield: JSOT Press, 1991.

________. *Exile and Restoration.* Philadelphia: The Westminster Press, 1968.

________. "God and People in the Chronicler's Presentation of Ezra." In *La Notion biblique de Dieu.* Ed. J. Coppens. Leuven: Leuven University Press, 1976.

________. *Studies in the Religious Tradition of the Old Testament.* London: SCM Press LTD, 1987.

Albright, W. F. "Jethro, Hobab and Reuel in Early Hebrew Tradition." *The Catholic Biblical Quarterly*, 25 (1963), 1–11.

________. "Some Remarks on the Song of Moses in Deuteronomy XXXII," *Vetus Testamentum*, 9 (1959), 339–346.

Anderson, A. A. *The Book of Psalms*, vol. 2. Grand Rapids: Wm. B. Eerdmans Publishing Company, 1972.

Anderson, Bernhard W. "Tradition and Scripture in the Community of Faith." *Journal of Biblical Literature*, 100 (1981), 5–21.

Asurmendi, Jesús. "En Torno a la Serpiente de Bronce." *Estudios Biblicos,* 46 (1988), 283–294.

Auld, A. Graeme. *Joshua, Moses and the Land.* Edinburgh: T. & T. Clark, 1980.

Bacon, Benjamin W. *The Triple Tradition of the Exodus.* Hartford: The Student Publishing Company, 1894.

Balentine, Samuel E. "Prayer in the Wilderness Traditions: In Pursuit of Divine Justice." *Hebrew Annual Review*, 9 (1985), 53–74.

Baltzer, Klaus *The Covenant Formulary*. Trans. David E. Green. Oxford: Basil Blackwell, 1971.

Barr, James. *Holy Scripture: Canon, Authority, Criticism*. Philadelphia: The Westminster Press, 1983.

Batten, Loring W. *The Books of Ezra and Nehemiah*. The International Critical Commentary. New York: Charles Scribner's Sons, 1913.

Beltz, Walter. *Die Kaleb-Traditionen im Alten Testament*. Beiträge zur Wissenschaft vom Alten und Neuen Testament, fünfte Folge, vol. 98. Stuttgart: Verlag W. Kohlhammer, 1974.

Bentzen, Aage. *Introduction to the Old Testament*, vol. 1. Copenhagen: G. E. C. Gad Publishers, 1959.

________. "On the Ideas of 'the Old' and 'the New' in Deutero-Isaiah." *Studia Theologica*, 1 (1948), 183–188.

Birch, Bruce C. "Tradition, Canon and Biblical Theology." *Horizons in Biblical Theology*, 2 (1980), 113–125.

Blair, Edward P. "An Appeal to Remembrance: The Memory Motif in Deuteronomy." *Interpretation*, 15 (1961), 41–47.

Blenkinsopp, Joseph. *Ezra–Nehemiah: A Commentary*. The Old Testament Library. Philadelphia: The Westminster Press, 1988.

________. *The Pentateuch: An Introduction to the First Five Books of the Bible*. New York: Doubleday, 1992.

________. *A Sketchbook of Biblical Theology*. London: Burns & Oats, 1968.

________. "The Structure of P." *The Catholic Biblical Quarterly*, 38 (1976), 275–292.

________. *Wisdom and Law in the Old Testament*. Oxford: Oxford University Press, 1983.

Boling, Robert G. *Joshua*. The Anchor Bible. Garden City: Doubleday & Company, Inc., 1982.

Boorer, Sue. "The Kerygmatic Intention of the Priestly Document." *Australian Biblical Review*, 25 (1977), 12–20.

Botterweck, G. Johannes. יָדַע. *Theological Dictionary of the Old Testament*, vol. 5. Ed. G. Johannes Botterweck and Helmer Ringgren. Trans. David E. Green. Grand Rapids: Wm. B. Eerdmans Publishing Company, 1986.

Bozak, Barbara A. *Life 'Anew': A Literary-Theological Study of Jer. 30–31.* Rome: Editrice Pontificio Istituto Biblico, 1991.

Bratcher, Robert G., and Barclay M. Newman. *The Translator's Handbook on the Book of Joshua.* New York: United Bible Societies, 1983.

Braun, Roddy L. "Chronicles, Ezra, and Nehemiah: Theology and Literary History." In *Studies in the Historical Books of the Old Testament.* Ed. J. A. Emerton. Leiden: E. J. Brill, 1979.

Briggs, C. A. *The Book of Psalms*, vol. 2. The International Critical Commentary. Edinburgh: T. & T. Clark, 1907.

Bright, John. *Jeremiah.* The Anchor Bible. Garden City: Doubleday & Company, 1984.

________. "Joshua." *The Interpreter's Bible*, vol. 2. Nashville: Abingdon Press, 1962.

Brown, Francis, S. R. Driver, and Charles A. Briggs. *A Hebrew and English Lexicon of the Old Testament.* Oxford: Clarendon Press, 1907.

Browne, L. E. "Ezra and Nehemiah." *Peak's Commentary of the Bible.* Ed. M. Black and H. H. Rowley. London: Nelson, 1962.

Brueggemann, Walter. *Abiding Astonishment: Psalms, Modernity, and the Making of History.* Louisville: Westminster/John Knox Press, 1991.

________. *The Creative Word: Canon as a Model for Biblical Education.* Philadelphia: Fortress Press, 1982.

________. "David and His Theologian." *The Catholic Biblical Quarterly*, 30 (1968), 156–181.

________. "The Kerygma of the Deuteronomistic Historian." *Interpretation*, 22 (1968), 387–402.

________. *The Land.* Philadelphia: Fortress Press, 1977.

________. *To Pluck Up, To Tear Down: A Commentary on Jeremiah 1–25.* Grand Rapids: Wm. B. Eerdmans, 1988.

________. "Wolff's Kerygmatic Methodology." In *The Vitality of Old Testament Traditions*. 2nd. ed. Ed. Walter Brueggemann and Hans Walter Wolff. Atlanta: John Knox Press, 1982.

________, and Hans Walter Wolff, Ed. *The Vitality of Old Testament Traditions*. 2nd. ed. Atlanta: John Knox Press, 1982.

Butler, Trent C. "An Anti-Moses Tradition." *Journal for the Study of the Old Testament*, 12 (1979), 9–15.

Cairns, Ian. *Word and Presence: A Commentary on the Book of Deuteronomy*. Grand Rapids: Wm. B. Eerdmans, 1992.

Campbell, Anthony F. "Psalm 78: A Contribution to the Theology of Tenth Century Israel." *The Catholic Biblical Quarterly*, 41 (1979), 51–79.

Campbell, Anthony F., and Mark A. O'Brien. *Sources of the Pentateuch: Texts, Introductions, Annotations*. Minneapolis: Fortress Press, 1993.

Carpenter, Eugene E. "Literary Structure and Unbelief: A Study of Deuteronomy 1:6–46." *Asbury Theological Journal*, 42 (1987), 77–84.

Carroll, Robert P. *The Book of Jeremiah*. The Old Testament Library. Philadelphia: The Westminster Press, 1986.

________. "Psalm LXXVII: Vestiges of a Tribal Polemic." *Vetus Testamentum*, 21 (1971), 133–150.

________. "Rebellion and Dissent in Ancient Israelite Society." *Zeitschrift für die Alttestamentliche Wissenschaft*, 89 (1977), 176–204.

Cassuto, U. *A Commentary on the Book of Exodus*. Trans. Israel Abrahams. Jerusalem: The Magnes Press, 1967.

Ceresko, Anthony R. "A Poetic Analysis of Ps. 105, with Attention to Its Use of Irony." *Biblica*, 64 (1983), 20–46.

Childs, Brevard. *The Book of Exodus*. The Old Testament Library. Philadelphia: The Westminster Press, 1974.

________. *Introduction to the Old Testament as Scripture*. Philadelphia: Fortress Press, 1979.

________. *Memory and Tradition in Israel*. Naperville: Alec R. Allenson, Inc., 1962.

________. "The Traditio-Historical Study of the Reed Sea Tradition." *Vetus Testamentum*, 20 (1970), 406–418.

Christensen, Duane L. *Deuteronomy 1–11*. Word Biblical Commentary. Waco: Word Books, 1991.

________. "Form and Structure in Deuteronomy 1–11." In *Das Deuteronomium: Entstehung, Gestalt und Botschaft*. Ed. Norbert Lohfink. Leuven: Leuven University Press, 1985.

Clements, Ronald E. *Deuteronomy*. Sheffield: JSOT Press, 1989.

________. *God and Temple*. Oxford: Basil Blackwell, 1965.

________. *Old Testament Theology: A Fresh Approach*. London: Marshall, Morgan & Scott, 1978.

________. *Prophecy and Covenant*. London: SCM Press, Ltd., 1965.

Clifford, Richard J. "In Zion and David a New Beginning: An Interpretation of Psalm 78." In *Traditions in Transformation*. Ed. Baruch Halpern and Jon D. Levenson. Winona Lake: Eisenbrauns, 1981.

Coats, George W. "The Book of Joshua: Heroic Saga or Conquest Theme." *Journal for the Study of the Old Testament*, 38 (1987), 15–32.

________. "Conquest Traditions in the Wilderness Theme." *Journal of Biblical Literature*, 95 (1976), 177–190.

________. "Despoiling the Egyptians." *Vetus Testamentum*, 18 (1968), 450–457.

________. "An Exposition for the Conquest Theme." *The Catholic Biblical Quarterly*, 47 (1985), 47–54.

________. "An Exposition for the Wilderness Traditions." *Vetus Testamentum*, 22 (1972), 288–295.

________. "The King's Loyal Opposition: Obedience and Authority in Exodus 32–34." In *Canon and Authority*. Ed. George W. Coats and Burke O. Long. Philadelphia: Fortress Press, 1977.

________. *Moses: Heroic Man, Man of God*. Sheffield: JSOT Press, 1988.

________. *Rebellion in the Wilderness*. Nashville: Abingdon Press, 1968.

________. "The Sea Tradition in the Wilderness Theme: A Review." *Journal for the Study of The Old Testament*, 12 (1979), 2–8.

________. "A Structural Transition in Exodus." *Vetus Testamentum*, 22 (1972), 129–142.

________. "The Traditio-Historical Character of the Reed Sea Motif." *Vetus Testamentum*, 17 (1967), 253–265.

________. "The Wilderness Itinerary." *The Catholic Biblical Quarterly*, 34 (1972), 135–152.

Coggins, R. J. *The Books of Ezra and Nehemiah.* Cambridge: Cambridge University Press, 1976.

Cooke, G. A. *The Book of Ezekiel.* The International Critical Commentary. Edinburgh: T. & T. Clark, 1936.

Cornill, Carl. *Introduction to the Canonical Books of the Old Testament.* Trans. G. H. Box. New York: G. P. Putnam's Sons, 1907.

Craigie, Peter C. *The Book of Deuteronomy.* Grand Rapids: Wm. B. Eerdmans, 1976.

Crenshaw, James L. *A Whirlpool of Torment.* Philadelphia: Fortress Press, 1984.

Cross, Frank M. *Canaanite Myth and Hebrew Epic.* Cambridge: Harvard University Press, 1973.

Dahood, Mitchell. *Psalms III: 101–150.* The Anchor Bible. Garden City: Doubleday & Company, Inc., 1970.

Darr, Katheryn Pfisterer. "Breaking through the Wilderness: References to the Desert in Exilic Prophecy." Ph.D. dissertation, Vanderbilt University, 1984.

Davies, G. Henton. *Exodus: Introduction and Commentary.* London: SCM Press, 1967.

________. "Glory." *The Interpreter's Dictionary of the Bible*, vol. 2. Ed. George A. Buttrick. Nashville: Abingdon Press, 1962.

________. "The Presence of God in Israel." In *Studies in History and Religion.* Ed. Ernest A. Payne. London: Lutterworth Press, 1942.

Davies, G. I. *The Way of the Wilderness.* Cambridge: Cambridge University Press, 1979.

________. "The Wilderness Itineraries: A Comparative Study." *Tyndale Bulletin*, 25 (1977), 46–81.

________. "The Wilderness Itineraries and the Composition of the Pentateuch." *Vetus Testamentum*, 33 (1983), 1–13.

DeRoche, Michael. "Jeremiah 2:2–3 and Israel's Love for God during the Wilderness Wanderings." *The Catholic Biblical Quarterly*, 45 (1983), 364–376.

De Tillese, G. Minette. "Sections 'tu' et sections 'vous' dans le Deutéronome." *Vetus Testamentum*, 12 (1962), 29–87.

De Vaulx, J. *Les Nombres*. Paris: J. Babalda, 1972.

De Vries, Simon. "The Origin of the Murmuring Traditions." *Journal of Biblical Literature*. 87 (1968), 51–58.

________. "A Review of Recent Research in the Tradition History of the Pentateuch." *SBL Seminar Papers*, (1987), 459–502.

Dodd, C. H. *The Apostolic Preaching and Its Developments*. London: Hodder & Stoughton Limited, 1936.

Dozeman, Thomas B. "Horeb/Sinai and the Rise of Law in the Wilderness Tradition." *SBL Seminar Papers*, (1989), 282–299.

Driver, S. R. *Deuteronomy*. The International Critical Commentary. Edinburgh: T. & T. Clark, 1902.

________. *An Introduction to the Literature of the Old Testament*. New York: Meridian Books, 1956.

________. *Exodus*. Cambridge: Cambridge University Press, 1911.

Eichrodt, Walther. *Ezekiel: A Commentary*. Philadelphia: Westminster Press, 1970.

Eissfeldt, Otto. *The Old Testament: An Introduction*. Trans. Peter R. Ackroyd. New York: Harper and Row, Publishers, 1965.

Ellis, Peter F. *The Yahwist: The Bible's First Theologian*. Notre Dame: Fides Publishers, Inc., 1968.

Engnell, Ivan. *A Rigid Scrutiny*. Trans. John T. Willis. Nashville: Vanderbilt University Press, 1969.

Fensham, F. Charles. *The Books of Ezra and Nehemiah*. Grand Rapids: Wm. B. Eerdmans Publishing Company, 1982.

________. "Covenant, Promise and Expectation in the Bible." *Theologische Zeitschrift*, 23 (1967), 305–322.

________. "Neh. 9 and Pss. 105, 106, 135 and 136: Post-Exilic Historical Traditions in Poetic Form." *Journal of Northwest Semitic Languages*, 9 (1981), 35–51.

Fishbane, Michael. "Sin and Judgment in the Prophecies of Ezekiel." *Interpretation*, 38 (1984), 131–150.

Flanagan, James. "History, Religion, and Ideology: The Caleb Tradition." *Horizons*, 3 (1976), 175–185.

Fohrer, Georg. *Introduction to the Old Testament*. Trans. David E. Green. Nashville: Abingdon Press, 1965.

Fox, Michael V. "Jeremiah 2:2 and the 'Desert Ideal.'" *The Catholic Biblical Quarterly*, 35 (1973), 441–450.

Freedman, David Noel. "The Chronicler's Purpose." *The Catholic Biblical Quarterly*, 23 (1961), 436–442.

Friedman, Richard E. "Sacred History and Theology: The Redaction of Torah." In *The Creation of Sacred Literature*. Ed. R. E. Friedmann. Berkeley: University of California Press, 1981.

Fretheim, Terence E. "The Theology of the Major Traditions in Genesis–Numbers." *Review and Expositor*, 74 (1977). 301–320.

Fritz, Volkmar. *Israel in der Wüste*. Marburg: N. G. Elwert Verlag, 1970.

Funk, Robert W. "The Wilderness." *Journal of Biblical Literature*, 78 (1959), 205–214.

Graffy, Adrian. *A Prophet Confronts His People: The Disputation Speech in the Prophets*. Rome: Biblical Institute Press, 1984.

Gray, John. "The Desert Sojourn of the Hebrews and the Sinai–Horeb Tradition." *Vetus Testamentum*, 4 (1954), 148–154.

________. *Joshua, Judges and Ruth*. The Century Bible. London: Thomas Nelson and Sons, Ltd., 1967.

Gray, George Buchanan. *A Critical and Exegetical Commentary on Numbers*. The International Critical Commentary. Edinburgh: T. & T. Clark, 1903.

Greenberg, Moshe. *Ezekiel 1–20*. Garden City: Doubleday & Company, 1983.

Greenstein, Edward L. "Mixing Memory and Design: Reading Psalm 78." *Prooftexts*, 10 (1990), 197–218.

Haglund, Erik. *Historical Motifs in the Psalms.* Lund: CWK Gleerup, 1984.

Hanson, Paul D. *The Diversity of Scripture: A Theological Interpretation.* Philadelphia: Fortress Press, 1982.

________. *Dynamic Transcendence.* Philadelphia: Fortress Press, 1978.

________. *The People Called: The Growth of Community in the Bible.* San Francisco: Harper & Row, Publisher, 1987.

Harrelson, Walter. "Guidance in the Wilderness." *Interpretation*, 13 (1959), 24–36.

________. "Life, Faith, and the Emergence of Tradition." In *Tradition and Theology in the Old Testament.* Ed. Douglas A. Knight. Philadelphia: Fortress Press, 1977.

________. "Traditions and the Tradition." *Perspectives in Religious Studies*, 6 (1979), 184–189.

Heck, Joel D. "A History of Interpretation of Genesis 49 and Deuteronomy 33." *Bibliotheca Sacra* 147 (1990), 16–31.

Helfmeyer, F. J. הָלַךְ. *Theological Dictionary of the Old Testament*, vol. 3. Ed. G. Johannes Botterweck and Helmer Ringgren. Trans. John T. Willis, Geoffrey W. Bromiley, and David E. Green. Grand Rapids: Wm. B. Eerdmans Publishing Company, 1978.

Hertzberg, Hans Wilhelm. *I & II Samuel: A Commentary.* Trans. J. S. Bowden. Philadelphia: Westminster Press, 1964.

Holladay, William L. *Jeremiah 2.* Minneapolis: Fortress Press, 1989.

Holmgren, Fredrick C. *Israel Alive Again.* Grand Rapids: Wm. B. Eerdmans, 1987.

Huffmon, Herbert B. "The Covenant Lawsuit in the Prophets." *Journal of Biblical Literature*, 78 (1959), 285–295.

________. "The Exodus, Sinai and the Credo." *The Catholic Biblical Quarterly*, 27 (1965), 101–113.

Hyatt, J. Philip. *Exodus.* Grand Rapids: Wm. B. Eerdmans Publishing Co., 1971.

________. "Were There an Ancient Historical Credo in Israel and an Independent Sinai Tradition?" In *Translating and Understanding the Old Testament.* Ed. H. T. Frank and W. L. Reed. Nashville: Abingdon Press, 1970.

Johnson, R. F. "Caleb." *The Interpreter's Dictionary of the Bible*, vol. 1. Ed. George A. Buttrick. Nashville: Abingdon Press, 1962.

Jones, Douglas Rawlinson. *Jeremiah.* Grand Rapids: William B. Eerdmans Publishing Company, 1992.

Kallai, Z. "The Wandering-Traditions from Kadesh-Barnea to Canaan: A Study in Biblical Historiography." *Journal of Jewish Studies*, 33 (1982), 175–184.

Kautzsch, E., and A. E. Cowley. *Gesenius' Hebrew Grammar.* Oxford: Clarendon Press, 1910.

Kirkpatrick, A. F. *The Book of Psalms.* Cambridge: Cambridge University Press, 1951.

Klein, Ernest. *A Comprehensive Etymological Dictionary of the Hebrew Language for Readers of English.* New York: MacMillan Publishing Company, 1987.

Klein, Ralph W. *Ezekiel: The Prophet and His Message.* Columbia: University of South Carolina Press, 1988.

________. *Israel in Exile.* Philadelphia: Fortress Press, 1979.

Knierim, Rolf. "The Composition of the Pentateuch." *SBL 1985 Seminar Papers.* Atlanta: Scholars Press, 1987, 393–415.

Knight, Douglas A. "Canon and the History of Tradition: A Critique of Brevard S. Childs' Introduction to the Old Testament as Scripture." *Horizons in Biblical Theology*, 2 (1980), 127–149.

________. "Revelation through Tradition." In *Tradition and Theology in the Old Testament.* Ed. Douglas A. Knight. Philadelphia: Fortress Press, 1977.

________, Ed. *Tradition and Theology in the Old Testament.* Philadelphia: Fortress Press, 1977.

Koch, Klaus, דֶּרֶךְ. *Theological Dictionary of the Old Testament*, vol. 3. Ed. G. Johannes Botterweck and Helmer Ringgren. Trans. John T. Willis, Geoffrey W. Bromiley, and David E. Green. Grand Rapids: Wm. B. Eerdmans Publishing Company, 1978.

________. *The Growth of Biblical Tradition.* Trans. S. M. Cupitt. New York: MacMillan Publishing Company, 1969.

Koehler, Ludwig, and Walter Baumgartner. *Lexicon in Veteris Testamenti Libros.* Leiden: E. J. Brill, 1958.

Kraus, Hans-Joachim. *Psalms 60–150: A Commentary*. Trans. H. C. Oswald. Minneapolis: Augsburg, 1989.

________. *Theology of the Psalms*. Trans. Keith Crim. Minneapolis: Augsburg Publishing House, 1986.

Labuschagne, C. J. "The Song of Moses: Its Framework and Structure." In *De Fructu Oris Sui: Essays in Honour of Adrianus Van Selms*. Ed. A. Van Selms. Leiden: E. J. Brill, 1971.

Lehmann, Manfred R. "Biblical Oaths." *Zeitschrift für die alttestamentliche Wissenschaft*, 81 (1969), 74–92.

Levine, Baruch A. *The JPS Torah Commentary: Leviticus*. Philadelphia: The Jewish Publication Society, 1989.

Liver, Jacob. "Korah, Dathan and Abiram." In *Scripta Hierosolymitana*, vol. 8. Ed. Chaim Rabin. Jerusalem: The Magnes Press, 1961.

Lohfink, Norbert. "Der Bundesschluss im Land Moab. Redaktionsgeschichtliches zu Dt. 28,69–32,47." *Biblische Zeitschrift*, 6 (1962), 32–56.

Lust, Johan. "Ez., XX, 4–26: Une paradie de l'histoire religieuse d'Israel." *Ephemerides Theologicae Lovanienses*, 43 (1967), 488–527.

________. "'Gathering and Return' in Jeremiah and Ezekiel." In *Le Livre de Jérémie: Le prophète et son milieu, les oracles et leur transmission*. Ed. P. M. Bogaert. Uitgeverij Peeters: Leuven University Press, 1981.

________. *Traditie, Redactie en Kerygma Bij Ezechiel*. Brussel: Paleis der Academiën, 1969.

Mann, Thomas W. "Holiness and Death in the Redaction of Numbers 16:1–20:13." In *Love & Death in the Ancient Near East: Essays in Honor of Marvin H. Pope*. Ed. John H. Marks and Robert M. Good. Guilford, Conn.: Four Quarters Publishing Company, 1987.

Mauser, Ulrich. *Christ in the Wilderness*. Naperville: Alec R. Allenson, Inc., 1963.

May, H. G. "Joshua." *Peake's Commentary on the Bible*. Ed. Matthew Black and H. H. Rowley. Hong Kong: Thomas Nelson and Sons, Ltd., 1962.

May, Herbert G. and Bruce M. Metzger, Ed. *The New Oxford Annotated Bible*. New York: Oxford University Press, 1973.

Mayes, A. D. H. *Deuteronomy.* Grand Rapids: Wm. B. Eerdmans, 1979.

Mays, James Luther. *Ezekiel, Second Isaiah.* Philadelphia: Fortress Press, 1978.

________. *The Story of Israel between Settlement and Exile.* London: SCM Press, Ltd., 1983.

McBride, S. Dean, Jr. "The Yoke of the Kingdom: An Exposition of Deuteronomy 6:4–5." *Interpretation,* 27 (1973), 273–306.

McCarthy, Dennis J. "Notes on the Love of God in Deuteronomy and the Father-Son Relationship between Yahweh and Israel." *The Catholic Biblical Quarterly,* 27 (1965), 144–147.

________. "Some Holy War Vocabulary in Joshua 2." *The Catholic Biblical Quarterly,* 33 (1971), 228–230.

________. "What Was Israel's Historical Creed?" *Lexington Theological Quarterly,* 4 (1969), 46–53.

McConville, J. G. *Law and Theology in Deuteronomy.* Sheffield: JSOT Press, 1984.

McDonald, James I. H. *Kerygma and Didache.* Cambridge: Cambridge University Press, 1980.

McEvenue, Sean E. *The Narrative Style of the Priestly Writer.* Rome: Biblical Institute Press, 1971.

McKane, William. *A Critical and Exegetical Commentary on Jeremiah, Vol. 1, I–XXV.* The International Critical Commentary. Edinburgh: T. & T. Clark, 1986.

McKenzie, John L. *Second Isaiah.* The Anchor Bible. New York: Doubleday & Company, Publisher, 1968.

Mendenhall, George E. "The Census Lists of Numbers 1 and 26." *Journal of Biblical Literature,* 77 (1958), 52–66.

________. "Covenant." *The Interpreter's Dictionary of the Bible,* vol. 1. Ed. George A. Buttrick. Nashville: Abingdon Press, 1962.

Mihelic, J. L. "Paran." *The Interpreter's Dictionary of the Bible,* vol. 3. Ed. George A. Buttrick. Nashville: Abingdon Press, 1962.

Miller, J. Maxwell, and Gene M. Tucker. *The Book of Joshua.* Cambridge: Cambridge University Press, 1974.

Miller, Patrick D., Jr. "The Gift of God: The Deuteronomic Theology of the Land." *Interpretation,* 23 (1969), 451–465.

Milgrom, Jacob. *The JPS Torah Commentary: Numbers*. Philadelphia: The Jewish Publication Society, 1990.

Mitchell, H. G. "The Use of the Second Person in Deuteronomy." *Journal of Biblical Literature*, 18 (1899), 61–109.

Moran, W. L. "The End of the Unholy War and the Anti-Exodus." *Biblica*, 44 (1963), 333–342.

Mowinckel, Sigmund. *The Psalms in Israel's Worship*, vols. 1 and 2. Trans. D. R. Ap-Thomas. Nashville: Abingdon Press, 1962.

Myers, Jacob M. *Ezra–Nehemiah*. The Anchor Bible. Garden City: Doubleday & Company, Inc., 1965.

________. "The Kerygma of the Chronicler." *Interpretation*, 20 (1966), 259–273.

________. "The Requisites for Response: On the Theology of Deuteronomy." *Interpretation*, 15 (1961), 14–31.

Nasuti, Harry P. *Tradition History and the Psalms of Asaph*. Atlanta: Scholars Press, 1988.

Newman, Murray L. *The People of the Covenant*. Nashville: Abingdon Press, 1962.

Nicholson, Ernest W. *Deuteronomy and Tradition*. Philadelphia: Fortress Press, 1967.

________. *Jeremiah: Chapters 1–25*. London: Cambridge University Press, 1973.

North, C. R. "The 'Former Things' and the 'New Things' in Deutero-Isaiah." In *Studies in Old Testament Prophecy*. Ed. H. H. Rowley. Edinburgh: T. T. Clark, 1950.

Noth, Martin. *The Chronicler's History*. Trans. H. G. M. Williamson. Sheffield: JSOT Press, 1987.

________. *The Deuteronomistic History*. Trans. Jane Doull and John Barton. Sheffield: JSOT Press, 1981.

________. *Exodus: A Commentary*. Trans. J. S. Bowden. Philadelphia: Westminster Press, 1962.

________. *A History of Pentateuchal Traditions*. Trans. B. W. Anderson. Atlanta: Scholars Press, 1981.

________. *The Laws of the Pentateuch and Other Studies*. Trans. D. R. Ap-Thomas. London: SCM Press, Ltd., 1966.

________. *Numbers: A Commentary*. The Old Testament Library. Trans. James D. Martin. Philadelphia: Westminster Press, 1968.

O'Connell, Robert H. "Deuteronomy VIII 1–20: Asymmetrical Concentricity and the Rhetoric of Providence." *Vetus Testamentum*, 40 (1990), 327–452.

Oesterley, W. O. E. *The Psalms*. London: SPCK, 1955.

________. *The Psalms, Book IV*. London: Society for Promoting Christian Knowledge, 1936.

Olson, Dennis T. *The Death of the Old and the Birth of the New: The Framework of the Book of Numbers and the Pentateuch*. Chico: Scholars Press, 1985.

Ottosson, Margnus. "Tradition and History, with Emphasis on the Composition of the Book of Joshua." In *The Production of Time: Tradition History in Old Testament Scholarship*. Ed. Knud Jeppesen and Benedikt Otzen. Sheffield: The Almond Press, 1984.

Perlitt, Lothar. *Deuteronomium (1:19–2:23)*. Biblischer Kommentar Altes Testament, vol. 2. Neukirchen-Vluyn: Neukirchener Verlag, 1991.

Pfeiffer, Robert H. *Introduction to the Old Testament*. New York: Harper & Brothers Publishers, 1941.

Phillips, Anthony. *Deuteronomy*. Cambridge: Cambridge University Press, 1973.

Plaut, W. Gunther. "Deuteronomy." In *The Torah*. New York: Union of American Hebrew Congregations, 1981.

Porter, J. R. "The Background of Joshua III–V." *Svensk Exegetisk Årsbok*, 36 (1971), 5–23.

Preuss, H. D. יָצָא. *Theological Dictionary of the Old Testament*, vol. 6. Trans. David E. Green. Ed. G. Johannes Botterweck and Helmer Ringgren. Grand Rapids: Wm. B. Eerdmans Publishing Company, 1990.

Rad, Gerhard von. "Deuteronomy." *The Interpreter's Dictionary of the Bible*, vol. 1. Ed. George A. Buttrick. Nashville: Abingdon Press, 1962.

________. *Deuteronomy: A Commentary*. The Old Testament Library. Trans. Dorothea Barton. Philadelphia: The Westminster Press, 1966.

________. *Genesis*. 2nd. ed. Trans. John H. Marks. Philadelphia: Westminster Press, 1972.

________. *Old Testament Theology*, vols. 1 and 2. Trans. D. M. G. Stalker. San Francisco: Harper & Row, Publishers, 1962.

________. *The Problem of the Hexateuch and Other Essays*. London: SCM Press Ltd., 1984.

________. *Studies in Deuteronomy*. Trans. David Stalker. London: SCM Press Ltd., 1953.

Rahner, Karl, and Karl Lehmann. *Kerygma and Dogma*. New York: Herder and Herder New York, 1969.

Ringgren, Helmer. *The Faith of the Psalmists*. Philadelphia: Fortress Press, 1963.

Rendtorff, Rolf. "The Concept of Revelation in Ancient Israel." In *Revelation as History*. Ed. Wolfhart Pannenberg. New York: Macmillan Company, 1968.

________. *The Old Testament: An Introduction*. Trans. John Bowden. Philadelphia: Fortress Press, 1986.

________. "Traditio-Historical Method and the Documentary Hypothesis." In *Proceedings of the Fifth World Congress of Jewish Studies*. Jerusalem: The Hebrew University Press, 1969.

________. "The 'Yahwist' as Theologian? The Dilemma of Pentateuchal Criticism." *Journal for the Study of the Old Testament*, 3 (1977), 2–10.

Richardson, Alan. *An Introduction to the Theology of the New Testament*. London: SCM Press, Ltd., 1958.

Riemann, Paul A. "Desert and Return to Desert in the Pre-Exilic Prophets." Ph.D. dissertation, Harvard University, 1964.

Ryle, Herbert E. *The Books of Ezra and Nehemiah*. Cambridge: Cambridge University Press, 1907.

Sabourin, Leopold. *The Psalms: Their Origin and Meaning*, vol. 2. Staten Island: Society of St. Paul, 1969.

Sailhamer, John H. *The Pentateuch as Narrative*. Grand Rapids: Zondervan Publishing House, 1992.

Sanders, James A. "Adaptation for Life: The Nature and Function of Canon." In *Magnalia Dei: The Mighty Acts of God. Essays on the Bible and Archaeology in Memoriam G. E. Wright.* Ed. F. M. Cross. Garden City: Doubleday & Co., 1976.

________. *Canon and Community.* Philadelphia: Fortress Press, 1984.

________. *From Sacred Story to Sacred Text.* Philadelphia: Fortress Press, 1987.

________. "Hermeneutics." *The Interpreter's Dictionary of the Bible*, suppl. vol. Ed. Keith Crim. Nashville: Abingdon Press, 1962.

________. *Torah and Canon.* Philadelphia: Fortress Press, 1972.

Sarna, Nahum. *The JPS Torah Commentary: Exodus.* Philadelphia: The Jewish Publication Society, 1991.

________. *Exploring Exodus: The Heritage of Biblical Israel.* New York: Schocken Books, 1986.

Sawyer, John. F. *From Moses to Patmos.* London: SPCK, 1977.

Schreiner, Joseph. "The Development of the Israelite 'Credo'." In *The Dynamism of Biblical Tradition.* Ed. Pierre Benoit and Roland E. Murphy. New York: Paulist Press, 1967.

Silver, Jacob. "Korah, Dathan and Abiram." In *Scripta Hierosolymitana.* Ed. Chaim Rabin. Jerusalem: The Magnes Press, 1961.

Simon, Ulrich E. *A Theology of Salvation.* London: SPCK, 1953.

Skinner, John. *Isaiah Chapters XL–LXVI.* Cambridge: Cambridge University Press, 1929.

Soggin, J. Alberto. *Joshua.* The Old Testament Library. Trans. R. A. Wilson Philadelphia: Westminster Press, 1972.

Sterling, S. David. "Joshua 24 Re-Examined." *Hebrew Union College Annual*, 58 (1987), 119–136.

Stock, Augustine. *The Way in the Wilderness.* Collegeville: The Liturgical Press, 1969.

Sturdy, John. *Numbers.* Cambridge: Cambridge University Press, 1976.

Talmon, Shemaryahu. "The 'Desert Motif' in the Bible and in Qumran Literature." In *Biblical Motifs: Origins and Transformations*. Ed. Alexander Altmann. Cambridge: Harvard University Press, 1966.

________. "Wilderness." *The Interpreter's Dictionary of the Bible*, suppl. vol. Ed. Keith Crim. Nashville: Abingdon Press, 1962.

Tate, Marvin E. *Psalms 51–100*. Word Biblical Commentary. Dallas: Word Books, Publisher, 1990.

Thompson, John A. *Deuteronomy*. London: Inter-Varsity Press, 1974.

________. *The Book of Jeremiah*. Grand Rapids: Wm. B. Eerdmans Publishing Company, 1980.

Thompson, Leonard L. "The Jordan Crossing: *Ṣidqot* Yahweh and World Building." *Journal of Biblical Literature*, 100 (1981), 343–358.

Thompson, Thomas L. *The Origin Tradition of Ancient Israel*. Sheffield: JSOT Press, 1987.

Throntveit, Mark A. *Ezra–Nehemiah*. Louisville: John Knox Press, 1992.

Tunyogi, Andrew C. "The Rebellions of Israel." *Journal of Biblical Literature*, 81 (1962), 385–390.

Van Leeuwen, Raymond C. "What Comes Out of God's Mouth: Theological Wordplay in Deuteronomy 8." *The Catholic Biblical Quarterly*, 47 (1985), 55–57.

Van Seters, John. "Confessional Reformulation in the Exilic Period." *Vetus Testamentum*, 22 (1972), 448–459.

________. "Joshua 24 and the Problem of Tradition in the Old Testament." In *In the Shelter of Elyon: Essays on Ancient Palestinian Life and Literature*. Ed. W. Boyd Barrick and John R. Spencer. Sheffield: JSOT Press, 1984.

Vink, J. G. "The Date and Origin of the Priestly Code in the Old Testament." In *Oudtestamentische Studiën*, vol. 15. Ed. P. A. H. De Boer. Leiden: E. J. Brill, 1969.

Walsh, Jerome T. "From Egypt to Moab: A Source Critical Analysis of the Wilderness Itinerary." *The Catholic Biblical Quarterly*, 39 (1977), 20–33.

Waltke, Bruce K., and Michael P. O'Connor. *An Introduction to Biblical Hebrew Syntax*. Winona Lake: Eisenbrauns, 1990.

Watts, John D. W. "Deuteronomy." *The Broadman Bible Commentary*, vol. 2. Ed. Clifton J. Allen. Nashville: Broadman Press, 1970.

________. "The Deuteronomic Theology." *Review and Expositor*, 75 (1977), 321–332.

________. *Isaiah 34–66*. Word Biblical Commentary. Waco: Word Books, Publisher, 1987.

Weinfeld, Moshe. "The Emergence of the Deuteronomic Movement: The Historical Antecedents." In *Das Deuteronomium: Entstehung, Gestalt und Botschaft*. Ed. Norbert Lohfink. Leuven: Leuven University Press, 1985.

Weiser, Artur. *The Psalms*. Trans. Herbert Hartwell. Philadelphia: Westminster Press, 1962.

Wellhausen, Julius. *Prolegomena to the History of Ancient Israel*. Gloucester, Mass.: Peter Smith, 1983.

Wenham, Gordon J. "The Deuteronomic Theology of the Book of Joshua." *Journal of Biblical Literature*, 90 (1971), 140–148.

Westermann, Claus. *Blessing in the Bible and the Life of the Church*. Trans. Keith Crim. Philadelphia: Fortress Press, 1978.

________. *Isaiah 40–66*. The Old Testament Library. Trans. David M. G. Stalker. Philadelphia: Westminster Press, 1969.

________. *Praise and Lament in the Psalms*. Trans. Keith R. Crim and Richard N. Soulen. Atlanta: John Knox Press, 1981.

________. "Psalms, Book of." *The Interpreter's Dictionary of the Bible*, suppl. vol. Ed. Keith Crim. Nashville: Abingdon Press, 1962.

Williams, Prescott H. "The Fatal and Foolish Exchange: Living Water for 'Nothings': A Study of Jeremiah 2:4–13." *Austin Seminary Bulletin: Faculty Edition*, 81 (1965), 3–59.

Williamson, H. G. M. *Ezra, Nehemiah*. Word Biblical Commentary. Waco: Word Books, Publisher, 1985.

Whybray, R. N. *Isaiah 40–66*. The New Century Bible. London: Oliphants, 1975.

Wilcoxen, Jay A. "Some Anthropocentric Aspects of Israel's Sacred History." *The Journal of Religion*, 48 (1968), 333–350.

Wolff, Hans Walter. "The Elohist Fragments in the Pentateuch." Trans. Keith Crim. In *The Vitality of Old Testament Traditions*. 2nd. ed. Ed. Walter Brueggemann and Hans Walter Wolff. Atlanta: John Knox Press, 1982.

________. "The Hermeneutics of the Old Testament." Trans. Keith Crim. In *Essays on Old Testament Hermeneutics*. Ed. Claus Westermann. Trans. James L. Mays. Richmond: John Knox Press, 1964.

________. "The Kerygma of the Deuteronomic Historical Work." Trans. Frederick C. Prussner. In *The Vitality of Old Testament Traditions*. 2nd. ed. Atlanta: John Knox Press, 1982.

________. "The Kerygma of the Yahwist." Trans. Wilbur A. Benware. In *The Vitality of Old Testament Traditions*. 2nd. ed. Ed. Hans Walter Wolff and Walter Brueggemann. Atlanta: John Knox Press, 1982.

Wright, G. Ernest. *God Who Acts: Biblical Theology as Recital*. London: SCM Press Ltd., 1952.

________. "The Lawsuit of God: A Form-Critical Study of Deuteronomy 32." In *Israel's Prophetic Heritage: Essays in Honor of James Muilenburg*. Ed. Bernhard W. Anderson and Walter Harrelson. New York: Harper & Brothers, Publishers, 1962.

Zimmerli, Walther. *Ezekiel 1*. Hermeneia. Ed. F. M. Cross, Klaus Baltzer, and Leonard Jay Greenspoon. Trans. R. E. Clements. Philadelphia: Fortress Press, 1979.

________. "I Am Yahweh." Trans. Douglas W. Stott. In *I Am Yahweh*, Ed. Walter Brueggemann. Atlanta: John Knox Press, 1982.

________. *Man and His Hope in the Old Testament*. London: SCM Press Ltd., 1971.

________. "The Message of the Prophet Ezekiel." *Interpretation*, 23 (1969), 131–157.

________. "Knowledge of God According to the Book of Ezekiel." Trans. Douglas W. Stott. In *I am Yahweh*. Ed. Walter Brueggemann. Atlanta: John Knox Press, 1982.

________. "Prophetic Proclamation and Reinterpretation." In *Tradition and Theology in the Old Testament*. Trans. and Ed. Douglas A. Knight. Philadelphia: Fortress Press, 1977.

Index of Hebrew Words

Index of Subjects